$20⁰⁰
3/96

Giving Glory to God
in Appalachia

Giving Glory to God in Appalachia

WORSHIP PRACTICES
OF SIX BAPTIST
SUBDENOMINATIONS

Howard Dorgan

The University of Tennessee Press

KNOXVILLE

Library of Congress Cataloging in Publication Data
Dorgan, Howard.
    Giving glory to God in Appalachia.
    Includes index.
    1. Public worship—Baptists. 2. Baptists—Appalachian
Region. 3. Appalachian Region—Church history. I. Title.
BX6337.D67 1987 264'.06'00975 87-5914
ISBN 0-87049-541-0 (alk. paper)

To Kathy, Kelly, and Shawn

Contents

Illustrations

Introduction

In summer 1973, Appalachian State University (ASU) hosted the Conference on the Rhetoric of the Contemporary South, the first of six annual scholarly exchanges designed to encourage research on rhetoric and public address in the contemporary South. The cosponsors of this conference—Carl Kell of the University of Western Kentucky, and I at ASU—felt that many sorts of public discourse in the contemporary South were being neglected and organized this meeting to call attention to areas that needed scholarly investigation.

Individual programs focused on specific topics of possible interest, particularly in popular culture, religion, and regional traditions. One of these sessions, "Folkways and the Rhetoric of the Contemporary South," was led by the late Cratis Williams of ASU and Lynwood Montell, then of Western Kentucky University, both eminent folklorists and recognized scholars in Appalachian studies. These leaders told the assembled rhetoric scholars that one figure in whom they might be interested was the Southern Appalachian preacher.

This idea was attractive to me. Having joined the ASU Department of Communication Arts in fall 1971, I had been in the mountains of Northwest North Carolina for two years. By then I had become fascinated by a style of preaching I had never heard in my native Louisiana or in any other area of the South where I had visited or resided. My introduction to this preaching had been entirely by radio, as I caught locally produced religious broadcasts over WATA in Boone, North Carolina; WKSK in West Jefferson, North Carolina; WMCT in Mountain City, Tennessee; and other small stations of the area. These colorful, emotionally charged, and eloquent regional broadcasts had generated a curiosity which was intensified by Williams's and Montell's remarks. As a result I resolved to visit some of the nearby mountain churches to learn more about this fast-paced, rhythmical style of preaching. On the Sunday following the close of the conference, I did just that. Thus began a field research project that has engaged me off and on for thirteen years.

Where to Start?

Although Williams and Montell inspired this study, they provided no direct connection with the phenomenon to be investigated, and I was somewhat at a loss where to begin my fieldwork. Limited access to the preaching could be gained simply by turning on a radio on Sunday mornings, but this method was not sufficient because the number of Appalachian preachers one could hear on the radio was limited. Nor did the method allow me to understand the total environment in which this preaching was taking place. I wanted to experience these church services directly, to sit in the small studios where the religious broadcasts were being produced.

The Southern Appalachian preacher with whom I was most familiar was Roscoe Greene, featured personality of "The Morning Star Gospel Program," broadcast (today, as it has been for the last thirty-five years) every Sunday morning at nine o'clock over WATA in Boone. Although the singing, preaching, and overall presentation of Greene's show is intriguing, it was the preacher's delivery that most interested me.

Greene spoke often of Bethany Baptist Church, where he was then pastor, and I thought I knew this church's location. As one drives north from Lenoir, North Carolina, toward Blowing Rock and Boone, a "Bethany Baptist" sign can be seen on the right just off Highway 321. I had noticed this sign numerous times during the two years I had been in the area. In addition, the mailing address that Greene gave over the air was a Lenoir route number. Therefore I assumed that this sign indicated the direction to Greene's church. I was mistaken, but that mistake was a profitable one for my growing interest in this area of study.

That first visit to a mountain church was undertaken with some hesitation, for in the back of my mind I feared that the congregation would be hostile to my presence. Up to that time I had made only limited contact with people indigenous to Southern Appalachia, and I held some simplistic, stereotyped views of these mountain folk, even to the point of thinking of them as steely-eyed "Hatfield and

Landmark Union Baptist Church, Alleghany County, North Carolina.
Photograph: Joel Poteat.

McCoy" types who sat on porches with rifles across their laps, ready
to fire at me for little or no reason. I also feared that they would
stereotype me, much as I had stereotyped them. I worried about
aspects of my professorial image: my clothes, my speech, my general
demeanor—and my beard. These were the protest years, and I had
a full chin of hair at the time. I even considered going to the church
clean-shaven and attired in work clothes. All of this indicated my
ignorance of the people of this region.

The church I attended that first morning was not the one Roscoe
Greene pastored. I discovered two weeks later that Greene's church
was in the Rominger community, a southwest section of Watauga
County, North Carolina. The church to which I found my way was
in Caldwell County, considerably southeast of there.

Liberty (Missionary) Baptist Church, Alleghany County, North Carolina. Photograph: Joel Poteat.

Nevertheless, that first visit to a Southern Appalachian church was a real success. It broke the ice for me, convinced me that if I continued this activity I would meet fascinating people who would not match my stereotypes, and introduced me to what has become one of my favorite mountain church buildings. The starkly simple, immaculately preserved white wood-framed structure was sitting on a small rise overlooking a beautiful valley, surrounded by a long-established graveyard and flanked by two well-kept out-

New Salem Regular Baptist Church, Alleghany County, North Carolina.
Photograph: Joel Poteat.

houses. Although the congregation that morning was small and the preaching not remarkably exciting, the church itself has remained the prototype of what I really want mountain churches to look like.

Many Southern Appalachian churches do not match my prototypical ideal, either because the buildings were not that aesthetically pleasing when originally constructed, or because congregations have remodeled or replaced their old church homes, producing those somewhat sterile but functional and easy-to-maintain brick facilities with which we are all familiar. Still, some mountain congregations do take pride in maintaining structures fifty, seventy, or a hundred years old. These are the picture-postcard churches one frequently sees on romanticized covers of gospel music albums. They rest on autumn-colored ridges or are tucked at heads of hollows amid lush flowering rhododendron or mountain laurel.

I prefer old clapboard structures with little or no architectural ornamentation, but possessing a sense of time and dignity. These picturesque facilities exist throughout Southern Appalachia, indeed throughout the South; but my own favorite concentration of such houses of worship lies around Sparta, North Carolina, the county seat of Alleghany County. Here travelers can find, by or near Highways 18 and 21, such traditional churches as Union Primitive Baptist, Landmark Union Baptist, Liberty Missionary Baptist, Meadow Fork Primitive Baptist, and New Salem Regular Baptist—all beautifully simple white frame structures that have been cared for lovingly over decades.

Limitations of the Study

This volume is not to be interpreted as "a study of Appalachian religion." My fieldwork has been too restricted to warrant such a characterization. I have limited this study to only six subdenominations of Southern Appalachian Baptists: Missionary Baptists, Free Will Baptists, Union Baptists, Primitive Baptists, Regular Baptists, and Old Regular Baptists.

When I began my Sunday morning wanderings, I concentrated exclusively on two counties in northwestern North Carolina, Watauga and Avery. Watauga County is heavily Baptist, with the strongest tradition—at least among the small mountain churches—being Missionary Baptist. So my work really began with these Missionary Baptist fellowships. Avery County, on the other hand, has been strongly influenced by the Holiness faith, and I visited a number of these churches during the early part of my work.

Before long, however, I made contact with traditional Appalachian churches in the two most northwestern counties of North Carolina, Ashe and Alleghany, and in Grayson County, Virginia. These contacts introduced me to four additional subdenominations of Baptists—Primitives, Union, Regular, and Free Will.

By the third and fourth years my fieldwork had become concentrated primarily in the summer months, and I moved into eastern Tennessee, deeper into southwestern Virginia, and into eastern Kentucky. In the vicinities of St. Paul, Wise, and Grundy, Virginia; Kingsport, Tennessee; and Jenkins, Kentucky, I contacted the last of the Baptist subdenominations I would study, the Old Regular Baptists.

During the late 1970s, to tighten the focus of my fieldwork, I ceased to study the Holiness, Church of God, Advent Christian, and other denominations I had occasionally visited, and concentrated on the six Baptist groups I have mentioned. The reader should realize, however, that these six do not constitute all the Baptist subdenominations of the Appalachian region. For example, two additional Baptists sects having fellowships in these mountains are the United Baptists and the Separate Baptists.[1] These groups are not well represented in the geographical area covered. The subdenominations discussed in this work are simply the most prevalent Baptist sects within the examined region.

That region's boundaries extend roughly from Boone, North Carolina, west and northwest to Johnson City and Kingsport, Tennessee; then north through St. Paul, Wise, and Grundy, Virginia, with a couple of spurs extending into Kentucky before the borderline drops southeast toward Galax, Virginia, and from there runs south around Sparta, North Carolina, and back to Boone. Were you to travel this region, you would encounter the coalfields near St. Paul, Wise, and Grundy. But were you to head southeast from these towns you would cross the valleys of the Clinch and Holston Rivers, progress to the North and South Forks of the New River, and in the process move through some of the most beautiful areas of the Southern Highlands.

This geographical area was not chosen because it contains any special concentration of mountain religious traditions. Instead, two factors forged the boundaries outlined above: (1) the need for a reasonable Sunday morning driving distance, and (2) serendipitous contacts that occurred. I can claim no other design.

A point that perhaps should be emphasized here is that my travels have taken me only peripherally into those parts of Appalachia notorious for their strip-mining ugliness, poverty, and rural decay. Although there are some pockets of want in my study region, it would be misleading to associate the farms, homes, churches, and scenery of this area only with media images of Appalachian poverty and environmental ruin. It may be that some of the socioeconomic characteristics of this particular segment of Southern Appalachia

1. See Frank S. Mead, *Handbook of Denominations in the United States*, 5th ed. (Nashville: Abingdon Press, 1970), 49–51; and James Owen Renault, *The Development of Separate Baptist Ecclesiology in the South, 1755–1976* (Ann Arbor, Mich.: University Microfilms, 1982), 206–10.

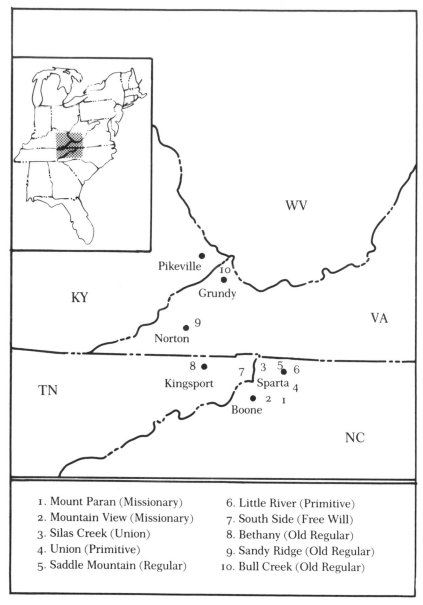

1. Mount Paran (Missionary)
2. Mountain View (Missionary)
3. Silas Creek (Union)
4. Union (Primitive)
5. Saddle Mountain (Regular)
6. Little River (Primitive)
7. South Side (Free Will)
8. Bethany (Old Regular)
9. Sandy Ridge (Old Regular)
10. Bull Creek (Old Regular)

Location of Selected Churches in the Study

are more favorable than would be the case in other regions of these mountains.

Fieldwork

During the 1973 conference on the contemporary South, Cratis Williams reminisced about some of the mountain preachers he had heard as a child in his native Kentucky. He argued that an initial need was simply to preserve samples of Appalachian preachers' rhetoric and speaking styles. He felt that much of the phenomenon already had been lost through passage of time and the changing cultural base, and he feared that what remained also might disappear, since most of the mountain preachers who maintained the distinctive pulpit styles of the region were growing old and their methods of preaching stood only a generation or two away from extinction.

Cratis convinced me that, whenever possible, I should audiotape these services. That idea gave me some concern, because I did not know how mountain congregations would respond to tape recorders or video cameras. Actually, only two of the six subdenominations of Baptists with whom I worked, the Old Regulars and the Primitives, expressed strong reservations about permitting services to be recorded; and these reservations were expressed on a church-by-church basis, so that some congregations have allowed taping and some have not. Those who have not allowed it generally have taken this position in such a way as to express approval of my work. Typically, however, congregations have been receptive to arguments in favor of recording for historic preservation.

There is, of course, a concern among some Southern Appalachian congregations that films, videotapes, or audiotapes of their worship services can be used in a manner that violates the spirit of the event being recorded. One member of the Bull Creek Old Regular Baptist Church of Maxie, Virginia, bluntly told me that he considered all Old Regular church activities to be sacred happenings and therefore not proper subject matter for taping or filming. He was familiar with the Appalshop film, *In the Good Old Fashioned Way*, having seen it on Kentucky Educational Television, and was disturbed that so many people had viewed the film while not in "the proper frame of mind." *In the Good Old Fashioned Way* is a 1973 documentary that was shot in cooperation with churches in the Indian Bottom Association of Old Regular Baptists. It shows, among other things, the intimate scenes of an Old Regular communion and footwashing.[2]

The gentleman quickly followed his statement, however, with an invitation to anyone who might wish to visit the Bull Creek church in a "proper spirit." During the exchange I never felt unwelcome; I was simply being spoken to in a very honest, straightforward fashion. I received essentially the same message from one member of the Little River Primitive Baptist Church of Sparta, North Carolina, and from the moderator and assistant moderator of Bethany Old Regular Baptist of Kingsport, Tennessee.

This same concern was at the heart of an exchange I had with one member of a church whose services were filmed.[3] I think of the church in question, Mount Paran Missionary Baptist Church in the Stoney Fork district of Watauga County, North Carolina, as a middle-of-the-road Southern Appalachian church. Neither very primitive nor very modern, it has preserved traditional modes of worship (footwashings, creek baptisms, and the like) while its members have progressed socioeconomically, particularly in income and education. Several years ago the congregation replaced the old wood-framed church with a small but modern brick structure. Since that time numerous embellishments have been added to both interior and exterior, including an outdoor picnic shed for homecomings, carpeted floors, upholstered pews, and airconditioning for the few times in the summer when these mountains get warm enough to warrant its use. All this has occurred while the members maintain worship styles many decades old. The traveler can reach Mount Paran by proceeding east from Boone on Highway 421 for about seven or eight miles, turning right onto Wildcat Road, and following this twisting course—which after about two miles becomes gravel—down the mountain until the church is spotted on the left.

Mount Paran is the home church of "Doc" Watson, a well-known bluegrass and country recording artist; and two other members of the congregation—Willard Watson and his wife—have won regional,

2. This film is distributed by Appalshop Films, Whitesburg, Ky.

3. The resulting documentary, *Mount Paran Baptist Church*, was filmed by Joseph R. Murphy and produced by Howard Dorgan, Richard Humphrey, and Joseph R. Murphy. It is available in the Appalachian Collection, Belk Library, Appalachian State Univ., Boone, N.C.

Mount Paran (Missionary) Baptist Church, Deep Gap, Watauga
County, North Carolina.

state, and even national recognition for their mountain crafts, having had their work displayed by the Smithsonian Institution in
Washington. Roscoe Greene, now the pastor of Mount Paran, moved
to that church in 1974.

All this outside recognition for some of its members has given
Mount Paran, and the entire Wildcat Road community, a sense of
importance, a sense that their culture does indeed possess qualities
highly valued by the more modern world. Nevertheless, there are in
this mountain community, as I am convinced there are throughout
Southern Appalachia, people who view this outside interest with
a certain degree of suspicion, fearing some violation of cherished
ways of life.

I was initially attracted to the Mount Paran church as a possible subject for a filmed documentary because of the openness of the congregation, because of my previous contacts with Roscoe Greene, and because this group was middle-of-the-road and could thus represent the average way of things in the religious practices of northwestern North Carolina. Preparatory to filming "Preacher Ros," as Greene's congregation frequently call him, invited me to speak to a midweek "sing" and prayer meeting.

My talk to the Mount Paran fellowship stressed the importance of preserving on film or videotape those elements of the mountain religious tradition in danger of becoming extinct. I mentioned the types of preaching styles and various ceremonies such as footwashings. As I spoke, it appeared that all members of the congregation were receptive to my ideas except one older woman who sat toward the front, looking rather stern. When I asked if the congregation had any questions, this woman was the first to speak: "Will you ever use this film to make fun of me?" It was a question I thought deserved my most thoughtful answer, and I told her so.

The woman had a small child, whom I presumed to be her granddaughter, sitting beside her. As I glanced at this child, I remembered a photograph taken of me when I was about her age. It was a sepia-colored snapshot taken one Easter morning in the late thirties, showing my two brothers and me as we stood on the steps of a small Methodist church in Castor, Louisiana. We were attired in short pants, white shirts with "Buster Brown" collars, and white coats, and were lined up to be immortalized as symbols of the pride my mother took in her children.

I told the woman about the photograph and of how I had often stared at it during my later youth, wanting to know more about what happened to me that one day of my life. I mentioned that most people—sometimes rather late in life—experience a desire to understand their cultural roots. I then suggested that were we able to make the proposed film, her granddaughter would have access to a more complete record of her day than I had of mine. This turned out to be a very successful argument, and the woman became a staunch supporter of the project.

Of course my statements did not really answer the woman's question about whether the film would ever subject her and the other members of the congregation to ridicule. In truth I had no guarantee to give in that regard. The fellowship would be submitting itself to the hazards of a good-faith bargain, one in which I would commit myself to a respectful attitude toward the intimate scenes to be recorded and in return they would trust the film crew enough to be natural.

By and large, the Southern Appalachian Baptist congregations I have visited have remained reasonably natural, even in the presence of distracting recording devices. Still, I have been aware of the degree to which these devices can change the phenomena being recorded. The best example of such a change occurred one Sunday evening in spring 1974. I had made contact with Brother Reeves Jones, pastor of the Scotsville (Missionary) Baptist Church, situated in the Scotsville community in northeastern Ashe County, North Carolina, not far from the Alleghany County line. I had been told that Jones's church was a "shouting church," that I could expect a great deal of emotionalism. Indeed, during my pretaping visit with Jones he expressed the hope that I would be able to capture his congregation in one of their most spirited worship sessions. Still, he delayed my attendance at his church for over a month, waiting for new pews that had been ordered. During this delay the congregation probably discussed my pending visit. Thus when the evening finally arrived they were more than ready for me—with special music, special flowers, and what appeared to be special clothing.

That evening Reeves Jones preached a very forceful sermon, trying hard to lift his congregation to a peak of emotional fervor, but they simply would not follow his lead. They held back, providing only a few timid "Amens" and one emotionally subdued testimonial, apparently feeling that the presence of a video camera demanded of them a special level of reserve. Five years later I returned to this church during one of their summer revivals. This time I had no camera or tape recorder, and I witnessed a much more spirited service.

By no means have I recorded all the mountain services I have attended in the last twelve years. In most cases I did not do any taping during a first visit to a church, choosing instead to allow congregations to know a little about me before I interjected a tape recorder into the scene. On a few occasions, however, particularly when my contact with the fellowship had led me to believe the congregation would not be offended, I did record on my first visit.

It was not always easy to guage the level of congregational offense, however, and on occasion I may have overstepped the boundaries of my welcome. I know this happened once with the Sandy Ridge Old Regular Baptist fellowship of St. Paul, Virginia. It was my third visit to this church, and I was feeling very comfortable with the congregation; this was the only Old Regular church so far that had permitted me to record its singing and preaching.

The service during which the problem developed was Sandy Ridge's annual communion and footwashing. I wanted photographs of the event and had secured the help of a photographer colleague, Joel Poteat. Prior to the service I checked with two elders—who in turn checked with other individuals—to see if it would be all right for Joel to photograph the events. These particular elders found no objections to the request, and Joel proceeded to photograph the preaching and singing parts of the service, being as unobtrusive as possible. During the break required to get set for communion and footwashing, however, one of these elders informed me of some complaints and requested that we not photograph the rest of the morning's events. I was disappointed, but I was also uneasy about having precipitated the complaints. Such circumstances are not conducive to the good relationships I always desire.

As has already been noted, my interest in these Southern Appalachian Baptist churches developed out of the study of southern rhetoric and public address and focused on regional preaching styles. When I visited services of these six Baptist groups, however, I saw and heard much more than sermons; I was introduced to all of the "old time way" traditions of these fellowships, and soon I found myself as fascinated by these added attractions as I already was with the rhythmic cadences of Appalachian pulpit elocution. I quickly became eager to relate my observations of all aspects of these colorful mountain church services.

This volume reports findings made during thirteen years of nosy but respectful probing into the worship customs of six Baptist sub-denominations. The book is, for the most part, a first-person descriptive account, a "this is what I have seen and heard" kind of narrative. The primary source materials for my analyses are my own notes on the Southern Appalachian church services and the audio and video recordings I made during visits to these churches "back in the hollow" or to local radio stations for their live Sunday morning broadcasts of mountain religious programs. It is a journal of observations, written by an "outsider looking in," from a perspective of deep respect for the people and traditions of this part of Appalachia. Frankly, I would be disappointed if the reader did not recognize in this work a bias in favor of my subjects, a bias in favor not of their respective beliefs, but of their tenaciousness of spirit in preserving traditional customs and values.

My role, as I perceive it, is to report, as vividly as possible, beliefs held and passions felt. While fulfilling that role I try to withhold theological or social judgments. My own beliefs are extraneous to the purposes of this work and should not influence the reader's reception of the doctrines, articles of faith, and worship practices to be presented here. The reader should avoid interjecting into her or his interpretations of these narratives any conclusions about the writer's religious convictions.

With the possible exception of parts of chapters 1 and 2, in which I report doctrinal differences and analyze preaching styles, the book is neither a historical nor a theoretical work. It is primarily descriptive, written to document religious customs so tied to the past that they may be in danger of extinction. Theory may come in later writings, as my own knowledge of these customs grows.

Acknowledgments

I would like to mention a few individuals who have been particularly helpful during my years of gathering information on the practices of Southern Appalachian Baptist churches.

Roscoe Greene, through his preaching style, was one of the early inspirations for this work. "Preacher Ros" has been very open with his thoughts, generous with his time, and liberal with his verbal support. He and his congregations welcomed me wherever I followed him, first at his radio broadcast, then at one of his revivals at Bethany Baptist, and finally at both Mount Paran and Mountain View. He has always been willing to trust me.

Elder Earl Sexton of Lansing, North Carolina, was my initial contact with the Union Baptist churches of Ashe and Alleghany Counties, North Carolina, and also welcomed me to his radio broadcast at WKSK in West Jefferson. Like Roscoe Greene, Sexton is an extremely open person, exhibiting no insecurities about who or what he is.

One of the individuals most valuable to this study has been Darvin Marshall of St. Paul, Virginia. Several years ago Marshall heard of my work with various Baptist subdenominations and called to invite me to the Sandy Ridge Old Regular Church. But not only did he assist me in making my first contacts with the Old Regulars, but he has spent hours helping me understand the customs of this particular group of Southern Appalachian Baptists. In addition, he read an earlier version of this work, closely checking my references to Old Regular doctrines and traditions. His suggestions and corrections have been most helpful.

Two other Old Regular elders whom I must not overlook are Elders Edwin May and Bill Campbell. May, of Abingdon, Virginia, is moderator of the Sardis Association of Old Regulars. He welcomed me into his home for an all-day visit, patiently fielding my endless questions. Campbell, of Vansant, Virginia, became my contact with the Bull Creek Old Regular fellowship and also has spent considerable time with me.

As pastor of the Saddle Mountain Regular Baptist Church, Elder Glenn Killon of Ennice, North Carolina, has seen to it that all the services of this fellowship have been open to my visitations. Barbara Roberts of this church provided me with a videotape of several Saddle Mountain services.

The assistance of Elder Walter Evans, moderator of the Mountain District Primitive Baptist Association, has been extremely valuable. He was particularly supportive when I visited two of the churches he pastors, Little River Primitive and Union Primitive, both in Sparta, North Carolina.

Brother Roland McClellan, former pastor of the South Side Free Will Baptist Church of Mountain City, Tennessee, was helpful in apprising me of some of the traditions in the Free Will subdenomination. Brother Gary Watson and his wife Vertie, of the Mountain View (Missionary) Baptist fellowship, patiently read my manuscript, offering suggestions for improvement and correction. Gaye Golds, a film librarian at Appalachian State and also a member of the Mountain View fellowship, provided me with background information concerning the flower service practiced at Mountain View and Mount Paran.

Although there are many other Southern Appalachian churchmen and churchwomen who helped me with this project, I cannot
name them all. But I haven't forgotten them, their contributions
of information, their friendliness in dealing with me, their warm
receptiveness to my proposals, and their general openness of spirit.

For years my colleague Dr. Richard Humphrey and I shared tapes
and observations, helping each other to appreciate better what we
were seeing and hearing in mountain churches. At that time he
chaired the Philosophy and Religion Department at ASU; he has
since returned to fulltime ministry in the Methodist Church.

The late Dr. Cratis Williams was instrumental in starting this
study, and he provided invaluable guidance along the way, including
advising me on the basic structure of and approach to this volume.

Notes, Tapes, and Association Minutes

I am placing in the Appalachian Collection of the Belk Library,
ASU, all of the tapes and notes I have preserved during this thirteen-
year study. I will also place there my collection of association minutes, including the minutes of the Union Association of Old Regular Baptists from 1898 to 1986 (on microfilm) and a two volume
compilation of New Salem Old Regular Baptist Association records,
1825–1983.[4] All other minutes quoted in the pages that follow will
be included in this collection.

My assortment of tapes includes both audio and video recordings,
but many of them have been edited for my earlier uses. In that
process there are a few sermon segments quoted in Chapter 3 that
have been preserved only in manuscript form. Those few quotations
will be identified in my footnotes.

---

4. *Burning Spring Baptist Association, 1813–1824; New Salem Old Regular Baptist
Association, 1825–1947*, ed. by Dexter Dixon and Walter Akers (2 vols.; Pikeville,
Ky.: Privately published by Dixon and Akers, 1983).

Giving Glory to God
in Appalachia

CHAPTER I

Baptists, Baptists, and More Baptists

This chapter has three objectives: (1) to advance a few observations concerning the physical churches being discussed; (2) to provide basic background on the doctrines and worship practices of each of the six Baptist subdenominations under consideration; and (3) to put forth a few ideas concerning the typical role of these churches in their respective Southern Appalachian communities.

The Church Buildings

There's poetry in the names of these Southern Appalachian Baptist churches. The names capture images of the late eighteenth- and early nineteenth-century mountain frontier, when geographical locations were identified by colorful references to creeks, rivers, ridges, bottoms, gaps, and valleys. So we have Appalachian Baptist churches with names such as Bear Creek, Panther Creek, Bee Branch, Bent Branch, Caney Fork, Pine Swamp, Peach Bottom, Deep Gap, Roaring Gap, Sandy Ridge, Laurel Springs, Rich Mountain, Willow Valley, Zion Hill, Gravel Lick, Ash Camp, Beaver Dam, and Old Pond. Other churches' names relate to biblical settings: Mount Carmel, Mount Zion, Mount Ephraim, Mount Ararat, Samaria, Lebanon, Calvary, Bethel, Antioch. Many Old Regular Baptist churches are named after biblical heroines, so many that occasionally one gets the idea that houses of worship are feminine in gender: Rebecca, Little Mary, Elizabeth, Little Sarah, Little Martha, Naomi, Little Ruth, Little Rachel, and so on. Finally, there are names that simply suggest repose, sanctuary, or escape from a busy, troubled, or perhaps evil secular world: Pilgrim's Rest and Zion's Rest, Pleasant Home and Sweet Home, Pilgrim's Hope

1

and Canaan's Hope, Little Flock and Little Dove, Mount Calm and Mount Pleasant.

These colorful names are posted on a wide variety of buildings, ranging from those idyllically picturesque churches mentioned in our introduction to those totally unadorned concrete block structures with tin roofs and metal-sashed windows. In general, the Baptist congregations discussed in this work are neither large nor affluent, and their religious facilities reflect architectural tastes dominant in their respective communities. Nevertheless, the buildings are always clean and usually in good to excellent repair, suggesting the care these fellowships regularly give their houses of worship. Individual homes may look neglected, but church structures generally do not. The interiors of these buildings are usually well preserved, and occasionally floors are carpeted, pews upholstered, and walls paneled, even when the concrete block or wood exteriors seem bare by comparison.

I have visited mountain churches—the Union Primitive Baptist Church of Sparta, North Carolina, being an excellent example—that have remained significantly unaltered, internally or externally, and maintained in good to exceptional states of preservation for over fifty years. And this was accomplished by the half-dozen families whose names flourished in each church's graveyard. In fact, so deep can this loyalty to a particular structure run that long after shifting population patterns, new roads, new churches down the way, or other factors eliminate the need for the particular church, one, two, or three elderly members go to great lengths to keep the small facility viable. Throughout our mountains, these two-, three-, or four-family churches testify to a determination to preserve that which is loved and considered sacred. For example, Horse Creek Primitive Baptist Church of Ashe County, North Carolina, founded in 1840, in 1986 possessed a membership of five elderly individuals who use the church building during summer months only.

Readers certainly should not picture the small Baptist churches treated in this study as structures rich in superfluous ornamentation. Old Regular, Regular, and Primitive Baptist church buildings in particular tend to be relatively plain, with virtually no purely decorative features inside or outside. There is often about them the stark simplicity commonly associated with New England/Puritan or Pennsylvania/Amish styles.

Horse Creek Primitive Baptist Church, Ashe County, North Carolina. Older Primitive churches such as this one had two front doors, one for the men and one for the women.

Customarily, Primitive churches are most severe in their decors, and Missionary and Free Will churches least so. Later in this chapter the reader will see that this contrast between Primitive and Missionary/Free Will groups extends into areas of doctrine and worship practices. For now, suffice it to say that typical Primitive houses of worship contain little more than is functionally required for services. Rarely do religious paintings or artifacts adorn the walls, and though woodwork in pews, pulpits, walls, and ceilings may show skill in craftsmanship, it contains no superfluous ornamentation. In contrast, the walls of a typical Missionary Baptist church in these mountains contain a number of religious paintings, prints, or plaques, plus a large framed copy of the church's covenant. In addition, Missionary Baptist sanctuaries may be embellished with color-tinted windows, paneling, carpeting, and upholstery.

Old Regular churches generally have more in common with Primitive than with Missionary structures. With one major exception, the walls of Old Regular houses of worship are also rather bare. This exception pertains to the subdenomination's practice of filling the wall immediately behind the "stand" (pulpit) with photographs of past moderators of the fellowship, forming a gallery of the church's patriarchs. Obviously, the older the fellowship, the more photographs displayed.

Another interesting feature of Old Regular churches is the way interiors are partitioned for congregational seating. These churches are traditionally rectangular in shape, with the pews laid out in a modified cruciform pattern. Approximately half the interior space is devoted to pews that run perpendicular to the long sides of the rectangle, divided by a center aisle and facing the stand. These seats are used by visitors, regular nonmember attendees, and members of other Old Regular fellowships who are unable to find seating in the section to be discussed next. The remaining half of the floor space is raised to the height of one or two steps and is further partitioned into three seating areas and the space occupied by the stand. To the right of the stand (the preacher's right) are several rows of pews that run lengthwise with the church and which are used by women church members. On the opposite side of the stand is a similar section of pews used by male church members. This assignment of gender areas, however, is sometimes reversed, with the women on the left of the preacher, or "elder," as he is called in this subdenomination.

Behind the stand, underneath the gallery of old photographs, are one or more other benches where the church's moderator (the elected leader) and the local and visiting elders (all ordained ministers) traditionally sit. When "in the stand" (a phrase often used to designate the act of preaching), an Old Regular elder is literally surrounded by his audience, with the result that he is frequently turning his back to the stand and the nonmember area as he talks

"Cast me not off in the time of
old age. Forsake me not when
my strength faileth. Psalms 71:9.

ELDER D. C. CHURCH

From the Collection of Church Patriarchs, Bull Creek Old Regular
Baptist Church, Maxie, Buchanan County, Virginia. Photograph:
Joel Poteat.

to fellow elders immediately behind him. In addition, because proximity to the stand appears important for all local or visiting elders
and deacons, the first row of the women's section may be occupied
by these gentlemen. This tends to intensify the "surrounded" effect
by placing a preaching elder within a tight horseshoe of masculine
support. In addition, it serves to indicate the secondary status of
women in Old Regular Fellowships.

Separation of the sexes is maintained in the side sections of the
raised area, but in the larger visitor and nonmember section families
or mixed-gender couples occasionally sit together. As a general rule,
however, even in this nonmember area, husbands and wives sit
apart, in the company of one or more individuals of their own sex.

Appalachian Primitive fellowships also maintain a high degree of gender separation, but not necessarily by the same patterning. Primitive churches visited for this study did not have sections reserved for the formal membership, but men and women did tend to sit on different sides of the main sitting area, particularly in the front pews. More will be said concerning Primitive gender separation in chapter 4, during discussion of the footwashing service at the Little River Primitive Baptist Church in Sparta, North Carolina.

In Union, Regular, and some Missionary churches, remnants of gender separation can be seen in the behavior of older worshipers. Younger couples or families may sit together, but elderly men and women tend to have special sitting areas, usually on opposite sides of the church. In other instances there may be one prominent front section where only the church leaders sit.

Missionary and Free Will churches usually have a piano and sometimes an organ, but Primitive, Regular, and Old Regular houses of worship traditionally have neither. All of the singing in the regular services of these last three subdenominations is *a cappella.* The term "regular services" is used here because Regular Baptist fellowships occasionally may tolerate guitars in informal singing services. Union Baptist churches vary in regard to use of musical instruments, with a few fellowships using a piano.

Although plain, many of these churches radiate a certain charm. Indeed, their charm lies in their unadorned simplicity, their settings, and their aura of "usedness." This invented term, "usedness," refers to a quality intrinsic to most of these small mountain Baptist churches. While in larger, more affluent churches everything appears new and unworn, the sanctuaries of most Southern Appalachian Primitive Baptist churches, for example, bespeak decades of wear. The picture is not one of disrepair, decay, and abandonment, however. Rather, in the discolored pews, scuffed floors, and virtually every feature of the building and its furnishings is visible that worn, grooved, polished quality we associate with objects long used—the old hoe handle with graining that has begun to separate but is still smooth and unsplintered.

Images of age are frequently associated with these churches even when the buildings are not old, because the activities transpiring within are "old," "dated," "traditional." Members of Sandy Ridge Old Regular Baptist in St. Paul, Virginia, meet the fourth Sunday of each month in a reasonably modern brick church, but when they sing hymns using the "lined" method, they preserve a worship style that originated long before organized European religion came to these mountains. The lining of hymns is a practice that supposedly began with the Westminster Assembly of Baptists in England in 1644 and was introduced to the American colonies in the 1690s.[1] More will be said later in this volume about the Old Regular, Regular, and Union Baptists' uses of "lining."

Another factor giving a feeling of antiquity to many of these churches, particularly those of the Missionary Baptists, is their graveyards. Crammed with headstones that may go back to the turn of the century or earlier, the graveyard is seldom far from the church building and thus is viewed as an integral part of the sacred scene. Even when the original building is being replaced by a modern structure, the congregation usually is reluctant to place its new building at some distance from the old cemetery. The gravestones help to maintain a sense of continuity in the church community, and also symbolize a belief that life is not solely temporal.

Grave markers sometimes abut the church structure itself, and may even surround it, at least on three sides. This encroachment of the headstones occasionally presents a problem when congregations wish to remodel or expand their facilities. If the Bethany Baptist Church, for example, were to be expanded in any direction, it would have to be moved out of its graveyard first: it is surrounded on three sides by gravestones and on the fourth by a road.

Because small family graveyards have been popular within these mountains, some Baptist churches—notably the Old Regulars— have not established cemeteries for the collective fellowship, but instead stage funerals and memorial services at a number of more restricted interment plots. The importance of these family grave sites to the larger church congregation, is not lost, however, for individual cemeteries are symbolically combined with the church location to form a network of sacred places.

Frequently a church is situated on one lofty point on a ridge and the cemetery on another nearby. The Mary Lou Church, for example, a member of the Old Friendship Association of Old Regular

1. George Hood, *A History of Music in New England* (1846; rpt. New York: Johnson Reprint, 1970), 47. Also see William Tallmadge, "Baptist Monophonic and Heterophonic Hymnody in Southern Appalachia," *Yearbook for Interamerican Musical Research*, vol. 2 (1975), 106–36.

Baptists, rests on one of the highest points on State Line Ridge Road running northwest off Highway 83 along the Virginia–West Virginia border; the Mary Lou Cemetery lies on a companion peak about a half mile away. Both these spots are inspiring locations for religious sites: a vast expanse of West Virginia can be seen in one direction and of Virginia in the other. It would be hard to find more beautiful natural surroundings than those in which some of these small churches are located.

The mountain Baptist churches discussed in this volume are not very large, in terms of either membership or size of physical structure. Nor is their outreach very expansive, since they tend to be relatively autonomous institutions affecting the lives of only those individuals who belong to the respective fellowship. Although most of the churches discussed have joined loosely structured "associations" of fellowships of their subdenomination, many are totally independent, owing allegiance to no larger governing body.

The Subdenominations

People occasionally speak of "the Baptists" of Appalachia as if all these individuals formed a monolithic religious unit. This is certainly not the case. In fact, there is as much disparity among the Southern Appalachian Baptist sects as there is within the general body of Christianity. There are, of course, significant areas of similarity between sects, but the areas of dissimilarity are also significant; in the history of the Baptist faith in these mountains, the general movement has been toward separation, not unity.

Let us now look at the principal Baptist subdenominations whose churches I have visited. The term "subdenomination" is used simply because most people think of the Baptists in general as a denomination.

The Primitives

It is somewhat easier to distinguish among other various Baptist groups when one has the Primitives as a basis of comparison. It is not being suggested, however, that the Primitives stand closest to any set of original Baptist doctrines.

Primitives trace their beginnings as a distinct Baptist subdenomination from that period in the 1820s and 1830s when debate erupted over Baptist missions.[2] The more strongly Calvinist Baptist theologians of those decades looked askance at the relatively new emphasis upon evangelism and missions, believing that human efforts to "win souls" ran contrary to established positions on predestination and unconditional election. If God had predestined the circumstances of each person's life and had from the beginning of time "elected" those who were to be the chosen people, then it was exceedingly arrogant for anyone to presume power to win new members to that elected body. Influenced by the antimission writings and preachings of ministers such as John Taylor and Daniel Parker,[3] the "Hard Shells" or "Primitives" opposed mission boards and missionary societies—and, by extension, Sunday schools, revivals, and other forms of evangelism and church outreach. Human effort to win souls through any of these non-biblically-sanctioned practices was viewed as improper, because God alone had the right to do such work.

The great "Antimission Split" occurred roughly between 1825 and 1845 and left the region's Baptists divided into two broad camps: those fellowships who believed in missionary work and who consequently were evangelistic, and those who were antimission and nonevangelistic. Although this highly simplified description ignores a multitude of other doctrinal issues that divided the Baptists before and after this great split, it does provide an initial framework for understanding our six subdenominations. With some exceptions, the beliefs and practices of Primitives and Old Regulars place these two groups in the antimissionary and nonevangelistic camp, while the beliefs and practices of Missionary and Free Will Baptists place them in the evangelistic camp. The Regulars and Union Baptists fall somewhere between.

Some Doctrinal Issues On the issue of predestination and the question of "the elect," Primitive churches have remained more Calvinist than any of the other five Baptist sects examined in this book. Primitive doctrinal positions on these issues can be found in "articles of

2. O.W. Taylor, *Early Tennessee Baptists, 1769–1852* (Nashville: Tennessee Baptist Convention, 1957), 177–201.

3. William Warren Sweet, *Religion in the Development of American Culture, 1765–1840* (Gloucester, Mass.: Peter Smith, 1963), 273–75.

faith" published in the minutes of various Southern Appalachian associations of this subdenomination:

> We believe in the doctrine of eternal, personal and unconditional election. . . .

> We believe in the doctrine of God's predestination in every sense as the Bible teaches it.

> We believe that all the elect . . . , chosen in Christ before the foundation of the world, shall be called, regenerated and sanctified by the regenerating power of God's grace, and shall ultimately enjoy heaven and immortal glory.[4]

> We believe in the doctrine of eternal and particular election.

> We believe that God's elect are called, converted, regenerated and sanctified by the Holy Spirit.[5]

> We believe in the doctrine of original sin and in Man's impotency to recover himself from the fallen state he is in by nature by his own free will or ability.

> We believe that sinners are called, converted, regenerated and sanctified by the Holy Spirit, and that all who are thus regenerated and born again by the Spirit of God shall never fall finally away.[6]

> We believe that God elected, or chose, His people in Christ before the foundation of the world. . . .

> We believe in the doctrine of original sin, and man's impotency to recover himself from the fallen state he is in by nature, by his own free will and ability.

> We believe that God's elect shall be called, effectually regenerated and sanctified by the Holy Ghost, and shall be preserved in grace and never finally fall away.[7]

The reader should note that these articles of faith are very specific relative to the "elect" doctrine, which claims that only a certain number of humans were chosen ("before the foundation of

4. Original Mates Creek Regular Primitive Baptist Association, *Minutes* (1976), 36–37.
5. Mountain District Primitive Baptist Association, *Minutes* (1983), 18.
6. Senter District Primitive Baptist Association, *Minutes* (1979), 14.
7. Mount Zion Primitive Baptist Association, *Minutes* (1975), 12.

the world") to become "people in Christ"; that this body of individuals has been regenerated from original sin through a special dispensation; that only God is responsible for calling, regenerating, and sanctifying these elect; and that, once chosen, the elect can never "finally fall away." Note that this "election" is a "particular election"; Primitives believe that specific individuals were elected before the beginning of time to constitute Christ's church. Evangelism, consequently, has no role in this theology, and in one way or another this nonevangelistic position affects the Primitives' attitudes toward revivals, Sunday schools, missions, church-sponsored radio and television shows, and all forms of church outreach.

The precise position of Primitives relative to "absolute predestination," is not always so clear, at least to judge by the informal rhetoric heard in contemporary Primitive fellowships. In talking with both Primitive ministers and laymen, I have found confusion concerning this doctrine. Does predestination, for example, apply solely to this elect issue, or to all world events? Historically, this has been a thorny question for Primitives, with some churches splitting over the issue. An interesting account of one such division is preserved in the little booklet, *In Defense of Truth, or Danville Church Division Investigated*, a committee's report on a predestination dispute that arose in the Danville, Virginia, Primitive Baptist Church in 1923.[8] The crux of the question has been whether God predestined only those aspects of the world that relate to his elect's being "called, converted, regenerated and sanctified," or whether he—or his dark counterpart, Satan—also predestined all the evils of the world. During the 1870s and 1880s, Primitive Baptist fellowships of eastern Tennessee were particularly troubled by the "Two Seed" controversy. This doctrine held both God and Satan to be "eternal, uncreated self-existent beings" who were responsible, respectively, for all the good and all the evil of the world. Both good and evil, therefore, were predestined, but by totally separate creative forces.[9]

Primitive pulpit rhetoric can be heard supporting all sides of the predestination question, but the official positions of Primitive associations whose articles of faith have been examined for this

8. R.H. Pittman, comp., *In Defense of Truth, or Danville Church Division Investigated* (Fort Royal, Va.: Buck Press, n.d.).
9. Taylor, *Early Tennessee Baptists*, 184–85.

work seem to apply the predestination principle only to the issue of election. The Original Mates Creek Regular Primitive Baptist Association does include in its articles of faith that cryptic clause, "We believe the doctrine of God's predestination in every sense as the Bible teaches it."[10] However, the Biblical passages Primitives usually employ to defend this doctrine seem to apply only to the question of election:

> And we know that all things work together for good to them that love God, to them who are the called according to his purpose.
>
> For whom he did foreknow, he also did predestinate to be conformed to the image of his Son, that he might be the firstborn among many brethren.
>
> Moreover whom he did predestinate, them he also called: and whom he called, them he also justified: and whom he justified, them he also glorified.
>
> Rom. 8:28–30

> Having made known unto us the mystery of his will, according to his good pleasure which he hath purposed in himself;
>
> That in the dispensation of the fullness of times he might gather together in one all things in Christ, both which are in heaven, and which are on earth; even in him;
>
> In whom also we have obtained an inheritance, being predestinated according to the purpose of him who worketh all things after the counsel of his own will.
>
> Eph. 1:9–11

The articles of faith of the two Primitive associations with which I have had the most contact—Senter District Primitive Association (nine churches in Ashe and Alleghany Counties, North Carolina) and Mountain District Primitive Baptist Association (eleven churches in Alleghany and Wilkes Counties, North Carolina, and in Grayson County, Virginia)—contain no statements confirming a belief in "absolute" predestination. These associations make formal pronouncements about predestination only as it applies to the doctrine of the elect.

In his small pamphlet, "What Do Primitive Baptists Believe?,"

10. Original Mates Creek Regular Primitive Baptist Association, *Minutes* (1980), 42.

Elder Lasserre Bradley, Jr., asks the question: "What is their [the Primitives'] position on predestination?" This is Elder Bradley's answer:

> They believe that God has predestinated a great number to be conformed to the image of His Son (Rom. 8:28–30). While some object to this doctrine because they say it is unfair, Primitive Baptists rejoice in it, for they see that had it not been for predestination, the whole human family would have been lost forever. Predestination is not the thing that condemns a man, or puts him in a ruined condition, but the very thing that gets him out of such a state. Predestination concerns not "what" but "whom." It is the great purpose of God to lift a people up from sin and corruption and make them like Jesus Christ. That's glorious! [11]

Apparently Bradley also hesitates to apply predestination to all world conditions—wars, famines, floods, and the like. Instead, he simply applies it to the question of who is to be lifted from the state of original sin, a state which he earlier characterized in the following fashion:

> What do Primitives believe about the fall of man?
> Answer: That Adam willfully transgressed the law of God and therefore plunged himself and his posterity into a state of guilt and corruption (Rom. 5:12–19). That now man in his natural state is dead in trespasses and sins (Eph. 2:1) and is unable to recover himself by an act of his own "free will" (John 1:13; John 6:44; Rom. 3:10–20; Rom. 9:16). [12]

It is, therefore, to the redemptive nature of the Christ figure that Bradley applies the predestination principle:

> Did not Jesus die for the whole human race?
> Answer: No, the scriptures will not support that idea. Jesus said He came into the world to do the will of His Father, and that will was that He should have all who were given Him (the elect) even before the world began (John 6:37–39). Jesus came to save HIS PEOPLE from their sins, and He did it (Matt. 1:21; Rom. 8:33, 34). He died for his sheep, not for goats (John 10:15). . . .
> Do Primitive Baptists deny that Christ died for the world?
> Answer: No, they believe that the world for which He died was the world of His elect. The world of souls for which He died do not have

---

11. Elder Lasserre Bradley, Jr., "What Do Primitive Baptists Believe?" (Cincinnati: Baptist Bible Hour, n.d.), 6–7.

12. Ibid., 5–6.

their trespasses imputed to them and therefore cannot be condemned (2 Cor. 5:18–19).[13]

I have the impression that many contemporary Primitives are mindful of the bitter disputes that developed over "absolute" predestination around the turn of the century, and that they would like to avoid such controversy in the future. The strategy, therefore, may be simply to bypass this issue, concentrating on the doctrine of the elect, for which there is much more general agreement.

There is also general agreement among Primitives on a number of principles less important theologically: that there should be no instrumental music in church; that choirs, quartets, and other special singing groups should not be allowed; that ministers should not be salaried; that congregations should not engage in formal tithing; and that churches should not establish Sunday schools.

The Primitive position concerning Sunday schools is particularly interesting, involving at least four supporting rationales. First, Primitives believe that since God does all the "calling," both to regeneration and to preach or teach, it would be wrong for a church to appoint teachers; that's God's work. Second, although they believe children ought to be raised "in the nurture and admonition of the Lord [Eph. 6:4]," they view this raising as a responsibility of the home. Third, they support Paul's advice that "women keep silence in the churches [1 Cor. 14:34]" and argue that most Sunday schools are taught by females. Finally, they reason simply that Sunday schools are another instrument for evangelism and thus involve people in a role they should not play.[14]

This opposition to evangelism, operating in conjunction with a distrust in an educated ministry and a belief that "the church" is a spiritual body and not a charitable organization, prevents Primitives from organizing to promote church outreach programs such as hospitals, orphanages, educational institutions, and electronic media activities. The result has been a high degree of insularity that influences not only the Primitives themselves but also outsiders' perceptions of this sect. For example, the author has encountered numerous individuals who seemed surprised that Primitive congregations would allow outsiders to visit their churches. In truth, in

13. Ibid., 7–8.
14. Ibid., 11–12.

the present study, these churches were found to be more open to visitors than anticipated.

Church Governance Factors   To a large degree, individual Primitive churches are autonomous religious units, but usually they are tied to associations composed of perhaps a dozen other fellowships in the respective geographical area. The term "usually" is employed here because there are quite a few independent Primitive churches—belonging to no association, but perhaps maintaining correspondence with one or more associations and even attending these associations' annual meetings. For example, at the 1976 session of the Mountain District Primitive Baptist Association, "visitors" were recognized from eight "sister associations" and from twenty independent "sister churches." [15]

These yearly association meetings constitute an important aspect of church governance. They generally last for three days and include a mixture of intense worship and traditional business deliberations. Standard items of business include the seating of delegates (or "messengers") from member churches (and visiting delegates from corresponding associations or from independent churches), the election of the association moderator and clerk, the receiving and consideration of committee reports and recommendations concerning such regular agenda items as arrangements and finance, the consideration of any "queries" concerning doctrinal orthodoxy or church decorum, the passing of resolutions of thanks for services rendered to the association, and the formulation of a memorial statement in honor of all recently deceased members of the affiliated churches, to be published in the minutes along with short obituaries and a photograph of each of the deceased.

In the past, deliberations over doctrines and decorum have elicited the most spirited debate and have, as noted above, occasioned some association splits. During the early 1860s, Primitive associations in eastern Tennessee and northwestern North Carolina were particularly plagued by disputes related to the Civil War. Some associations split at that time because member churches took different sides in that conflict. [16]

15. Mountain District Primitive Baptist Association, *Minutes* (1976), 1–3.
16. Lawrence Edwards, *The Primitive Baptists* (a published version of Edwards' masters thesis [n.p, n.d.], Univ. of Tennessee, May 1940), 51–53.

In recent years, at least to judge by minutes examined for this study, association meetings have been relatively quiet, with only an occasional debate over doctrine or decorum. An example of a contemporary associational deliberation—one which apparently engendered no great controversy—was reported in the 1978 minutes of the Mountain District Primitive Baptist Association. That year this association agreed to reword one of its articles of faith. The article had read: "We believe that the scriptures of the Old and New Testament is [sic] the written word of God and the only rule of faith and practice." The change resulted in the following: "We believe that the scriptures of the Old and New Testament, as translated in 1611 into the King James Version of the Holy Bible, is the written word of God and the only rule of faith and practice."[17]

The discussion of this particular resolution apparently was peaceful. Nevertheless, because heated controversy has occasionally erupted in these meetings, "Rules of Decorum" have been developed to provide a framework for proper debate. One can easily imagine the past improprieties these rules were designed to correct. Consider, for example, the Senter District Primitive Baptist Association decorum rules:

1. The Association shall be opened and closed by prayer.

2. A Moderator and Clerk shall be chosen by the suffrage of the members present.

3. Only one person shall speak at a time, who shall rise from his seat and address the Moderator when he is about to make his speech.

4. The person thus speaking shall not be interrupted in his speech by anyone except the Moderator till he is done speaking.

5. He shall strictly adhere to the subject, and in no way reflect on the person who spoke before, so as to make remarks on his slips, failings or imperfections, but shall fairly state the matter as nearly as he can so as to convey his light or ideas.

6. No person shall abruptly break off or absent himself from the Association without liberty obtained from it.

7. No person shall rise and speak more than three times on one subject without liberty obtained from the Association.

8. No member of the Association shall have liberty of laughing during the sitting of the same, nor whispering in the time of public speech.

17. Mountain District Primitive Baptist Association, *Minutes* (1978), 3–4.

9. No member of the Association shall address another in any other appellation than the title of brother.

10. The Moderator shall not interrupt any member or prohibit him from speaking till he gives his light on the subject except he break the Rules of this Decorum.

11. The names of the several members of the Association shall be enrolled by the Clerk and called over as often as the Association requires.

12. The Moderator shall be entitled to the same privileges of speech as any other member, provided the chair be filled, and he shall not vote unless the Association be equally divided.

13. That any member who shall willingly and knowingly break any of these rules shall be reproved by the Association as they shall think proper.[18]

All of our six groups have such rules of decorum to govern the deliberations of both association sessions and local church meetings. It is easy to see that these various sets of procedural rules go back to some common origin. For example, the rule that forbids mocking or ridiculing a previous speaker (number 5 in the Senter Association rules) can be found in virtually all of these parliamentary documents, often in the same or similar wording.

Historically, individual Primitive churches have been proud of their relative autonomy and watchful to see that their associations do not grow powerful enough to control the local fellowships unduly. Such concerns can be seen in the constitutions instituted to govern various associations. Consider, for example, the third article of the constitution adopted by the Mountain District Primitive Baptist Association: "The members thus chosen and convened shall have no power to lord it over God's heritage, nor shall they have any ecclesiastical power over the churches, nor shall they infringe on any of the internal rights of any church in the union."[19]

Similar clauses are included in the constitutions of the Senter, Mount Zion, and Original Mates Creek Associations, and I presume in the constitutions of numerous other associations. The "internal rights" referred to above include such local church powers as the final right to determine church membership. Ultimately, it is the local church that decides whether or not any individual will be

18. Senter District Primitive Baptist Association, *Minutes* (1978), 11–12.
19. Ibid. (1979), 12.

admitted to formal fellowship in the Primitive Baptist faith, since each church "holds the key" to its membership and uses that key judiciously.

It should be noted that we are dealing with a sensitivity not restricted to Primitive fellowships. Such clauses frequently can be found in the constitutions of Regular, Old Regular, and Union associations. Later in this chapter, we shall see specific evidence of this sensitivity in Union Baptist association deliberations.

How does one become a member of a Primitive church? As in most Protestant fellowships (although it must quickly be added that Primitives do not consider themselves to be Protestants[20]), one initially becomes a member of a local Primitive church by one of two ways. One is either received by expression of faith and baptism, or received by letter. In the latter case, the letter in question would be from another Primitive church in the same association or from a church in another association (or a purely independent Primitive fellowship) with which "correspondence" is maintained. If one association "corresponds" with another association, this means, among other things, that the two recognize each other's doctrinal legitimacy.

One ceases to be a member of a local Primitive church by being dismissed by letter to another church, by dying, or by being "excluded." This exclusion, often referred to in the mountains as being "churched," is an act by which an errant member is literally expelled from fellowship. This may occur simply as a consequence of doctrinal errancy or of a lack of attendance and involvement, but occasionally it may come in response to a lifestyle not acceptable to the membership: frequent drunkenness or overt adultery; lying, cheating, and other forms of social maleficence; blatantly unacceptable dress codes; and even gossiping, backbiting, hypocrisy, and general troublemaking. An examination of recent minutes of the various mountain Primitive associations will reveal that exclusion still is practiced, though perhaps not as liberally as it was in the past. In 1975 five members were excluded from churches in the Mount Zion Association. Between 1976 and 1978, six members were excluded from churches in the Mountain District Association. In 1979 the minutes of the Senter District Association recorded four exclusions,

20. Bradley, "What Do Primitive Baptists Believe?," 13.

while minutes of the 1980 meeting of the Original Mates Creek Association reported twenty-four exclusions in its eighteen churches. Of my collection of Primitive minutes, the most recent set to report exclusions (the 1983 minutes of the Mountain District Association) records three such actions.[21]

Primitive fellowships tend to be more reserved in their religious enthusiasm and passion than are Regular, Old Regular, and Union Baptist fellowships. In both preaching and congregational response, Primitives are less emotional than these other subdenominations. Indeed, a basic solemnity prevails in Primitive worship services, standing in sharp contrast to the joyous crying and shouting of Old Regular services. This is not to say that Primitives never show emotion. The women, particularly, do indeed. However, as we shall see in our discussion of footwashing services, in comparison to these other fellowships Primitive behavior is reserved and solemn.

The Primitives of Southern Appalachia appear to be sharply diminishing in number, if not dying. The most striking impressions the visitor receives when visiting Primitive churches are that their memberships are small and that the members are primarily elderly people. Generally speaking, there is a notable absence of children, teenagers, and young married couples; and the buildings, though modest in size, are only scantily occupied. Furthermore, many Primitive congregations of the region have been reduced to only a handful of members. At the 1985 meeting of the Senter Association, one fellowship (Horse Creek) reported only 5 members, while five other churches (Bear Creek, Beaver Creek, Big Helton, Meadow Fork, and North Fork) claimed memberships of less than 20. The 1983 statistical table for the Mountain District Association also showed one affiliate fellowship (Rook Creek) with only 7 members, and another (Saddle Creek) with only 11 members. In fact, between 1976 and 1983 the Mountain Association as a whole suffered a twenty-eight percent membership loss, dropping from 384 members in eleven churches to 274 in nine churches. Two fellowships (the Cranberry and Bartons Cross Roads affiliates) disbanded for lack of members.[22] It may also be significant that while these Primitives have been losing ground, the nation in general has been experiencing a religious revival.

The Old Regulars

The Old Regular subdenomination can also be traced to the 1820s, specifically to the 1825 formation in Kentucky of the New Salem Association. This New Salem body of churches—in conjunction with the Union Association, founded in 1859—were responsible for the early formulation of the particular set of beliefs and worship practices that we now see in Old Regular fellowships.[23]

This study has brought me into direct contact with several churches in the Union, Sardis, and Old Friendship Associations, and into indirect contact with the Indian Bottom and New Salem Associations.[24] In 1985 the Union Association reported a membership of 3,326 individuals, distributed over sixty-nine churches located between Ypsilanti, Michigan, and Green Cove Springs, Florida, with the major concentration of fellowships in eastern Kentucky and southwestern Virginia.[25] That same year the Sardis Association reported a membership of 1,287 in twenty-nine churches, all but two of them in Kentucky and West Virginia. The two exceptions were both in Florida: Southern Home in Citra and Okeechobee in Okeechobee. In 1985 the New Salem Association claimed 3,090 members in fifty-seven fellowships, and the Old Friendship Association reported ten churches and a membership of 713.[26] Three other associations hold correspondence with one or more of the groups I have already mentioned: Philadelphia, Northern New Salem, and Mud River.[27]

The differences between the doctrines of the Old Regulars and

22. Senter District Primitive Baptist Association, *Minutes* (1985); Mountain District Primitive Baptist Association, *Minutes* (1976) and (1983).

23. Ron Short, "The Old Regular Baptist Church," *Southern Exposure*, 4:3 (1975), 60–65.

24. An elder from one association will frequently visit the services of churches in other associations; consequently, I have met a number of Indian Bottom and New Salem elders.

25. Union Association of Old Regular Baptists, *Minutes* (1985), 26–27.

26. Sardis Association of Old Regular Baptists, *Minutes* (1985), 67; New Salem Association of Old Regular Baptists, *Minutes* (1985), 108–9; and Old Friendship Association of Old Regular Baptists, *Minutes* (1985), 50.

27. New Salem Association of Old Regular Baptists, *Minutes* (1985), 4.

Members Gather after Church to Socialize at Bent Branch Old Regular Baptist Church, Meta, Pike County, Kentucky. Many Old Regular churches have only "Regular" in their names.

the doctrines of the Primitives are not great, but both groups feel strongly about the differences that do exist. Perhaps the best way to compare the beliefs of these two faiths is to examine the articles of faith of two associations.

Mountain District Primitive Baptist Association

1. We believe in only one true and living God, and that there are three persons in the Godhead, the Father, the Son, and the Holy Ghost.

2. We believe that the scriptures

Sardis Association of Old Regular Baptists

1. We believe in only one true and living God, the Father, the Son, and Holy Ghost; and these three are one, equal in power, essence, and glory.

2. We believe the Scriptures of

Communion Sunday at Little Martha Old Regular Baptist Church, Leemaster, Buchanan County, Virginia.

of the Old and New Testament, as translated in 1611 into the King James Version of the Holy Bible, is the written word of God and the only rule of faith and practice.

3. We believe in the doctrine of eternal and particular election.

4. We believe in the doctrine of original sin.

the Old and New Testaments of the Authorized King James Version of the Bible are the written words of God and are the only rules of faith and practice.

3. We believe in the doctrine of election by grace, for by grace are ye saved through faith.

4. We believe in the doctrine of original sin and of man's inability to recover himself from the fallen state he is in by nature, therefore

5. We believe in man's impotency to recover himself from the fallen state he is in by nature of his own free will and ability.

6. We believe that sinners are justified in the sight of God only by the imputed righteousness of Jesus Christ.

7. We believe that God's elect are called, converted, regenerated and sanctified by the Holy Spirit.

8. We believe the saints are preserved in Jesus Christ and called and shall never fall finally away.

9. We believe that baptism and the Lord's Supper are ordinances of Jesus Christ, and that true believers are the only subjects of these ordinances, and that the true mode of baptism is by immersion.

10. We believe in the resurrection of the dead, both of the just and unjust, and a general judgment and the punishment of the wicked will be everlasting and the joys of the righteous will be eternal.

11. We believe that no minister has the right to administer the ordinances only such as are

the Saviour is needed for our redemption.

5. We believe that sinners are called to repentance and believe in the Gospel and regeneration of the soul and sealed with the Holy Spirit of promise, and none shall fall away and be lost.

6. We believe that sinners are justified in the sight of God only by the imputed righteousness of Jesus Christ.

7. We believe that baptism is the ordinance of God's Church on earth and [in] the mode of IMMERSION, back foremost, so as to cover all over.

8. We believe that the Lord's Supper is the command of the Saviour, and that by the use of bread and the fruit of the vine; and feet washing should be kept up until His second coming by His believers.

9. We believe in the resurrection of the dead, both of the just and unjust, and that the joys of the righteous and the punishment of the wicked shall be eternal.

10. We believe that no Minister has the right to administer the ordinances and commands of the Gospel except such as are regularly ordained and baptized, and that by immersion by a legal administrator of the Gospel comes under the hands of a regularly chosen presbytery of the Church.

11. We believe it to be the duty of all Church members to contribute for defraying all

regularly called and come under the imposition of hands by the presbytery, and in fellowship with a church of our faith and order.[28]

reasonable expenses of the Church, never forgetting the poor according to their several abilities.

12. We believe that every doctrine that goes to encourage or indulge people in their sins or cause them to settle down on anything short of saving faith in Christ for salvation is erroneous, and such doctrine will be rejected by us.

13. We believe that the Church of Jesus Christ is a congregation of faithful believers in Christ who have obtained fellowship with the Lord and one another, and have given themselves to the Lord and have agreed to keep up a Godly discipline according to the rules of the Gospel.

14. We believe that Jesus Christ is the Head of the Church and the government thereof is upon His Shoulders.

15. None of the above Articles shall be considered as to hold with particular election and reprobation so as to make God partial, directly or indirectly, nor to injure any of the children of men; nor shall any of these Articles be altered without legal notice and free consent.[29]

It should be obvious that these two sets of articles of faith are in many cases very similar. The one really significant difference lies between Article 3 of the Mountain District Primitive Association and Articles 3 and 15 of the Sardis Association of Old Regulars. The Primitive doctrines uphold "eternal and particular election," while the Old Regular doctrines renounce "particular election," substitut-

28. Mountain District Primitive Baptist Association, *Minutes* (1983), 18–19.
29. Sardis Association of Old Regular Baptists, *Minutes* (1983), 57–58.

ing in its place "election by grace." The words "eternal and particular election" denote the idea that the "elect" have been chosen before the beginning of time as the "particular" individuals who will be redeemed from original sin. As we have already seen, this doctrine holds that the elect are known to God as specific individuals chosen for salvation.[30]

"Election by grace" is a more liberal doctrine. Note the exact wording of Article 15 of the Sardis Association: "None of the above Articles shall be considered as to hold with particular election and reprobation so as to make God partial, directly or indirectly, nor to injure any of the children of men. . . ." By this doctrine God has not chosen either to save or condemn any "particular" person before the event. Instead, salvation through "grace," which anyone may seek, becomes both the process and the end result of election.

Here "grace" is used as an unmerited divine assistance given to people for regeneration and sanctification. According to Old Regular theology, it is God who does the electing for this regeneration and sanctification: individuals may seek "salvation," but it is God who grants it. That is where the "grace" comes in. Indeed, only God, according to this doctrine, can teach the way to this salvation. "The doctrine of Christ is a sacred doctrine," says Elder Edwin May of the Bent Branch Old Regular Church in Meta, Kentucky, "and if there are any here who desire to know the doctrine of Christ, I humbly beg you to ask the Lord to teach you that doctrine."[31]

Old Regulars, therefore, belong squarely within the antimission, nonevangelistic camp of mountain churches. "There is no pressure from church members to stimulate others in the community to join. There are no revivals and no membership drives; no undue influence is brought on family and friends."[32] In addition, there are no Sunday schools, no church-sponsored radio shows, and no other forms of community outreach.

In these respects Old Regular churches are like the Primitive fellowships we have already discussed; nevertheless, there are numerous ways in which the two subdenominations differ. In general, Old Regular fellowships are much more exuberant and impassioned

30. Bradley, "What Do Primitive Baptists Believe?," 6.
31. Sardis Association of Old Regular Baptists, *Minutes* (1983), 14.
32. Short, "The Old Regular Baptist Church," 62.

in all their worship practices than are their reserved cousins, the Primitives, and there are a large number of precise differences in the actual methods of worship. Some of these differences will be examined closely in chapters 4 and 5 when we look at such special services as communions, footwashings, memorials, and union meetings.

Are Old Regulars fairing any better than the Primitives in terms of growth and vitality? They appear to be. Their services have remained viable, in both attendance and emotional energy, with their numbers holding steady or dropping slightly. For example, between 1979 and 1983 the Union Association grew in membership from 3,419 to 3,599, then dropped to 3,506 the next year and the next year to 3,326. The Union Association's statistics on baptisms in recent years also fail to provide a decisive picture of either growth or decline: 1979 (135), 1980 (219), 1981 (175), 1982 (142), 1983 (127), 1984 (122), and 1985 (110). The Sardis Association shows a similar picture. It realized very slight growth between 1982 and 1983, from 1,302 to 1,311, then slid to 1,287 by the 1985 association meeting. Baptisms also experienced a bit of a drop between 1982 and 1985, from 59 to 32.

A number of fellowships in these two associations do appear to be struggling for survival. The 1985 minutes of the Union group, for example, showed that the Hurricane Church of Wise, Virginia, had only seven members, while thirteen other churches claimed memberships of less than twenty. The 1985 minutes of the Sardis group indicated much the same situation: Little Tavie Church of Point Pleasant, West Virginia, reported only fourteen members, and five other fellowships had memberships of less than twenty. Even the larger churches in these two associations claimed memberships ranging only from 100 to 196 in 1985.

Such statistics are misleading, however, if they suggest that attendance at services of these churches is limited to these numbers. Old Regular fellowships (like the Primitives and most Union and Regular Baptists) have regular Sunday services only once a month. The particular Sunday will be set as the Sunday following the first, second, third, or fourth Saturday. Members are encouraged to visit each other's churches and do so quite regularly in the spring, summer, and fall, when mountain roads are usually quite passable.

Consequently, during these good travel periods, a church with a formal membership of only twenty or so may see attendance rise to seventy, eighty, ninety, or even a hundred or more, particularly for special services such as union meetings, memorials, communion, and footwashings. The Bull Creek Old Regular Church of Maxie, Virginia, in 1983 reported a membership of 124; but during this fellowship's memorial service on June 10, 1984, the church was crowded to overflowing with more than four hundred worshipers. Visitors came from Tennessee, Virginia, West Virginia, Kentucky, and probably other states as well. Winter tends to be an almost dormant period for many of the more isolated Old Regular fellowships, so during spring and summer these people really enjoy traveling to each other's services. During the meetings and the dinners-on-the-ground that always follow, new friendships are made, old friendships are continued, and acquaintanceships that may have been interrupted for years are renewed.

A large number of the Old Regular church members are growing old, and while young people are certainly more visible at Old Regular services than at Primitive meetings, there doesn't seem to be that supply of children and teenagers required for substantial longterm growth.

One phenomenon, however, should be considered when examining Old Regular membership and growth. Individuals generally come to membership in the Old Regular faith much later in life than they do in the Missionary Baptist tradition. In the more evangelistic Baptist sects, it is expected that baptism will occur around the age of accountability or soon thereafter; thus young Missionary Baptists will "go down to the water" at twelve to fifteen years of age. It is not unusual for Old Regulars, on the other hand, to be baptized in their forties or fifties. Evidence of this can be seen over and over again in the obituaries published in association minutes. These obituaries generally tell when the individual was baptized and by whom. It is not uncommon for persons to attend an Old Regular church—faithfully or in a "hit or miss" fashion—for years before finally deciding that they have been called to membership. Individuals, then, may pass through the uncertainties and instabilities of young adulthood, and even express some early passions and radical behaviors, before they begin to settle down.

Regular Baptists

It may seem confusing to discuss both "Old Regular" and "Regular" Baptists. Such a division is necessary, however, since a number of churches in the geographical area studied are identified by this second title. I know of three associations of Regular Baptists in the region—Little Valley, Mountain Union, and Little River—but my direct contact has been only with the Little River group of churches.

The Little River Regular Baptist Association is composed of six small churches, five of them in Alleghany and Surry Counties, North Carolina, in the general vicinity of Sparta and Mt. Airy; and the sixth in York County, Pennsylvania. At one time there were eight churches in the group, but Rich Hill and Saddle Mountain (lying close to each other, near the Virginia line in Alleghany County) have since left the association. The Saddle Mountain departure involved a serious split over doctrine which will be examined shortly. In 1982, the membership of the six remaining churches totaled only 361, the largest church having 98 members and the smallest having 32.[33]

Much earlier in the history of all these Baptist subdenominations, Regulars were, in terms of their doctrine, very much like the present-day Primitives. In fact, Regular Baptists once were known also as "Particular" Baptists, since they held to the doctrine of "sovereign, eternal, particular, personal and unconditional election."[34] Today, however, Regulars generally agree with Old Regulars on the doctrine of "election by grace." In other respects, however, they tend to be more evangelistic and slightly more contemporary than Old Regulars. For example, Regular Baptists hold revivals and strongly encourage the establishment of "Sabbath schools."[35] Another difference has to do with the singing practices of the two groups. Old Regulars hold staunchly to the "lined" technique of hymn singing; while Regulars perform more contemporary hymns by more popular gospel-singing methods, including the beat and harmony techniques prevalent at any given moment in the Nashville gospel sound. Regular Baptists, however, still—for the most part—do not allow musical instruments in their formal church services. Infor-

33. Little River Regular Baptist Association, *Minutes* (1982), 13.
34. Taylor, *Early Tennessee Baptists*, 31–35.
35. Little River Regular Baptist Association, *Minutes* (1971), 4. See also the names of the original eight churches, p. 12.

mal "sings" constitute a different situation and may involve guitars, accordions, autoharps, and the like.

The Regular Baptist fellowship with which I have had most contact, the Saddle Mountain Regular Baptist Church, is not a typical one. Led for the last fifty-two years by Elder Royal Glenn Killon, the Saddle Mountain church has developed a set of doctrines and methods of worship that place this church closer to the Missionary Baptists—and, to some degree, to the Free Will Baptists—than to the churches in the Little River Association. In fact, the Little River churches became so concerned about the doctrines and practices of the Saddle Mountain brotherhood that in 1971 they voted to exclude the errant congregation until the fellowship dropped their "present Elders" (mainly Killon) and "set themselves in order." However, the exclusion resolution may have been only an act of reciprocity, since the Saddle Mountain church sent no delegates or letter of correspondence to the 1971 association session.[36]

Apparently the major dispute arose over Killon's freewheeling interpretation of Regular Baptist doctrine, and particularly his very liberal treatment of the communion service. "Elder Glenn" appears to have rejected all remnants of the "elect" doctrine, preaching instead an Arminian, universal-atonement, "free will" theology. In addition, he confounds traditional Regular Baptists by opening his communion services to all "baptized [by any method] Christians." When I visited his communion and footwashing service in August, 1984, he insisted that I participate in the communion, and never asked about my denominational affiliation. In these respects, therefore, Killon is more in line with Free Will Baptists than with orthodox Regular Baptists.

There is also a charismatic and mystical element in Killon's beliefs that is best demonstrated by his account of his own salvation and call to preach. According to Killon, he was "saved" and baptized during a revival at the old Saddle Mountain Church in early September, 1931. Killon relates that the night he was converted there were several other individuals at the altar attempting to "pray through" to regeneration. After being satisfied of his own salvation, he "returned to the altar to pray for others left there." At that moment "a vision was revealed to him of a huge pit with smoke rolling up and going

36. Ibid., 5.

back down. On the edge of this pit was an old man with a cane in his hand just ready to slip down in." At this moment, Killon claims, the first vision disappeared and another took its place, an image "of the book stand [pulpit lectern] at Saddle Mountain Church." Now, according to Elder Killon, God spoke to him and said, "This is your place to warn the people of that awful place of torment."[37]

In February, 1932, Elder Killon was licensed to preach, a preliminary step in the ordination process. That month began his half century of ministry to the Saddle Mountain fellowship. Born on August 25, 1905, Elder Killon is now over eighty years old. He has not been the only elder (ordained preacher) at this church during all this period, for the Regulars—like the Primitives, Old Regulars, and Union Baptists—may have a number of these individuals within one fellowship. Nevertheless, in recent years "Elder Glenn" has been the main force at this church, guiding the congregation in all questions of doctrine, finance, and methods of worship.

Elder Killon's story exemplifies what has often happened in these small mountain churches. A fellowship will come under the long-term influence of a dynamic and perhaps charismatic preacher whose strong feelings about doctrine and worship procedures result in a slow pulling away from orthodoxy, perhaps by steps that are wholly unintentional. Indeed, the congregation may not even realize that it has slipped into "heresy" until called to task by other fellowships in the association. One result of this process is that there are numerous independent churches throughout these mountains whose doctrines or behaviors differ from those of their progenitor traditions, although they may have kept the respective denominational name (Regular, Old Regular, etc.). Perhaps a similar process explains, at least partially, why there are so many subdenominations of Baptists in these mountains in the first place.

Evidently this problem was more pronounced years ago when individual churches were more isolated than they are today. Extended periods elapsed between visits of the associaton's moderator or elders from other churches. In the interims, fellowships occasionally went astray in matters of doctrine or worship methods. Old

37. Quotations from the printed program for a special memorial service held at Saddle Mountain Regular Baptist Church, 29 July 1984. The service celebrated Killon's 52 years of leadership at the church.

Regular groups apparently had so much trouble of this sort that they mandated "union services" to be conducted by each church in the association. At these annual events, the object was to hear the preaching of several visiting elders, with the purpose of watching for doctrinal irregularities.

The Original Mates Creek Regular Primitive Baptist Association also holds union services. I mention this group because its name suggests that it lies halfway in between the Regulars and the Primitives. However, its minutes show it to hold correspondence only with Primitive fellowships, and its articles of faith (particularly the one treating the doctrine of election) place it squarely in the Primitive theological camp.

The eighteen churches of the Original Mates Creek Regular Primitive Association are located for the most part in eastern Kentucky and western Virginia, with two fellowships in Ohio, one in Michigan, and one in Indiana. The 1980 minutes of this association reported a total membership of 1,264, slightly down from its 1976 count of 1,301.[38]

Union Baptists

During the years immediately prior to the Civil War, Baptists of eastern Tennessee and northwestern North Carolina were frequently torn by disputes over slavery and related issues that divided the nation at the time.[39] These disputes, of course, also rent the larger population of Baptist fellowships, with the result that the Southern Baptist Convention was formed in 1845 from promissionary Baptist churches supportive of the Southern cause. The internecine quarrels were particularly intense in the mountains of North Carolina, Tennessee, and Virginia, where pockets of strong Unionist support existed. In Ashe County, North Carolina, the Unionist-Rebel split was so intense that the discord divided many area churches and ultimately resulted in the formation of a new mountain Baptist subdenomination, the Union Baptists. This group is not to be confused with the United Baptists, who were moderately strong in the 1800s and who still maintain some churches in eastern Kentucky.

---

38. Original Mates Creek Regular Primitive Baptist Association, *Minutes* (1976) and *Minutes* (1980).

39. Edwards, *The Primitive Baptists*, 51–53.

The particular quarrel that led to the birth of the Union Baptist sect erupted in 1858 at the annual meeting of the Senter Primitive Baptist Association, held that year at the Silas Creek Church in Ashe County. Since the Silas Creek fellowship sympathized strongly with the Unionist position on slavery, the association's deliberations soon moved to issues related to the growing national dispute.[40] There was no split in the Senter Association that year, but seeds of discontent were planted that were nurtured during the war itself. It wasn't until 1867, however, that the Mountain Union Association was founded. This was the first Union Baptist association and was composed of fellowships that had been pro-Union during the war.[41]

There are now four associations functioning in the geographical area touched by my study that apparently are Union in affiliation: the Mountain Union Association, the Union Baptist Association, the Primitive (Union) Baptist Association, and the Friendship (Union) Association. I have had direct contact only with churches in the first two of these groups, whose affiliate fellowships exist primarily in Ashe and Alleghany Counties, North Carolina, and in Grayson County, Virginia. These congregations long ago forgot the ideological disputes that precipitated the formation of their subdenomination. They know only that they differ from some other Baptist groups on certain theological and behavioral issues.

The two other associations with whom I have not had contact, Primitive and Friendship, may not think of themselves as Union Baptists. Although they hold correspondence with Union and Mountain Union, they call themselves Regular Baptists. So we have one association named "Primitive," that corresponds with two "Union" associations but calls its churches "Regular."

In terms of both doctrine and worship practices, the Union Baptists are very much like Regular Baptists. They are less Calvinistic and more evangelical than the Primitives and Old Regulars; they promote Sunday schools in their churches; they hold revivals, though mostly to benefit their members rather than to increase the fold; they occasionally sponsor radio broadcasts, thus engaging to some degree in community outreach; they hold to the doctrine of

40. J.F. Fletcher, *A History of the Ashe County, North Carolina and New River, Virginia Baptist Association* (Raleigh, N.C.: Commercial Printing, 1935), 30.
41. Ibid., 31–34.

Silas Creek Union Baptist Church Today, Ashe County, North Carolina.

election by grace; and they are generally more open to outsiders than are the Primitives and Old Regulars.

Even more than the Regulars, Union Baptists tolerate a wide range of diversity in their churches. The Union Baptist Association, for example, contains two churches that stand only a couple of miles from each other in Alleghany County, and which differ considerably in worship habits. In terms of building style and the worship practices employed inside, the Landmark Church is very traditional, while the Whitehead Church is much more contemporary. The Landmark Church is very plain externally, white and wood-framed, while inside it possesses chestnut plank pews that have been in the church for decades and unadorned interior walls of the original tongue-and-groove hardwood planking. Unfortunately, the members have painted both the walls and the pews, rather than leaving their original natural tones.

Another indication of the tolerance of this subdenomination is the considerable association between Union Baptists and other Baptist groups of northwest North Carolina and southwest Virginia, particularly the Regular Baptists in Alleghany and Wilkes Counties, North Carolina. Members of Union and Regular fellowships often attend each other's services and occasionally share preachers. Dan Edwards of Sparta, North Carolina, is one of the elders at Whitehead Union Baptist, but he also preaches for a Regular Baptist fellowship in the vicinity.[42] Furthermore, the obituaries published in the 1983 minutes of the Union Baptist Association give frequent indication of crossover attendance and shared or cooperating ministers, not only between Union and Regular churches but also between Unions and Primitives, Unions and Missionary Baptists, and even in one instance between a Union fellowship and a United Methodist fellowship.[43] Such interdenominational relations would not be tolerated by Old Regulars, who exclude preachers who share pulpits with ministers from other Baptist groups.

Union associations hesitate to demand complete conformity among member churches either in precise interpretation of doctrine or in worship practices. This hesitation was exemplified at the forty-sixth annual session of the Union Baptist Association, when the Resolutions Committee put forth a series of resolutions they hoped the association would adopt, including one statement calling for the use of only the King James Version of the Bible in all worship services. The committee prefaced their resolutions, however, with the following statement:

> We believe in every Church having the God-given right to sustain or not to sustain and to hold their own keys, therefore these Resolutions

42. Interview with Elder Dan Edwards, Whitehead Union Baptist Church, 15 Jan. 1984.
43. Union Baptist Association, *Minutes* (1983), 18, 19, 20, 23, 29, 30, 33, 35.

are not binding on the Sister Churches in Our Union, because according to our Constitution the Association has no right to Lord it over God's heritage, or infringe over the internal right of any Church, therefore we are submitting the following which we feel is good advice to the Churches.[44]

I mentioned earlier in this chapter that when one divides all these small Baptist subdenominations into missionary or antimissionary camps, Union Baptists fall with the antimissionary group. That's somewhat of an oversimplification, for Union Baptists are not so much antimissionary as they are nonmissionary. Their associations are small, a dozen or so churches with memberships ranging from 25 to 150; and they are formally connected to other associations only through that loosely structured relationship of being in correspondence, which means little more than that they generally accept each other's doctrines and worship practices. One result of this small size and disjointed character is that Union Baptists don't have the sophistication of structure needed for the establishment of home or foreign missions, or of schools, hospitals, and orphanages.

The worship practices of Union Baptists tend to be just as spirited and emotional as those of Old Regulars and Regulars. There is not the stern, almost cold solemnity that one occasionally finds among the Primitives. Most of the Union fellowships still do not use musical instruments in their regular Sunday services, but they do occasionally employ them in their special singing services. The actual singing tends to be a mixture of very traditional and more modern Nashville-sound gospel music, but there are no choirs, quartets, or other special singing groups. All singing is strictly congregational, except on those occasions when a single individual decides to testify by song.

This practice of using singing as a form of personal testimony is prevalent in all these mountain Baptist sects, with the possible exception of the Primitives. During moments of intense emotional fervor, individuals may choose to communicate their joy by breaking into a solo rendition of some old hymn. During footwashings, for example, it is not unusual for one or more individuals to roam among the celebrants testifying by song. Other worshipers may join them, but no-one feels obliged to do so. The individual in question is

44. Ibid., 6.

simply making her or his own statement, but making it in song. Such scenes occur often in Regular, Old Regular, and Union worship, and occasionally in Missionary services. One qualification: in the case of Old Regulars, only men do the solo singing.

Union Baptist fellowships have preserved a small remnant of the old practice of lining hymns, a hymnody technique already mentioned as the primary singing method employed in Old Regular services. Union congregations usually sing one hymn by the lined method just prior to communion, a once-a-year event. This custom of reserving the "old-time way" exclusively for the communion service is not limited to Union Baptists, as I have witnessed the same practice in communion services at Saddle Mountain Regular Baptist Church and at Little River Primitive Baptist.

In the lining method, a song leader (always one of the elders) stands before the congregation with a words-only hymnal and speaks the lines of a given hymn, usually one couplet at a time. After he says each couplet, the congregation then sings the words. Members of the congregation have no words or music before them and depend on their prior knowledge of the melody. In Old Regular worship services, the liner chants a highly compressed tune, and the congregation follows with a very slow, stretched-out, almost wailed rendition of the same words and melody. However, in all of the Union, Regular, and Primitive services I have attended in which this method was used, the liner did not sing or chant the couplets, but simply read them in a slightly more rapid pace than normal. The method was very useful in early Southern Appalachian churches, where congregations had no hymnals or couldn't read them when they were available.

Free Will Baptists
Apparently Welsh in origin, the theology that undergirds the beliefs and practices of Southern Appalachian Free Will Baptist fellowships was brought to the American colonies at the very beginning of the eighteenth century and nourished in an area of Pennsylvania known as the "Welsh Tract." One authority contends that the church was organized in the South in 1727 and in the North in 1780.[45] The volume that seems to stand as the authorized his-

45. Frank S. Mead, *Handbook of Denominations*, 42.

Dunham Free Will Baptist Church, Dunham, Letcher County, Kentucky.

tory of the Northern branch of this subdenomination, *History of the Freewill Baptist: A Study in New England Separatism*, credits the 1780 efforts of Benjamin Randall in New Hampshire with the official origin of the faith.[46] Other authorities place the Free

46. Norman Allen Baxter, *History of the Freewill Baptists: A Study in New England Separatism* (Rochester, N.Y.: American Baptist Historical Society, 1957), 25.

Will movement in eastern North Carolina, under the leadership of Paul Palmer, some time before the middle of the eighteenth century.[47] The establishment of this fellowship in the mountains of North Carolina, Tennessee, and Virginia apparently can be traced to the creation of the Toe River Association of Free Will Baptists, on November 15, 1850, at Jack's Creek Church in Yancey County, North Carolina.[48] In 1911 the northern branch of the subdenomination united with the American Baptist Convention,[49] while many of the southern Free Will churches have been organized into the National Association of Free Will Baptists, with offices in Nashville, Tennessee. Not all of the mountain Free Will fellowships, however, belong to this group. For example, the John-Thomas Association of Freewill Baptists contains ninety-nine churches in Virginia, Kentucky, Ohio, and Indiana. These John-Thomas churches held their fifty-ninth annual meeting in Coeburn, Virginia, in 1981, and there reported a membership of 7,483.[50] Although this subdenomination spells its name two ways, I have chosen to use "Free Will" rather than "Freewill," unless the latter spelling is used by a specific church or association.

As their name implies, Free Will Baptists believe in a doctrine of atonement not constricted by any election theology. They think that the opportunity for "redemption" is available to all who exercise free will to believe and practice the Christian faith, and that the Gospel call is universal, open to all persons in all cultures. As a result, these churches generally have been committed to both home and foreign mission work, with only a few of the independent mountain fellowships in the past showing an influence of the antimission and anti–Sunday school sentiments.[51] Commitment to missionary doctrine, however, does not necessarily mean participation, since many of these fellowships are small and independent, and lack the broader organizational ties needed for broad missionary efforts.

47. Elmer T. Clark, *Small Sects in America* (Nashville: Abingdon Press, 1965), 204; and Paul Woolsey, *God, a Hundred Years, and a Free Will Baptist Family* (Chuckey, Tenn.: Union Free Will Baptist Association, 1949), 4.
48. Woolsey, *God*, 165, 193.
49. Baxter, *History of the Freewill Baptists*, 153–82; and John A. Hardon, *The Protestant Churches of America* (Garden City, N.J.: Image Books, 1969), 63.
50. John-Thomas Association of Freewill Baptists, *Minutes* (1981), 37.
51. Woolsey, *God*, 165, 193.

In mountain Free Will churches—and apparently in many of the rural and more traditional southern Free Will fellowships— footwashing is mandated as an extension of the "Lord's Supper" service. These congregations consider footwashing to be a "Gospel ordinance," in the same sense that they view baptism as an ordinance. As is the case with the other subdenominations we have been discussing, Free Will Baptists view an ordinance as a practice instituted by God via the acts of Christ or one of his disciples. The practice, therefore, is to be kept alive because it has been ordained by one or more divine precedents. A statement adopted in 1916 by the North Carolina state conference of Free Will Baptists, as part of the articles of faith for that branch of the church, still stands as the official position of many of the mountain Free Will fellowships on ordinances: "We believe, as touching Gospel Ordinances, in believers' baptism, laying on of the hands, receiving of the sacrament in bread and wine, washing the saints' feet, anointing the sick with oil in the name of the Lord, fasting, prayer, singing praise to God and the public ministry of the Word, with every institution of the Lord we shall find in the New Testament."[52]

The ordinance of "anointing the sick with oil," which these churches faithfully follow, is justified by James 5:14: "Is any sick among you? Let him call for the elders of the church; and let them pray over him, anointing him with oil in the name of the Lord." Laying on of the hands—applicable to Free Will ceremonies for both ordination and baptism—is explained by Acts 8:17 and Acts 19:6: "Then laid they [Peter and John] their hands on them, and they received the Holy Ghost"; and "when Paul had laid his hands upon them, the Holy Ghost came on them; and they spake with tongues, and prophesied." As justification for the footwashing ordinance, Free Will Baptists turn to John 13:4–17, the only Gospel account of Christ's washing the feet of his disciples. Mark 16:15 becomes the scriptural basis of the "public ministry" ordinance: "And he said unto them, Go ye into all the world, and preach the gospel to every creature." Free Will and Missionary Baptists wonder how the Primitives and other antimissionary sects miss this verse. Darvin Marshall, my original contact with the Old Regular fellowships,

52. *Church Discipline of the Free Will Baptists* (Ayden, N.C.: Free Will Baptist Press, 1930), 8.

answers this argument by charging that although Christ instructed his disciples to go "into all the world," he did not tell them "to appoint others to do the same."[53] Nevertheless, the command, "Go ye into all the world," is used by Free Will Baptists to justify not only foreign missions but also home evangelism, including the revival.

Mountain Free Will Baptists have spirited revivals, but while Missionary Baptists "hold" or "schedule" these events, Free Will Baptists "experience" them. The Missionary fellowship will plan one or two revivals annually, placing the event on the church calendar long in advance. It is common for Missionary Baptist fellowships in northwest North Carolina to have two revivals a year, in the spring or early summer and the other in the fall. This means that the congregation will have a revival, ready or not.

Free Will Baptists, on the other hand, do not feel that a revival can be planned. I first learned this one Sunday in 1983 when I was visiting the South Side Free Will Baptist Church in Mountain City, Tennessee. After the service I talked to the minister, Rev. Roland McClellan, and asked him when their next revival would be, thinking that I might want to attend one or more of the sessions. McClellan's answer was that he did not know when the event would occur but that the congregation had been praying for a revival and had recently begun to feel one to be imminent. These Free Will fellowships believe a revival should just break out as a natural consequence of a growing spiritual intensity that a church might be experiencing. Such spontaneous outpourings of the spirit, of course, cannot be planned.

In several other respects Free Will worship practices are similar to those one might encounter in the numerous small independent Missionary Baptist churches of the region. Both these subdenominations encourage the establishment of Sunday schools. Both generally have abandoned a more traditional hymnody in favor of a contemporary gospel sound, although mountain congregations in each group frequently employ the old shaped-note hymnals. The preachers in both sects, as we shall see in the next chapter, have developed delivery styles that are very similar, if not identical. Finally, both have preserved several traditional services or ceremonies, such as footwashings, creek baptisms, decoration days or memorial ser-

53. Letter to the author from Darvin Marshall, 18 Aug. 1985.

vices, and homecomings—the types of ceremonies that have been kept alive by many rural Baptist churches throughout the South.

Missionary Baptists

Frank S. Mead's *Handbook of Denominations in the United States* lists twenty-seven subdenominations of Baptists; *The Protestant Churches of America*, by John A. Hardon, mentions twenty-three distinct Baptist groups; and Elmer T. Clark's *Small Sects in America* briefly discusses sixteen of the lesser-known Baptist divisions. But none of these volumes acknowledges the existence of a faction known as Missionary Baptists.[54] Nevertheless, in the mountains of North Carolina, Tennessee, and Virginia—and elsewhere—there are multitudes of small independent Baptist fellowships that identify themselves by this term. Only occasionally do they have the word "Missionary" in their posted names—Mount Paran Baptist, Mountain View Baptist, Bethany Baptist, Mount Ephraim Baptist, Rock View Baptist—but if we ask these congregations what kind of Baptists they are, they tell us, in their attempt to distinguish themselves from Primitives, Regulars, Old Regulars, Union Baptists, and so on, that they are "Missionary Baptists."

This type of mountain Baptist church is a small independent fellowship—independent at least in the sense that it is not affiliated with the Southern Baptist Convention. It believes in an evangelistic mission, and in the past probably separated from a more Calvinist antimission association. Indeed, the fellowship may possess a spotty affiliation history, perhaps having originated as a member of an association that split during the controversies over election and predestination. Then this church may have gone through periods of total independence, alternating with periods of association with churches of like character.

The Mount Paran fellowship, mentioned in the introduction, is a good example of this type of church. The church was founded by a group that split from Stoney Fork Baptist Church because the mother church had become too modern. For decades Mount Paran existed as an independent, traditional Missionary Baptist fellowship. Then the church affiliated with the Three Forks Baptist

54. Mead, *Handbook of Denominations*, 31–51; Hardon, *Protestant Churches*, 42–69; and Clark, *Small Sects*, 196–208.

Association, a group of Watauga County, North Carolina, congregations who belong to the Southern Baptist Convention. After several years in this relationship, however, Mount Paran again became disenchanted with the growing modernism of the Three Forks Association churches and the entire Southern Baptist Convention. As a result, Mount Paran has returned to independent status, calling herself a Missionary Baptist church.

The term "Missionary Baptist" of course originated in that period in the 1820s and 1830s when numerous Baptist churches and associations did split over the issue of missionary societies. Many promission churches affiliated with the Southern Baptist Convention when it was formed in 1845, but a significant number of Southern Appalachian congregations remained either totally independent or only associated with other small promission churches.

In some instances a church is referred to as Missionary Baptist by its older members, while its younger members speak of themselves as Southern Baptists. What has happened, of course, is that while the church began as Missionary Baptist, later it joined an association affiliated with the Southern Baptist Convention. The oldtimers in the congregation then held to the original name.

In summer 1983 I attended the homecoming of such a church, Proffit's Grove Baptist in the Meat Camp community of Watauga County. During the "dinner on the ground" that followed the morning service I interviewed a retired preacher, Rev. Carl Triplett, who had served as the church's minister back in the early 1940s. At one point in our conversation Triplett referred to the Proffit's Grove fellowship as being Missionary Baptist. Later that afternoon I was talking to a younger current member of the church and mentioned something about the institution's being Missionary Baptist. "No," said the individual, "we're Southern Baptist." The Proffit's Grove church is a Southern Baptist affiliate and a member of the Three Forks Association. But the 1982 minutes of this association reveal that Proffit's Grove originally was instituted as a Missionary Baptist fellowship.[55]

If a church does belong to the Southern Baptist Convention I do not consider it as falling into the genre being discussed in this section. These Missionary Baptist churches of the Appalachian re-

55. Three Forks Baptist Association, *Annual* (1982), 35.

gion are traditional "old-time-way" churches that preserve practices (such as footwashings, creek baptisms, some old-way singing styles, and numerous other ways of worship) rooted in the nineteenth century. Occasionally the church is so small that it shares a minister with one or two other congregations, with the result that some Sundays are devoted only to Sunday school. These fellowships do not pay their ministers much, if anything. A few of the smaller and more traditional congregations use the "love offering" method of pastoral support, occasionally taking up special collections for the preacher and his family. Even in this practice, however, Missionary fellowships differ sharply from Old Regulars, whose preachers refuse all monetary offerings except when in dire circumstances.

The title "Missionary Baptist" has lost its original meaning to a large degree, since these small independent churches are not extensively involved in mission work, particularly with foreign missions. They do not have the funds and organizational structures needed to carry out such large-scale evangelistic projects. They nevertheless differ from the Primitives in the sense that they believe fervently in the duty of the individual church to "spread the gospel," to "save souls," to evangelize. This belief translates into sponsorship of locally-produced evangelistic radio broadcasts, support for revivalism, some active proselytism, and a host of other activities in which the object is to win converts.

The beliefs of these Missionary Baptist churches are not as liberal theologically as those of the Free Will Baptists, particularly with regard to baptism and communion. They also are not as liberal as the typical Southern Baptist church, with regard to everything from social issues and national politics to worship practices. These Missionary congregations, for example, demand the use of the King James Version of the Bible; take staunchly conservative stances on such issues as alcohol sales, abortion, prayer in the public schools, and sex education; challenge the value and/or legitimacy of indoor baptisteries, robed choirs, seminary educated ministers, and women preachers; and hold tenaciously to those practices that they believe to be Gospel ordinances, such as footwashing.

Furthermore, there is a decided difference in emotional spirit between the services of these Southern Appalachian Missionary Baptists and those of the typical Southern Baptist congregation. The latter will often appear very reserved, even stilted, compared with the exuberant vocal and physical displays that typify many Missionary services. Missionary Baptist congregations take great joy in their faith and generally are not at all reserved in communicating that joy. Responsive shouting occasionally undergirds and intensifies the preaching. There is joyous crying during footwashings, flower services, and the like; and frequent embraces, handshakes, and other forms of warm tactile contact. And impassioned singing plays a vital role in all of the meetings of this subdenomination.

The Role of These Churches in Mountain Communities

One Sunday morning during Roscoe Greene's "Morning Star Gospel Program" on station WATA in Boone, I went on the air and asked listeners to contact me with stories indicating how important that program had been to them over the last thirty-five years.

One call I received in response to my request came from an elderly gentleman who lives in the Triplett community, an area of Watauga County just south of U.S. Highway 421 between Boone and Deep Gap. This gentleman wanted to tell me about "Preacher Ros's" broadcast, but he also wanted to talk generally about the mountain religious practices of an earlier time.

The caller's very picturesque and vivid verbal imagery conjured up scenes of days when mountain communities had little in the way of inspiration and entertainment other than religious services. He spoke of the social as well as the religious aspects of these church activities and told how church fellowships or pastors often became arbiters of community quarrels as well as of intracongregational disputes.

One of the caller's stories dealt with a method used to build attendance during summer revivals. The small congregation would gather and begin to sing, with windows thrown open so the sounds could float over the valley. The preacher would urge the gathering to "sing them in." The result, claimed the caller, would be a steady trickle of late arrivals, as holdbacks at home caught the faint but joyous evangelistic swells of song, augmented later in the evening by impassioned preaching and equally impassioned congregational responses. By the third or fourth night of the revival, this lodestone effect had built the congregation of saved, or would-be saved, from the initial handful to a church-bulging crowd of worshipers who now added their own voices to the call. In this way revivals occasionally grew into movements that lasted far longer than anticipated.

This caller's observations illustrate the social and religious influence these churches once had, and to a large degree still have, over mountain communities. A retired Baptist preacher of Zionville, North Carolina, Brother Roby Eggers ("Uncle Roby" to his close friends) talked about mountain revivals of the past during an interview in spring 1974. Eggers had remarked that these revivals would just break out at times and take over an entire community. In fact, one of the dangers of this kind of happening was that people would get so caught up in the whole affair that they would stop working at their regular jobs.

One night after a revival service, Preacher Eggers recalled, he had lingered in the church talking to a few members of the fellowship, when someone came into the sanctuary and said that a certain brother down the road appeared to need help. He had been in church during the service but on his way home had collapsed in a ditch in a state of considerable emotional upheaval.

Eggers immediately left the church to check out the situation and did indeed find the man lying in the ditch praying and crying. The preacher assumed that the man's needs were purely spiritual and proceeded to minister to him in that vein. It turned out, however, that what was agitating the emotionally torn brother was a situation that had developed between him and his neighbor—in fact, between their respective families.

Apparently the families had lived side by side in relative peace for years, but recently there had been a rupture in the relationship due to a dispute over land, a road, or the behavior of some farm animals. The gentleman in the ditch was experiencing deep remorse for the role he had played in the situation, and he wanted Eggers to go with him immediately to visit the neighbor. That night Preacher Eggers walked with the distraught man up to the neighbor's house and initiated a purgative confrontation that eventually involved both families. The session extended into the early hours of the morning, but eventually all was settled amicably.[56]

56. Videotaped interview with Rev. Roby Eggers, Zionville, N.C., 12 Apr. 1974;

This story suggests the role these mountain churches and their pastors occasionally play in mediating purely social interpersonal conflicts. "I try to help them live together as well as worship together," Roscoe Greene once told me. "They've got their problems that I can sometimes help them negotiate."

In the past, mountain religious fellowships frequently played quasi-judicial roles, settling disputes that otherwise might have involved the civil or criminal justice system. That the churches were instrumental in setting standards of acceptable behavior for their members is evident from the early minutes of many of these churches.

Cove Creek Baptist Church in Sugar Grove, North Carolina, for example, was founded in 1799 and was originally affiliated with the Mountain Association, a forebear of numerous Baptist fellowships in the northwestern counties of North Carolina. However, this church later split from the Mountain Association during the mission-antimission controversies, and in 1841 it became one of the charter members of the Three Forks Association, then and now a promission group. At present the church is a fairly large, semirural fellowship affiliated with the Southern Baptist Convention.[57]

Minutes of the Cove Creek church document the case of Emsey Gragg. It was July 1863, and Brother Gragg was absent without leave from the Confederate Army, having come home to put in a crop since his family had been "suffering for the want of something to live on." The fact of Gragg's desertion, however, was brought before the fellowship, and a delegation of members was appointed to check the situation. The committee did just that and reported to the membership that Gragg's wife had earlier written to her husband the news of the family's destitution. In turn, the young Confederate soldier had come home to see what he could do.

Deliberations on this case took place over a four-month period. In October 1863, Emsey Gragg appeared before the fellowship, acknowledged his desertion, and promised to return to his regiment just as soon as he could do so without harm to his family. The congregation apparently was satisfied with this statement and closed

housed in the Appalachian Collection, Belk Library, Appalachian State Univ., Boone, N.C.

57. "History of Cove Creek Baptist Church, 1799–1974," mimeographed (Cove Creek Baptist Church, 1974), 7.

the deliberations, taking no action against Brother Gragg.[58] He was not, therefore, excluded from the fellowship, and the fact that there was no further mention of the incident suggests that he did return to his military duty.

Some of the issues or situations deliberated by early Cove Creek fellowships seem humorous today, but they were discussed, no doubt, with great seriousness. Brother William Whitlow was brought before a monthly business meeting to explain why he had taken another brother's mare and tied her in the woods, but when Whitlow explained that this had been the only way he could keep the animal out of his corn the church decided not to exclude him. Brother Archibald Macalray appeared at a meeting and brought a charge against himself "for getting very drunk and behaving very much out of character." The church accepted the charge and waited three months for Macalray to repent and request forgiveness for the offense. When no statement of repentance or request for forgiveness was forthcoming, the fellowship voted to exclude Macalray on the grounds of his own self-indictment.

One brother brought a charge against his own mother-in-law, and the committee appointed to investigate was unable to bring about a reconciliation between the two. Shortly thereafter, the man moved away, without a letter of dismissal from the church, leaving his mother-in-law behind. For this offense, and because the man's wife had left an unpaid bill at a local store, the church voted to exclude the brother.

One young couple found themselves in trouble with the congregation because it was alleged that they played "cat-ball" on Sunday. This apparently was a double offense, since the game was frowned upon when played together by members of both sexes, and since it was not the sort of thing one did under any circumstances on Sunday. Cited for their misdoing, the two were admonished to appear at the next month's business meeting to justify their behavior. However, before this meeting occurred, the two were married, an act that apparently alleviated the pressure on them for their previous conduct. One month later, nevertheless, the two were excluded for "neglect and folly."[59]

58. Ibid., 10.
59. Ibid., 6. These stories come from church minutes of the 1800s.

The preceding stories, with the possible exception of the charge of drunkenness, represent situations that probably would not be deliberated at meetings of contemporary mountain Baptist churches, but other issues enliven business sessions of local churches and annual association gatherings today—issues that relate to behavioral standards for both church and community. Consider, for example, three questions deliberated at the 1983 session of the Sardis Association of Old Regular Baptists.

The first question was originally introduced in 1975 by the Dix Fork fellowship: "Does the Sardis Association believe in Sisters wearing pants, slacks or shorts?" In 1983 a motion was passed to have the response to that original query reprinted in the new session's minutes. The issue apparently had been broached again on the local level, perhaps by one of the more conservative fellowships, and the association was taking this action to remind all member churches what had been decided before. However, the 1975 association action really had dodged the issue by tossing the matter back to the individual fellowships. This had been done by referring the query to a special advisory council, which in turn had produced the following statement:

Brethren:
In answer to the Query from the Dix Fork Church asking "Does the Sardis Association believe in Sisters wearing pants, slacks or shorts?" We, as an Advisory Council and not as a law-making body, say:

To answer this Query in the affirmative would be interpreted by some Brethren too liberally and they would say we have laid down the gate and opened the doors to anything and everything.

To answer this Query in the negative would be interpreted by some Brethren too strictly and they would say we have shut the door on everything and Committees would flow from Church to Church like water.

We believe the Sardis Association should advise the Churches to advise their members—both Brethren and Sisters—to dress soberly and modestly and to conduct themselves in a manner that becometh a Child of God. We believe that each Child of God will adorn themselves in such a manner that they can easily be identified from the World. We feel the Bible, the infallible Word of God, sets forth and the Spirit will teach us how we should dress and conduct ourselves.

We believe, and the Association has so stated in the past, that each Church in the Sardis Association holds the key to its own door and is the sole judge of the conduct of its members as long as they follow the

Association Meeting, Union Association of Old Regular Baptists, Wise, Wise County, Virginia, Elder John Layne Moderating.

orthodox principles of religion and keep up a Godly discipline according to the rules of the Gospel as laid down in the Scriptures. In fact, Article 3 of our Constitution guarantees that the Association shall not infringe on any internal right of the Churches.

> Elder Wayne Herald
> Brother Ralph W. E. Varney, Jr.
> Brother James M. Ray[60]

By refusing to be definitive on the question, the advisory council may have avoided a church-splitting controversy, but it also may

60. Sardis Association of Old Regular Baptists, *Minutes* (1983), 8–9.

have kept the issue alive. Debate on the matter must have continued; otherwise, why would there have been a need to reprint the statement eight years later?

The same issue was debated in 1979 at the annual meeting of the Union Association of Old Regular Baptists. That year a request for a dress code was presented by the Little Martha Church of Leemaster, Virginia:

> We the Little Martha Church of Old Regular Baptists of Jesus Christ met at our regular session. . . . After being fully discussed and by a move and second, . . . we send a request to the Union Association not to allow Sisters to wear pants or pantsuits. We ask them to be as our Sisters of Old, only to be worn as for safety, or if they are working on a job that require them to be worn. Even at this they should be worn loose not in a way to show their bodies in an ungodly manner.
>
> We also ask that the Brothers and Sisters not to wear Bathing suits or shorts for any reason, also ask the Brothers not to wear their hair long enough that it might be an offense to another Brother or Sister.
>
> We are asking that all Moderators advise their Churches that if any Brother or Sister is guilty of the above that they be advised to stop such practice and if they refuse to do so that they be excluded, until such time that they have stopped such practice, then the Church from which they were excluded may restore them to full fellowship.
>
> We the Little Martha Church is sending this request not to tear the Churches apart, but to try to unite them into full fellowship with each other to be united as one.
>
> Signed by Order of the Church
> Elder John C. Layne, Moderator,
> Elder Russell Hicks, Assistant Moderator,
> Brother Hufford Coleman, Clerk[61]

The next issue considered by the 1983 session of the Sardis Association again dealt with the decorum of sisters in the respective churches. The question arose as to whether these sisters should be allowed to have short haircuts. Here the answer from the assembled delegates was fairly precise: "The Association, by regular move and second, said that if a Sister has cut her hair, she should be asked to let it grow out; if she fails to do so and cuts her hair again, she will be excluded."[62]

61. Union Association of Old Regular Baptists, *Minutes* (1979), 6.
62. Sardis Association of Old Regular Baptists, *Minutes* (1983), 9.

The third area of debate was how member churches of the Sardis Association should treat individuals who are divorced and remarried. This discussion centered around three separate motions, the first of which read as follows: "By motion and second it is ordered that we advise our Ministers of our Association not to marry people into adultery, where either man or woman has a living wife or husband."

The next two motions arose out of a query advanced by the Rebecca fellowship: "In the receiving of members having more than one living companion, does the criteria of receiving the innocent party also apply to the receiving of members by other than baptism (restoration, recommendation, letter)?" The association's answer:

> On regular move and second, the word "receive" . . . is defined to include "any means of receiving members."
>
> In answer to the question, "Shall we receive into fellowship men or women having more than one wife or husband?" The Association by regular move and second said, "We advise the Churches not to receive into their fellowship any such, except those who have put away their companion for the cause of fornication, such cases to have Gospel or Church evidence of the same."[63]

With these three motions, the Sardis Association of Old Regulars created a policy on divorce and remarriage that appears to say the following: "We frown upon remarriage after divorce and advise our ministers not to perform such marriages; but should there already have been a remarriage for the innocent party of a divorce (the individual who put away her or his partner for reason of fornication), we advise our churches to receive that individual into membership 'by any means of receiving members.'"

Many readers will view these pronouncements by the Sardis Association and the Little Martha Church—particularly those treating the dress and hairstyles of women members—as unduly confining and tyrannical. Nevertheless, these actions represent attempts to establish acceptable codes of behavior for church members, and all codes of behavior—whether for church members, high school students, employees, or corporate executives—are potentially tyrannical. Unfortunately, women of the Sardis Association cannot be

63. Ibid.

delegates to the various sessions and therefore never can vote on the resolutions that restrict their behaviors.

One aspect of the social influence of Southern Appalachian churches seems, at least on its surface, very healthy. Perhaps because these fellowships have been plagued in the past by spiritually and temporally damaging splits, congregations and preachers have been cognizant of the need to mend small rifts between individuals or factions within the church community before they grow to damaging proportions. Later we shall see how some of the major services, particularly the footwashing ceremony, provide opportunity for conflict resolution. But in a majority of these mountain churches (with the possible exception of the Primitive fellowships) males and females alike tend to do a great deal of warm and friendly—even loving—touching. The beginnings and endings of services, and frequently moments during the meeting, are marked by emotional hugs, handshakes, and kisses. In Holiness churches of the region, males kiss each other on the lips (the "Holy kiss"), but in the fellowships covered by this study, males usually confine themselves to warm bear hugs and handshakes, with an occasional cheek-to-cheek embrace. Accompanying tears or joyous laughter intensify both male and female exchanges.

The emotional expressiveness characteristic of Southern Appalachian Baptist worship services stands out sharply for visitors accustomed to the greater formality of the typical Protestant or Catholic church. In spring 1980, Appalachian State University sponsored the Appalachian Studies Honors Semester, an academic program hosting honors students from all over the United States. I took a class to several local revival meetings. In the group was a young Lutheran lady from the upper Midwest. Coming back to the campus one night after attending the revival at Boone Fork Baptist, a small Southern Baptist church south of Boone, this student wanted to talk about the behavior of the men of this church. She had never seen men so publicly emotional and tactile, and she confessed that she had found the experience somewhat unsettling.

I wonder how the student might have reacted had she observed an even more emotional church service such as a footwashing at Silas Creek Union Baptist or Saddle Mountain Regular Baptist, a Memorial Service at Bull Creek Old Regular Baptist, or a Flower

Service at Mount Paran (Missionary) Baptist. At each of these events both men and women, in states of great joy, move throughout the congregation embracing fellow communicants with little or no reserve of enthusiasm, sometimes singing, sometimes shouting, and sometimes testifying. During sermons at these churches preachers move out into the congregations, shaking hands as they go or throwing their arms around brothers and fellow elders. And at the close of these services comes a final outpouring of emotion, as worshipers circulate for one last round of embraces.

A striking example of this mountain religious emotionality happened at that same 1980 service at Boone Fork Baptist Church. My student group had attended three of the revival services that week at the Boone Fork church to hear the preaching of Brother Pete Tester, then the minister of Howard's Creek Baptist in the Meat Camp area of Watauga County. The attendance for Tester's sermons had been steady but relatively sparse, and during the evenings we were there, no-one had responded to the preacher's altar calls. On this last night, therefore, Tester changed his tactics and employed a somewhat different final plea. He said he sometimes preached revivals at churches where no-one needed to be "saved," because all of them already were. Nevertheless, he argued that there wasn't any church that did not need some kind of revival of loving fellowship. He suggested that at Boone Fork there were certain to be some members who had fallen out with each other and needed a reconciliation. Tester then said that instead of the usual altar call he would be asking these individuals or couples to take this opportunity to reach out to each other, to ask forgiveness if necessary, and to become reunited in spirit and brotherly love.

The pianist played the customary "Just As I Am," and Tester waited for something to happen. During that first verse of the hymn, nothing did. And, in spite of the minister's renewed invitation to action, nothing happened during the second verse. Then the congregation began to sing the third verse: "Just as I am, tho' tossed about, with many a conflict, many a doubt, fightings and fears within, without, O Lamb of God, I come! I come!" At this, one couple arose from their pew down front and moved toward a second couple near the back of the church. The crying began before the couples met, and it continued as the four embraced and, I assume, asked forgiveness for wrongs of which I knew nothing. What I did know was that these people were being reconciled, and I had the feeling that my student group was witnessing a reconciliation that had been long in coming. Then, the ice broken, other couples and individuals met in a like spirit, and the service ended on this very emotional note.

CHAPTER 2

Hanging Their Toes
in the Heavens

When I moved to the mountains of North Carolina, it was the pulpit prowess of Brother Roscoe Greene that first stimulated my interest in Southern Appalachian religious practices, and since that first introduction to this preaching art, I have never lost my fascination with the colorful performances of mountain exhorters. In the summer of 1973 I thought I had found the prototype of the Southern Appalachian sermon style in Brother Greene's pulpit artistry. Later I realized that although Greene's rhythmical style had much in common with other indigenous pulpit delivery forms, it was only one of several broad variations within the genre: and that, in fact, no two preaching styles are exactly alike. Every visit to a Southern Appalachian worship service allows me to hear more preaching. Even when traveling through Appalachia on Sunday mornings, perhaps on my way to some church in Virginia, Tennessee, or Kentucky, I check the offerings available on my car radio, always listening for that preacher who will give a new twist to the basic style.

This chapter examines preaching styles and methods, while the next chapter focuses on content. First, a general view of the southern mountaineer's customary mode of homiletic delivery is presented. Next, several style variations and techniques are examined. And the chapter closes with a look at the preacher himself.

In discussions such as this, there is always a danger of generalizing too much. Thus the reader is cautioned not to take any of my descriptions as absolute or universal in the region. Mountain sermons are the creations of individuals who add their own flourishes to the basic art form. Furthermore, some aspects of preaching style tend to characterize one subdenomination but not another. The prototypical delivery mode I am about to describe is found more frequently among Missionary, Free Will, and Regular Baptists than among Primitive, Union, and Old Regular Baptists. There is, however, such a mixing of styles within these groups that you can find the delivery variations of one subdenomination used by preachers of any of the other five subdenominations.

The Archetypal Southern Appalachian Sermon Style

Intensely emotional, extremely rhythmical, and highly physical, the typical Southern Appalachian Baptist sermon pours out in furious volleys of rhetoric that build, hold for ten or twelve minutes on high plateaus of exuberance, subside, and then build again, over and over. Extending from forty-five minutes to two hours in length, this prototypical sermon is delivered with a passion that demands all the energy a preacher can muster. This fervor engenders in many mountain congregations a type of responsive behavior seldom seen outside of rural black churches.

In general, these Southern Appalachian Baptist preachers begin their sermons slowly. They may say a few words about the joys of the day—the blessings they and their congregations have received "at the hands of the Lord." They may issue a special welcome to someone present who has been ill or just away from the fellowship for a while. Indeed, these preachers may talk about anything of a spiritual or congregational nature as they gradually warm to the occasion.

If they are Old Regulars, they may perfunctorily apologize for the fact that the moderator chose them to speak, suggesting that other brethren might have much more to say. Indeed, these Old Regular elders may spend two or three minutes complaining that they do not as yet have the spirit, stating bluntly that they are not at all confident that they will find any message to deliver.

Preachers from all six of the subdenominations frequently ask congregations to pray that they might "find the Lord's voice," and occasionally they denigrate both their speaking abilities and their spiritual worthiness, suggesting that if anything of value comes from their messages, it should be credited solely to God.

These typical sermons are impromptu; the speakers use no notes or prepared texts. In fact, most of these preachers do not formulate, ahead of time, any theme around which a sermon will be developed. "I believe," states Darvin Marshall, "that most [Old] Regular Baptist preachers will say that they do not think of what they will say next, and I have heard some say that they have little or no knowledge of what they have said during their preaching. If they are present with the Lord in spirit, they are absent from the body."

"I don't prepare," says Roscoe Greene, "because if God is with me I don't need to. If God isn't with me, I shouldn't be up there." [1]

The central assumption behind this impromptu style appears to be that complete preparation precludes any on-the-spot inspiration by God. A corollary to this premise is that to have spoken well isn't to the preacher's glory, but "to the Lord's." Likewise, if on a particular occasion the exhorter's eloquence falters and his sermon does not rise to inspirational heights, it is because on that day God chose not to use this man. The speaker tried; he made himself available; but the inscrutable deity opted to work in another way. The critical question becomes: did the preacher, on that occasion, earnestly seek to do God's will, to be his instrument; or did this temporal, fallible, sin-cursed man allow his vanity, his own self-will, to intervene? To exhort well is to be with God; not to exhort well is to be absent from God. No wonder these preachers worry when they hit a temporary slump in inspiration: they believe that God has abandoned them.

Beginning these sermons, preachers struggle to get the spiritual fire started. Sometimes they employ scripture readings to start their ascensions, cautiously testing voice, tempo, and "spirit." This is often the roughest part of an Appalachian preacher's performance, since he tends not to be a good reader. He may stumble over words, misplace emphases, and confuse meanings. In addition, he frequently seems uncertain of where he will end, glancing ahead once or twice to see what thought the next verse might introduce. Nevertheless, he generally reads with fervor and conviction, even when he misreads. Polished fluency can sometimes be sacrificed; intensity, passion, earnest zeal are essential. The young preacher just developing his oratorical skills is usually willing to forfeit fluency

1. Letter to the author from Darvin Marshall, 18 Aug. 1985. Roscoe Greene statement from an informal conversation between author and Greene, 21 Nov. 1975.

and a degree of intelligibility for speed and rhythm, knowing that speed and rhythm are associated with "spirit." His congregation will pardon a lack of verbal skills but not a lack of zeal.

Not all of these preachers, however, employ scripture readings as foundations of their messages. Union, Old Regular, and some Regular elders just start speaking, slowly meandering their way into a theme, integrating memorized Bible passages as they go. In this initial building process, the elder who is preaching is prone to play off the encouraging responses of other elders sitting behind or beside the "stand." These churchmen cheer on their brother with "Amens'" and similar exclamations, stoking his fire, helping him catch the spirit.[2]

Frequently Old Regulars will warm up for exhortation not by talking but by singing. On these occasions the elder in question will move slowly to the pulpit, thumb meditatively through the pages of a song book, and then begin to sing in a solo performance without any instrumental accompaniment, that serves not only as a transition to reverence, but also as an inspiration to eloquence. Having completed his hymn, this preacher will then allow the moment to deepen into a quiet, subdued mood, a mood that he will violate only slightly as he begins to speak, keeping his voice low, almost inaudible. From this level the exhorter will begin gradually to increase his volume and intensity until he finally finds his stride in those impassioned, rhythmical, and highly physical exhortations that will occupy him for the next thirty to sixty minutes.

Occasionally there's a false start or two as a preacher attempts to move from his scripture, or from any other preliminary speaking or singing, to the more rapid rhythmical delivery of the main body of his sermon. At these moments he may subside, fumble awkwardly in search of inspiration, read another verse or two of scripture, talk briefly to one or two brethren, then catch the spirit and begin his ascent once more.

By the time this spirit and the homiletic theme have developed— usually three to five minutes into the sermon—the preacher's delivery will have accelerated in pace, volume, and intensity until it

2. In reference solely to Old Regular preaching, Darvin Marshall stated: "None of the Old Regulars would agree that they could help anyone catch the spirit. They are only agreeing with his statement or showing an agreement with his usage of the scripture." Letter to the author, 18 Aug. 1985.

reaches a climactic plateau from which the speaker can climb no further. The physical limits of his voice and the mental constraints imposed by impromptu speech at such speed usually hold him at this plateau. He may drop down to rest or to gain inspiration, but for the most part here he will remain, "hanging his toes in the heavens"—an expression I once heard a preacher use to describe these moments of peak exuberance. Meanwhile, his congregation capitulates to the fervor of his delivery, responding with "Amen" after "Amen."

Now speaking at rates often exceeding two hundred words per minute, intoning his message in staccato bursts of rhetoric similar to the irregular lines of unrhymed verse, with an occasional phrase that rises like an auctioneer's chant and approaches song, the preacher pours out such a torrent of words that at the end of each linear segment he emits a sharp "huuh" or "haah," as he quickly exhales and inhales preparatory for his next flow of rhetoric. This "huuh" or "haah" constitutes the dominant beat of his rhythm and is usually thought of as the hallmark of the Southern Appalachian sermon style.

The explosive "haah," followed by a quick, silent or gasping inhalation, does not always come at the close of a regularly constituted sentence. Instead, it breaks the overall content into short, rhythmic lines that only occasionally coincide with what would be the natural punctuation of the preacher's sentences. The effect is a hypnotic rhythm that tends to dominate content, with congregations, like audiences at rock concerts, responding more to beat than to lyrics.

In addition to its effect upon preacher and congregation, this choppy, rhythmic style of delivery allows preachers to speak rapidly while meeting the physical and mental demands of their sermons. By breaking their rhetoric into short, staccato sentence segments, the preachers systematically provide times for both breathing and thinking. Air intake is forced into patterns that coincide with the rhythmic flow of words. Thus the preacher avoids the awkward straining for air that otherwise might accompany the completion of long sentences. In addition, these brief breaks, in which exhorters quickly exhale their remaining air and inhale fresh oxygen, provide vital seconds for thought about what is coming next.

An energetic physical delivery style usually accompanies and accentuates the vocal rhythm. Often this style includes swinging

Preaching at Sandy Ridge Old Regular Baptist Church, Wise County, Virginia. Author in pew at left. Photograph: Joel Poteat.

movements of the arms, forceful strokes of the hands, springing strides or toe jumps, slapping of hands or thighs, and thrusting forward the upper torso while crouching, with one or both arms stretched out to the side, to the front, or above the head. In such cases the dominant physical action often coincides with a "haah," "huuh," or shout, and thus reinforces the beat.

One physical feature of the delivery frequently seen is this: the preacher cups his right hand lightly over his right ear, or places the fingers of that hand slightly below that ear, and rocks forward in rhythm with the beat. At such times the speaker may appear to have closed his eyes and to be rhythmically moving and speaking in a trance-like state. Indeed, the preacher seems entranced by his own

Preaching at an Outdoor Memorial Service, Lonesome Dove Old Regular Baptist Church, Canada, Pike County, Kentucky.

sound—hearing it, feeling it, savoring it, as if enclosed in a system of reciprocally responding stimuli.

Nevertheless, he is not in a closed system, since the congregation also feels and responds to his rhythm. Its response is manifested both vocally and physically. With "Amen," "Praise God," "Bless him" and other such exclamations, and with movements that tend to complement those of the preacher, the audience provides a kind of counter-rhythm. In Old Regular, Regular, and Union services the responses come primarily from fellow elders, from deacons sitting in the male membership pews, and from a few older females who become notable for their "shouting and praising." "Shouting" is a rising, high-pitched, wailing "holler" that usually brings the woman in question to her feet, arms thrown high above her head, hands bent sharply back at the wrists, palms thrust toward heaven, fingers apart and slightly curled. The body sways with forceful jerks; the head is forced backward in a neck-straining, eyes-toward-heaven position; and the hands are occasionally pulled quickly downward for two or three loud claps, before being thrown skyward again. "Praising" is generally accompanied by the same set of physical behaviors, but now one or two exclamatory phrases replace the shouts: "Oh what a sweet Jesus we have!" or "Oh children, I'm going home!"

One of the most dramatic events that can be observed in Old Regular churches is the phenomenon of an elder using his histrionics literally to orchestrate the crying jubilations of a group of rejoicing women, as he nurtures their passionate, soaring outcries and builds them into a crescendo of sound and spirit. Furthermore, these high-pitched "Holy Ghost" exclamations have their own power to energize or enthrall, electrifying congregations into ardent reciprocal responses or mesmerizing them into rapture.

Old Regular men do not engage in "shouting," except when preaching, but they do contribute substantially to the intensity and to the actual rhetoric of sermons, by calling out full-sentence responses to the preaching elder's declarations, often completing his biblical quotations or briefly extending his arguments. Such interventions result in a spirited, fast-paced, loud dialogue between the main speaker and several other elders or deacons who are clustered near the "stand." This dialogue can build to the point that one has the sense of hearing a group-delivered sermon.

In Missionary, Union, and Free Will churches there may be shouters, but the congregational responses are more commonly short verbal exclamations—"Amen," "Praise God," "Bless him, Lord," and the like—that originate primarily from males, build in intensity with the sermon, and fall at the end of individual lines in the preacher's rhythmic pattern. Audience responses in the Primitive churches I have visited typically are more subdued, giving the service an aura of puritannical reserve.

Sermons are generally divided into several cycles, each composed of one of those slow-paced, struggling, talk-to-the-congregation starts, followed by a rapid rise to an intense, rhythmic, fast-paced, "hanging-toes-in-the-heavens" plateau. Once there, the preacher remains on this plateau until he has exhausted his energy, his inspiration, and/or his ideas and has to descend for a breather. During these brief breaks before another rise starts, the speaker will relax his physical movements, keep talking slowly, perhaps take out a handkerchief and wipe his brow or the back of his neck, catch his breath, move back to the pulpit and fumble with the Bible as if looking for insight in other scriptures, sometimes talk directly to a church member or another preacher, and just generally await the spark that ignites another explosion of high-plateau rhetoric. A complete sermon may include five or six of such cycles.

Variations in the Basic Pattern

First Variation

There are at least four distinct variations in the rhythmic style just discussed. The first of these, though the least complicated, is certainly not the least spirited. The sermon's rhetoric is broken into the standard short, staccato sentence fragments, each segment ending with the quick exhaling-inhaling process that produces the "haah" or "huuh" sound. But here no lines are chanted or sung. The delivery is fast, forceful, and fervid, placing great demands upon the exhorter's vocal prowess. Of the four variations, this tends to be the most rapid in number of words emitted, but occasionally it lacks the aesthetic qualities present in our second and third delivery modes.

This first style is popular among mountain Missionary and Free Will Baptists, and among some Regular and Union Baptists. It is not prevalent in Old Regular circles. A number of Southern Appalachian Primitive preachers employ it, but generally they do so with less fire and passion than is found in Missionary preaching.

Although the least complicated of the four variations, this style is far from easy to master with any degree of polish; for one must get the rhythm going and keep it consistent, while both speaking extemporaneously and controlling the flow of words and oxygen exactly. If too little fresh air comes in, one needs oxygen; if too much is taken in, one hyperventilates.

In this fastest-paced of the variations, a highly adept practitioner of this oral art form can, at peak moments, keep rhetoric flowing at between 200 and 230 words per minute without loss of fluency or train of thought. And he can maintain his speed and rhythm without having to back up frequently and start over, and without working himself into sentence structures that have no way of being completed. Of course the rhetoric is highly colloquial; however, it is reasonably fluent within that linguistic framework.

Use of the pronoun "him" in the discussions of these mountain Baptist preachers does not imply that the author is sexist. In fact, all preachers in these six subdenominations are male, and these fellowships view with considerable disdain any movement to place females in the pulpit. Holiness churches in these mountains have some female preachers, but none of these Baptist subdenominations has followed their lead.

One of the best of the pulpit artists employing this first style is Roscoe Greene, pastor of Mount Paran (Missionary) Baptist Church at Deep Gap, North Carolina. In top form Greene is a master of his style, captivating mountain congregations with sermons appreciated for both sound and substance. Although now in his late sixties, Greene has maintained a passion and energy seldom topped by preachers in this first category.

The passage to come, an example of this first rhetorical style, came at the close of one of Greene's high-plateau segments, one which had peaked at a delivery speed of approximately 225 words per minute. At the very end of this sermon segment, Greene dropped from that plateau, slowing his pace and reducing his volume, and prepared to talk very quietly to his congregation for a moment before beginning another climb.

Keep in mind three things. First, Greene's physical delivery keeps him seldom behind his pulpit; rather, he moves out toward his congregation with surging strides punctuated by occasional foot-stamping or quick jumps and by abundant dramatic arm and hand movements. Second, his vocal style is loud, vibrant, and impassioned. And third, he delivers a vocal "punch" at the end of each linear segment with his quick exhalation and inhalation. In the passages quoted in this chapter, "haah" at the end of each line indicates where this punch occurred.

> Now, brethren, one time (haah)
> I was hoping to get saved. (haah)
> Now, brethren, (haah)
> I'm not trying to get saved. (haah)
> But I have a hope (haah)

that one day (haah)
the Lord Jesus will descend from heaven, (haah)
and with a shout (haah)
will void the dark kingdom. (haah)
And with the trump' of God, (haah)
the dead in Christ will rise first. (haah)
And then we who are allowed to remain (haah)
shall be called together (haah)
and will be told (haah)
how to meet the Lord in the air. (haah)
And so shall (haah—dropping down)
we go to be with the Lord. (coming all the way down)[3]

Given the impromptu nature of these messages, the preacher must maintain his rhythmic form while composing the sermon as he goes. The accomplished mountain preacher is able to sustain his rhythm even when integrating scripture into his sermons or when shifting from one unit of thought to another. In fact, once the speaker reaches a high plateau, everything runs together as if it were one continuous long thought. The more fluent preachers do seem to order their expressions so that the rhythmically emphasized line breaks occur where commas, periods, question marks, or other punctuation would fall, but that is not necessarily the case. Especially noteworthy is the fact that once the rhythm is established, all of the preacher's rhetoric flows in a relatively unbroken stream, at least until he slows the pace and comes down from his very intense "hanging their toes" segment.

When the preacher begins an ascent, he moves to his elevated level very quickly. Once he reaches that lofty plateau he generally just "hangs" there without any major variations in rhythm, tempo, or volume. Then he descends as quickly as he ascended. Greene, however, will occasionally break his high-plateau pattern with an abrupt shout or two. At these times he does a quick little jump, followed by a movement toward or away from his congregation. These moments tend to be points of peak exuberance.

In addition to this fast-paced rhythmic style and the accompa-

3. Recorded 21 Nov. 1975, at Mount Paran Baptist Church, Deep Gap, N.C. Unless otherwise noted, all sermon passages in this chapter and in ch. 3 are taken from audiotapes or videotapes housed in the Appalachian Collection, Belk Library, Appalachian State Univ.

nying physical dynamics, Greene's sermons are also notable for their intense emotionalism, their colorful linguistic forms, and their traditionalism in dogma and values. These characteristics will be examined, at least indirectly, in the next chapter.

Second Variation

The passage cited next illustrates the second oral style to be discussed. The sermon segment in question was delivered by Elder Earl Sexton of the Silas Creek Union Baptist Church, located near the town of Lansing in Ashe County, North Carolina. Silas Creek, affiliated with the Mountain Union Association, is one of the original churches that formed the Union Baptist subdenomination.

Elder Sexton has served for a number of years as the Mountain Union Association's moderator. Now in his middle to late sixties, like Roscoe Greene he has maintained a high level of physical exuberance and natural eloquence.

In this second sermonic mode, as in the first one, the preacher breaks his rhetoric into short staccato lines, each ended with "haah" or "huuh." But he also intersperses lines that quaver or warble on the opening sound, rise rapidly in modulation immediately thereafter, and then alternately fall and rise in a definite singing pattern. The words on which the ascensions are made are stretched out so that the preacher's voice slides upward as he proclaims that term and then glides downward. Some lines peak twice in this process, and some peak only once.

In this delivery mode there are ear-pleasing flourishes that sound like the more tuneful and melodious moments of a tobacco auctioneer's chant, particularly those closing chant lines when the auctioneer announces a sale by allowing his voice to soar quavering upward before floating downward in an elongated glide. These tend to be the lines of the auctioneer's peak passion, and he invariably accompanies them with body movements of appropriate zeal.

The preacher may speak for some time without adding one of these lines of rising inflection, and then he might interject several in the course of a brief period. The result is a rhythmic style more varied in both tone and meter than the previous variation, and one which produces sounds that often can be described as psalmody. This mode, which can be very pleasing to the ear, is popular among

Union and Regular Baptist fellowships and also can be found in the
pulpit artistry of some Missionary and Free Will preachers.

In this passage from Elder Sexton's sermon, the height of emotion
came near the end of the excerpt, when the preacher began to let
his voice soar on the chanted lines.

> But thank God that light (haah)
> has shined down into our hearts, (haah)
> that guiding morning star (haah)
> that Jesus said He was (haah)
> there in the Book of Revelations. (haah)
> Read that "I am the bright and Morning Star." (haah)
> And again He said, "To him that overcometh (haah)
> will I give the Morning Star." (haah)
> Thank God for that Morning Star today! (haah)
> We read of wearied and down, (haah)
> in a world of darkness. (haah)
> And things are getting darker every day. (haah)
> But praise God this morning, (haah)
> amid all this darkness, (haah)
> any child of God (with rising inflection and warbled on "any")
> that can see the Morning Star (haah)
> because it's a-shining in your heart . . . (haah)
> But thank God this morning (haah)
> the Morning Star is shining. (haah)
> And we come on up to the time (haah)
> when Jesus built the church here in the world. (haah)
> He went away for a period of time. (haah)
> He's not come back yet. (haah)
> But He's coming one of these days. (haah)
> He told the disciples when He gathered them there, (haah)
> just before He went to the Father. (haah)
> He said, "Let not your heart be troubled. (rising inflection and warbled
>   on "let")
> Ye believe in God. (with rising and falling inflection)
> Believe also in me. (with rising and falling inflection)
> In my Father's house there are many mansions. (haah)
> If it were not so I would have told you. (haah)
> I go and prepare a place for you. (with rising and falling inflection)
> And if I go I come again (rising inflection and warbled on "And")
> and receive you unto myself, (haah)

that where I am (haah)
there you may be also." (haah)[4]

Twice in this Sexton passage, slight shifts were made in the rhetoric's direction: first with the line, "We read of wearied and down"; and next with "And we come on up to the time." When these shifts occurred, there were absolutely no changes in the pacing, no pauses to denote new directions of thought. In other words, all of the sentences were run together in one continuous rhythmic chain of sounds.

Moreover, at the close of the above sample of rhetoric, when Sexton quoted John 14:1–3, he did so without altering the rhythmic pattern he had created. The fact that this biblical passage was not read, but was produced from memory, illustrates not only the impressive ability of many of these preachers to remember extensive segments of scripture but also their skill at quickly plucking these passages from their mental storehouses for extemporaneous employment in the momentary rhetorical flow.

Elder Sexton does not use very loud "haah" or "huuh" sounds. The rhythm is there, and the breathing pattern is present, but the audible "punch" at the end of each linear segment is more subdued than Roscoe Greene's explosive "haah." While in Greene's delivery this explosive "haah" is the main histrionic feature, the rising-inflection line, with its extended warble on the beginning word, is the main histrionic feature in Sexton's style. In this mode the preacher seems always to be moving toward that sung line, even readying his body for the accompanying surge of physical activity. The soaring sound constitutes a high point of passion and is generally accentuated by an appropriately strong movement of the arms and/or upper torso and head.

Third Variation
The third variation of this rhythmic style moves the preacher even more into a singing mode. In this "singing style," the preacher again breaks the general flow of speech into short segments that accommodate the regularity of his breathing. The big difference, however,

4. Recorded 17 July 1977, in the studios of WKSK, West Jefferson, N.C. The excerpt was taken from Sexton's radio broadcast that morning. I am indebted to Richard Humphrey for this tape.

is that the typical Roscoe Greene line—fast-paced and dominated by the explosive "haah" or "huuh"—is subdued, replaced in vocal emphasis, emotion, aesthetics, and general importance by a slower line that derives its charm from an exhilarating rising and falling cadence decorated by quick modulated slides and by warbles, trills, and quavers, all accentuated by sudden increases or decreases in volume. While Greene's style is rapid-fire, forceful, pounding, explosive, this singing style is smoother, lyrical, more melodious.

Now the preacher adds entire sermon segments that are virtually sung or at least chanted in a manner somewhat similar to the way a priest intones the litany of a high mass. The "haah" sound might still be present (see below), but the focal characteristic, the one that marks the preacher's performance at his moments of highest exuberance, is the singing.

Preachers who adopt this mode tend to develop their own styles in the pattern followed for rising or falling lines. For example, one speaker might utilize a line format that opens on an ascending inflection, peaks in the middle, and closes on a descent. Others might employ two basic line patterns, one which steadily rises in inflection, and one which steadily falls, with both including internal trills, warbles, or quavers.

The first example given here builds primarily on an inflection pattern that rises at the beginning, peaks in the middle, and falls at the end. Elder Danny Miller, of the Union Baptist subdenomination, is the speaker, and this passage was extracted from a prayer Miller delivered during Elder Earl Sexton's regular Sunday morning radio program. Sexton's program, a thirty-minute broadcast over station WKSK of West Jefferson, North Carolina, has become a tradition in Ashe County and will be discussed in more detail in a later chapter of this volume.

A brief segment of this prayer will show how the rhetoric was divided for the basic breathing pattern and suggest at least an impression of Miller's chanting inflection. The "haah" sounds are noted, but the reader needs to envision a vocal punch that is much more subdued than that present in Roscoe Greene's style.

Oh God, we see, Lord, (haah—rising sharply on "Oh God," and then falling)
so many, Lord, who're afflicted, (haah—rising to peak on "Lord")

so many down and out, (haah—rising to peak on the second syllable of
  "many," then falling)
so many, God, that (haah—rising to peak on "God")
have this body (haah—rising to peak on "body")
and infirmities in it. (haah—steadily falling)
Oh God, we ought to lift up holy hands (haah—rising sharply on "Oh
  God," falling, then rising again on "holy")
and thank you, God, that your grace (haah)
has been sufficient, Lord, (haah)
to bring us safe thus far and will (haah)
take us all away. (haah)[5]

Upon closer examination of any of these lines, we discover that
the complicated inflection patterns enrich the basic rhythmic style
and establish not only a distinct chanting or singing mode but also
a set form for emotional expression. For example, in the part of
Miller's prayer from which I extracted the lines quoted above, six
lines began with "Oh God," each of them opening on an initial high
pitch only to rise quickly in additional pitch, intensity, and volume
before falling in an elongated slide that fused the impassioned salu-
tation with the remainder of the chanted line.

Of all the phrases in the prayer, these "Oh Gods" received by far
the most energy, emphasis, and intense feeling, with Miller stretching his body upward as the words soared, lifting the corporal self as
he lifted his voice, attempting to push himself and his appeals into
greater proximity with the deity.

Since the patterns of rising and falling inflections vary from practitioner to practitioner, let us examine another example of this style
category. This passage is from a sermon delivered by Elder Ward
Brooks, to the Whitehead Union Baptist Church in the Pine Swamp
community of Alleghany County, North Carolina. Brooks' preaching mode serves as a bridge between the singing patterns of Danny
Miller and the "spiritual-holler" of the fourth style to be discussed
next.

Brooks is one of six elders who serve the Whitehead church, and
on this particular morning the congregation was distraught over the
fact that another elder, Jimmy Joines, had suffered a serious heart

5. Recorded 24 July 1983.

attack the day before. Brooks did not know if his fellow elder would survive.

As Brooks warms to an occasion, he first moves into a pattern dominated primarily by an elongated slide on the closing word of each line. The main direction of these slides is upward, but occasionally there will be lines that slide downward in inflection. Then at the peak of his exuberance, Brooks moves into a delivery mode in which he takes the beginning word of a line, lifts it up, and stretches it out into a prolonged and passionate "holler."

The following passage was delivered at an early moment in Brooks's sermon. He had just begun to build in intensity when he spoke the following lines. No "haah" is included at the close of each line, because that sound does not exist in Brooks's vocalizations.

If the Lord was (building in intensity)
to call him out
of this life tonight, (sliding up on "tonight")
or today, (sliding down on "today")
there wouldn't be (building again)
no point
in mourning for him.
He's gone on, (sliding up on "on")
his troubles are over. (sliding up on "over")
His sorrows (sliding up on "sorrows")
and his heartaches, (sliding up on "heartaches")
they're all past. (sliding up on "past")
They're gone. (sliding up on "gone," with special emphasis)
Then he's gone to sleep (sliding down)
in the arms
of the crucified redeemer.
But, brother, right now's (sliding up on "now's")
the time we can weep. (sliding up on "weep")
We can mourn. (sliding up on "mourn")
We can ask God to help him. (sliding up on "him")
While he's alive (sliding down)
and has his being here,
I hope that
the Lord will bless him
to come back
and preach for us.
We don't know. (sliding up on "know")

> Oh, but we can ask God (sliding up on "God")
> to reach down (sliding up on "down")
> from his eternal throne (sliding up on "throne")
> in glory (sliding down)
> to bless him
> and to keep him
> down here in this world.
> I don't want you to weep
> for me
> when I'm gone. (sliding up on "gone")
> When I'm gone (sliding up on "gone")
> it won't do any good. (sliding up on "good," with emphasis)
> But while I'm here (sliding up on "here")
> I'd like for you (sliding up on "you")
> to ask God (sliding down)
> to help me along
> in this life.[6]

As illustrated by this passage, Brooks breaks his rhetoric into very short lines. He makes up for his abbreviated content, however, by the elongated closing slides. The result is a delivery that is full of sound but is actually slower than the style employed by Roscoe Greene. At his most rapid, Brooks emits only about 190 words per minute, while Greene averages around 200 and occasionally speaks much more quickly. In addition, Brooks's delivery was slowed by a sad-sounding, lamenting tonal quality—the "Methodist whine" found in preaching styles of rural Louisiana Methodist preachers I heard as a child.

Brooks's style follows a rising and falling inflection pattern much different from the one that dominates Danny Miller's delivery. A typical line in Miller's delivery either opens with an elevated inflection and falls to the end, or opens on a low inflection, rises to the middle, and falls at the end. But a typical line from Brooks's sermon has two ascensions, one at the middle and one at the end. In addition, Brooks frequently links a number of lines together, with each successive linear unit ascending higher than the previous one in crescendo fashion, gaining intensity as Brooks increases his passion and pitch. Then he may follow this sequence with several lines that close with descending slides, gradually diminishing the intensity.

6. Recorded 15 Jan. 1984, at Whitehead Union Baptist Church.

Now let us examine a sequence a little later in Brooks's sermon. By the time he delivered this passage he had reached a very high level of emotionalism; motivated by this depth of feeling, he employed two special-intensity couplets that built on spiritual "hollers."

> One of these days
> God's gonna call. (rising on "call")
> The hand of death (rising on "death")
> is gonna reach down (rising on "down")
> into your home. (falling on "home")
> If the death angel
> has not come your way,
> well, one of these days (an elongated holler on "well")
> it's gonna come your way. (rising on "come" and "way")
> It's gonna call
> somebody out of your midst.
> And if you're here without God, (rising on "God")
> and without a hope today, (rising on "today")
> that's the time (an elongated holler on "that's")
> when the spirit of the Lord (rising on "spirit" and "Lord")
> moves in your life. (falling on "life")
> Now's the time to get ready
> for that day.
> You know,
> if you never make that preparation,
> you'll never get there. (rising on "there.")

These extended rising-inflection endings create the impression of a *wail*. Each dramatic wail is accompanied by an equally dramatic physical movement, usually a graphic posturing with the head thrown back and the arms stretched out to the sides, or a quick, forceful, and deep genuflect, with head up, eyes closed, and one hand thrust high and forward. At these moments Brooks's face is flooded with an expression of intense, earnest passion, and occasionally he gives the appearance of crying.

Groups hearing recorded segments of Brooks's sermon frequently comment that Elder Brooks's style is extremely mournful, while Roscoe Greene's style sounds much happier. The elongated, wailing upward slides of Brooks's delivery suggest images of heavy grief, even when the preacher is speaking of issues far less oppressive than death. Greene's spirited vocal style, on the other hand, captures images of vigor, positive affirmation, even joy. These differences in mood do not originate in the theological bases of the respective subdenominations; they are simply matters of style related to the personalities of these particular preachers.

As a whole, Elder Brooks's sermon developed around a series of alternating high- and low-intensity passages. The entire series of lines first quoted above was part of his initial high-intensity segment. As in the prototypical model set forth earlier, he had started rather slowly and rather prosaically as he talked casually with the Whitehead congregation about the circumstances of Elder Jimmy Joines' heart attack. Then he moved into his first high-intensity, wailing sermon segment, later to return briefly to his original low-intensity level before building again. But each high-intensity unit was also subdivided into line series that linked in either an ascending or a descending pattern. In short, the overall structural format was quite complicated.

Fourth Variation

This fourth major style, the "clapping and shouting 'spiritual holler' sermon," combines a wailing holler, similar to that employed by Elder Brooks, with a rhythmic hand-clapping that accentuates both meter and content. I have heard versions of this style in a Missionary Baptist church in Johnson County, Tennessee; in a Regular Baptist church in Alleghany County, North Carolina; in a Union Baptist church in Ashe County, North Carolina; in the Sandy Ridge Old Regular Church just north of Coeburn, Virginia; and in a number of other Old Regular churches.

One of my visits to Sandy Ridge occurred on the fourth Sunday in June, 1983. Three elders preached on that occasion, but it was the second speaker, a nameless gentleman in his late sixties or early seventies whose delivery style caught my attention. A typical Old Regular service involves three to five sermons, while a special service such as a communion and footwashing may involve as many as seven. These sermons tend to be shorter than the ones preached in Missionary Baptist fellowships, but are not necessarily so. Old Regulars are known for their long services.

At Sandy Ridge the elder in question began his sermon very haltingly, pointedly telling the congregation that he didn't think he had the spirit or the physical energy to preach that morning. "I'll tell you now," he said very slowly, "that I'm gonna have to feel much better than what I do before there'll be any preaching from me this morning. I don't have it. My arms are too short and my cries are too weak to bring this thing down from God out of heaven."

In a manner traditional among Old Regular preachers, this elder suggested that the moderator should not have chosen him that morning, that other elders would have done better than he. About five minutes later, however, after some initial stumbling about to find a theme, the speaker was clapping, shouting, jumping, waving his arms, and thrusting his body forward in a very vigorous manner, all to emphasize his message, an apocalyptic warning of impending "bondage."

Compared to Roscoe Greene, this elder was not particularly rapid in his delivery; during the passage below he was averaging only 136 words per minute. However, he sounded faster than that, because he filled every moment with sound, whether words or vocal segregates—"uh"s, "um"s, and the like. In addition, unlike Ward Brooks, this elder did vocalize his gasps for air, his explosive exhalation followed by a quick inhalation.

The main feature of this preacher's style, though, was the holler. The exhorter could be seen moving toward that dramatic explosion of sound, tensing his body, preparing for the physical surge he would make when he reached that moment. His eyes would close. His head would be thrown back, his hands lifted high. Then it would come, the elongated holler, the fervid wail, that would rise to an absolute peak of passion, energy, and volume, sometimes a mournful cry, sometimes an urgent plea, sometimes an angry exclamation. His body would lunge forward and down, his arms stretched out, hands tense, fingers rigidly apart, the perfect picture of a raging prophet harried by his own urgent warnings. The elder literally would hurl himself toward his audience, much as an athlete might do in a climactic effort to achieve. And, indeed, the preacher would achieve, as his congregation responded forcefully to all this drama.

One Union Baptist elder who uses this style, a gentleman whom I heard at the Silas Creek church, approaches his holler by lifting his right foot high in the air, his knee bent as in a drum major's prance. Then as he hollers he thrusts that leg forward, coming down on his left knee, both arms stretched out directly in front of him, his head first bent forward, then pulled upward as the exclamation peaks.

The Old Regular elder at Sandy Ridge had a habit of directing many of his hollers at one of the other elders sitting behind him, a delivery technique often seen in this subdenomination. His bowing thrusts were then made either squarely into the face of the respective elder or to an area of the pew beside this man. The result was that the speaker occasionally ended up being physically supported by his colleague, usually with an accompanying "Amen!" or "That's right!" from the second elder.

Clapping sequences usually consist of only one to three sharp claps at the close of a line, coinciding with the gasping air intakes. There might be only one clapping line between several non-clapping ones, or there might be two or three in a row, each gaining in fervor.

These clappings are employed as part of the dramatic buildups that precede the hollers. They provide an opportunity for the physical exertions preliminary to the even larger, more dynamic, and explosive movements of the holler. Arms are held low, knees are bent in a slight crouch, hands are out front, and the claps are accompanied by slight jumps that spring the body upward. If the claps are immediately followed by the surging movements of the holler, then these jumps are punctuated by the hands being thrown high above the head, preparatory for the lunging bow or genuflection that comes with the "holler." To visualize this sequence of actions, notice the placement of the clapping lines relative to the hollers in the next passage. If a non-clapping line falls between claps and a holler, this usually means that this line is delivered while the hands are held high in the air.

> Listen, my friends, (haah)
> today. (haah)
> I'll never see it, (haah)
> I know. (haah)
> But my little grandchildren (haah)
> and maybe some of my children (haah)
> and a few of you (haah)
> are going to be in bondage (haah)
> in the United States of America (haah—clapping)
> before God comes back. (haah—clapping)
> I believe that, Brother Francis, (haah)
> with all (hollered)
> my heart! (hollered)

Why? Because (haah)
the people here have strayed (haah)
far from God. (haah)
It ain't all right (haah)
if you don't want God to rule and reign in your heart (haah—clapping)
after a while! (hollered)
Because, (hollered)
Brother Francis, (haah)
I preach my mind. (haah—clapping)[7]

In this style the hollered phrases, and sometimes the other lines, are extremely difficult to understand. I played this particular tape several times before locating this forty-second segment that I could understand well enough to transcribe. All of this suggests either that my ear is still not properly attuned to these Southern Appalachian preaching styles, or that these congregations also don't always completely understand these sermons. The latter case would indicate that precise content is sometimes not as important as the dramaturgy of sound and action, and that congregations respond more emotionally to impassioned rhythms, modulations, and dynamic movements than to clearly articulated subject matter.

Some Additional Stylistic Factors

The factors just mentioned may suggest that no significant attention is ever focused on sermon content, by either the preacher or his audience. Of course, as we shall see in the next chapter, such is not the case. Nevertheless, one problem mountain preachers face is the difficulty of maintaining these rhythms, claps, hollers, and a pace of up to 200 words per minute, while speaking with any degree of coherence. Congregations do appear to value highly these energetic, fast-paced, rhythmical styles, but I feel certain that, given an option, they would like to have both style and intelligible substance. How, then, can the preacher do all this and still keep his thoughts reasonably organized, particularly when orating extemporaneously?

7. Recorded 12 June 1983, at Sandy Ridge Old Regular Baptist Church.

Repetitions

One answer to this question is that the preacher slows down the development of his rhetorical content by interjecting repetitious words and phrases that serve both to maintain the rhythm and to fill time while the speaker thinks about what might come next. Elder Danny Miller, discussed earlier, appeared to be doing just that with his "Oh God," "dear God," "our Father," etc. Take, for example, a segment of Miller's prayer that went as follows:

Oh God, we pray, Lord,
bless those, dear God,
listening in this morning.
Bless those, dear God,
dear Father, that's not able
to get out to Thy house.

Note the number of nouns of direct address to the deity in this short segment. At least two things were achieved by these repetitions: (1) the lines were filled out to the desired lengths, and (2) the actual development of content was slowed, giving Miller more time to compose his thoughts.

A more complete example of this technique can be seen in a sermon delivered by Brother James Simms, a minister who pastors churches in northeastern Tennessee and northwestern North Carolina. The passage in question was part of a message delivered during Simms's radio broadcast over Station WMCT in Mountain City, Tennessee. Note the pattern of repeated exclamations and admonitions.

Neighbor, when the outside gets saved
the inside does, too.
    Come on, Church! Amen! Hallelujah!
You can't wash teacups
unless you get the outside clean.
    Come on, Church! Amen!
If you put it in the water—
    Glory to God! Amen! Hallelujah!
If you repent before God—
    Amen! Hallelujah!
If you repent before God
and go down in the water
of baptism in Jesus's name,
you got to be clean.

> Come on, Church! Amen!
> That's what's wrong
> with a bunch of people today.
> They go down a dry sinner
> and come up a wet sinner.[8]

Simms employed his repetitious exclamations both to slow the development of his content and to urge his congregation toward reciprocal responses. When he would say, "Come on, Church!", he usually would receive a chorus of replies: "Praise God," "Bless him, Lord," "Amen," etc. Thus, the exclamations whipped the congregation toward a paroxysm of religious fervor.

The "Amen"s and "Hallelujah"s that Appalachian Baptist preachers interject into their rhetoric are not necessarily intended as affirmations of statements that immediately precede the respective exclamations. In fact, the preacher might be in the middle of indicting some social or theological evil when he throws in a "Praise God." Taken literally, the "Praise God" pronounces approval of the evil. This, of course, is not the preacher's intent. Notice how this principle works in the passage that follows. The excerpt was taken from a radio sermon that was sponsored by the Full Gospel Fellowship Church of Creston, North Carolina, and broadcast over station WMCT. The preacher was called simply "Brother Priest."

> So many people, Amen,
> are just a-preaching for money.
> The love of money—
> Amen!—is all they're after.
> Not for the soul of man.
> Praise God!
> If we lay aside
> the lust of luxury
> and all these things
> and get with the work of the Lord—
> Amen! I'm a-talking,
> Amen, to the preachers
> out in this land and country.
> Amen! If you're out there,
> Amen, and a-preaching for money,

8. Recorded 18 Nov. 1973. I am indebted to Richard Humphrey for this tape.

Amen, and not for the soul,
Amen, you're
a-bound for hell,
Praise God,
just as sure
as I'm standing here
this afternoon.
Amen![9]

Notice that Priest said "Praise God" after "you're a-bound for hell." Surely he was not praising God because some poor soul was bound for perdition; this phrase and his other repeated exclamations more likely were mere stylistic fillers that served the additional purpose of encouraging congregational responses.

"Commonplaces"
Not all mountain preachers rely on these "Amen"s or "Praise God"s to maintain their steady flow of language. Some are able to maintain their 200-plus words per minute while remaining reasonably coherent and avoiding the disjointed quality given to rhetoric by frequently repeated exclamations.

Roscoe Greene, for example, can speak as rapidly as 225 words per minute without stumbling verbally, losing his train of thought, or backing up to rephrase—all this while orating improvisationally. Greene does employ a technique, however, that helps him in this regard. This is the classical rhetorical device known as a "commonplace."[10] A line of argument, example, anecdote, bit of scripture, colorful phrasing, dire admonition, or other rhetorical element is held in the memory intact, to be quickly retrieved and integrated with similar "commonplaces" to forge endless varieties of a particular chain of thought.

All experienced speakers do this, but the Southern Appalachian Baptist preacher, given his usual rapid pace, appears to be conspicuously dependent upon this technique. One of Greene's anecdotes, which I have heard him use on three occasions, is employed when Greene wants to make a point about church unity, about temptation,

9. Recorded 18 Nov. 1973. I am indebted to Richard Humphrey for this tape.
10. Lane Cooper, *The Rhetoric of Aristotle* (New York: Appleton-Century-Crofts, 1932), 15.

about devotion to church principles, or about being tested by God.
In the sermon quoted below, "Preacher Ros" had just come down
from one of his intense periods of rapid delivery and was talking
quietly to his audience for a moment. As he developed the narrative,
he began to climb to yet another high plateau of rapid-fire speech,
where he stayed for the duration of this sequence.

> God gave me a service test
> about three months after I got saved.
> I could take the Devil and rub his nose over the place God saved me.
> I could take him back and rub his nose over the place where God gave
>   me a service test,
> the first one God ever gave me.
> Hallelujah! (shouting)
> It was right down here on the mountain—
> right out there on the other side of Brother Dallas's.
> I got my nose turned up at church.
> I made a statement
> that I wouldn't have nothing to do with that bunch of people.
> And, beloved, listen to me!
> I never got by even the whole week.
> I went down there to pick chinkapins.
> But instead of picking chinkapins,
> God had me on my face, and my face
> right down in the dirt.
> And He said, "Listen,
> you didn't realize that you said
> you wouldn't have nothing else to do with me."
> And I said, "Lord, I didn't realize it."
> But He said, "You did."
> And I said, "Lord, if that be the truth,
> give me grace to go back and get the cross."
> Praise God! (shouting and leaping)
> I went back and got the cross
> and I haven't laid it down, by the grace of God,
> from that time 'til today.[11]

Note that in this passage Greene claimed to have had a first-
hand encounter with God. Taken literally, this claim places Greene
alongside the most renowned saints of religious tradition. It is un-

---

11. Recorded 30 Nov. 1975, at Mount Paran Baptist Church.

certain, however, whether Greene's congregation accepted their pastor's words this way, or—more likely—interpreted them in some metaphorical sense. These Baptist preachers often report having obtained a particular spiritual truth in such a manner. And mountain congregations might allow such claims under some right of ecclesiastical poetic license.

Although these regional orators are not notably effective in their oral readings of the Bible, most of them—particularly the older ministers—hold a large number of scriptural passages in their memories. Consequently, they are able to pull forth a Bible verse or two at almost any point to support or develop an argument. These extemporized scriptural renditions and subsequent interpretations constitute "commonplaces," in the sense that the preacher probably has employed these exact combinations of rhetoric time and time again.

Recall the passage quoted earlier in which Elder Earl Sexton was speaking metaphorically of Christ as "the Morning Star" (a reference to Rev. 22:16). Then he shifted to a slightly different line of thought, ending this segment by quoting John 14:1–3. The quote from John was produced from memory, as was every other biblical passage Sexton used that morning. Sexton only reads scripture at the very beginning of his sermons, and sometimes not even then.

Closing Observations

Two factors place all of these Southern Appalachian Baptist preachers into a common category. First, none of them has received any formal seminary training; and second, none is, strictly speaking, salaried for his ministerial duties. Their training usually has consisted solely of self-directed Bible study and preaching practice, plus the informal tutelage of older preachers. If they have received any remuneration at all for their preaching services, it probably has come in the form of "love offerings."

A majority of these Appalachian exhorters firmly believes that if God did indeed "call" them to preach, they ought to be willing to do so for free. Furthermore, they are convinced that a true call is accompanied by "gifts of the spirit" that provide the chosen preacher with all the basic knowledge and skills necessary to that call. He should study the Bible, of course; but every man and woman should do that. His main jobs are to seek the will of God through constant prayer, and to relay that will to the people.

Experience has taught these churches to be suspicious of the seminary-trained minister. Vital traditions and doctrines are inevitably lost, they believe, when seminaries get hold of a "God called" man. Besides, such training is totally unnecessary; not only does God provide the talents requisite for preaching, but also the formal process of being ordained is controlled at the local church level. Therefore a prospective preacher does not have to obtain a degree in homiletics and then appear before a bishop—or any hierarchical body—to receive permission to exhort for God. Instead, he has only to convince a local church of the genuineness of his call.

Even the associations usually accept judgments of local churches when it comes to either granting ordination or withdrawing it. Old Regular association minutes, for example, frequently report action to withdraw, at the request of a local church, a name from the official roll of ordained ministers.[12]

These brethren believe that one learns to preach above all, by preaching. One Regular Baptist elder expressed the argument in these words:

Oh listen, my friend,
today.
You can go to the seminary
and get an education,
or you can read the Bible,
and you can learn
to stand up before
men and women
here,
and you can utter the words
that are in this Bible.
Amen![13]

Emphasis is placed, then, on a kind of on-the-job training, a period during which the would-be preacher develops his skills while

12. See action taken by Cedar Bottom Church against Elder Chester Belcher, Union Association of Old Regular Baptists, *Minutes* (1983), 6.

13. Recorded 12 June 1983, at Sandy Ridge Old Regular Baptist Church.

giving the local church a chance to judge whether he has indeed "received a call." The implication is that if, after a reasonable period of time, the neophyte has not developed at least modest preaching skills, then perhaps he is mistaken about his call.

All of the six subdenominations of Baptists have a formal status for such preachers-in-training. The Sardis Association of Old Regulars, for example, calls these men "liberated brethren." The names of individuals holding this title are published in the association's minutes, to let affiliate fellowships know that it is acceptable to call on these men to preach. Then when a local church ordains a "liberated brother," his name is moved to the minutes' "Ordained Ministers" list.[14]

A majority of these churches believes strongly in an unpaid ministry. Therefore most of these ministers accept as a given that they will have to support their families by working at other jobs. Roscoe Greene, for example, for much of his life has operated a small sawmill where he rough-cuts short hardwood stock for use in the North Carolina furniture industry. Elder Edwin May, moderator of the Sardis Association of Old Regulars, proudly claims never to have accepted any monetary reward for preaching; until he retired a few years ago, he operated a lumber business in Meta, Kentucky. Elder Glenn Killon, one of the two pastors of the Saddle Mountain Regular Baptist Church, has worked as a carpenter and small-operations building contractor. Bill Campbell, an elder at Bull Creek Old Regular Church, owns a television repair shop in Grundy, Virginia. Brother T.J. Jackson, whose preaching is examined in the next chapter, for years has worked in Boone, North Carolina, as a service station operator and automotive repairman, to allow himself the avocation of being a Missionary Baptist preacher. Brother Roland McCellan, pastor of the South Side Free Will Baptist Church in Mountain City, Tennessee, spends his weekdays as a groundskeeper for a children's home in Avery County, North Carolina. And Elder Walter Evans, who pastors three Primitive Baptist churches in and around Sparta, North Carolina, is a retired farmer.

Many of these preachers do, nevertheless, regularly receive money from their congregations, not as fixed monthly salaries but as love offerings provided in a variety of ways. Sometimes the

14. Sardis Association of Old Regular Baptists, *Minutes* (1982), 55; (1983), 60.

offering is formally procured, with a collection plate being passed. But often individual male church members simply slip the preacher a few dollars after a service. I saw this process in action at the close of a meeting at Union Primitive Baptist Church in Sparta, North Carolina. When I went to the front of the church to shake hands with Elder Walter Evans, who had preached the sermon, I noticed that two gentlemen passed bills to him as they shook his hand.

The monetary rewards these men receive for preaching, however, cannot be very large, certainly not enough to compensate them for their time, energy, and emotional involvement. None of the individuals I have met in these visitations is becoming wealthy through service to his church(es), and in that respect these preachers contrast sharply with that breed of churchmen who are using national cable television so effectively to promote themselves and their institutions.

By several standards these mountain Baptist preachers are rather humble folk. As their spheres of influence and power are relatively small, they could easily be passed over as inconsequential in terms of the larger workings of the world. They believe passionately, however, in the importance of what they are doing. They tend to be the opinion leaders in their fellowships, and they often figure prominently in the broader sociopolitical structures of mountain communities—as secular leaders, as arbiters of disputes, and as judges of ethics and morality. In this sense, therefore, they are persons of some importance. Moreover, through their preaching styles they have developed an indigenous art form which is itself worthy of study. An immensely creative lot, they have managed to preserve some rich rhetorical traditions that otherwise might have passed from the American scene.

CHAPTER 3

Naming the Sin
and Sometimes the Sinner

The last chapter may have left the impression that style is the only meaningful aspect of Southern Appalachian Baptist sermons and that the substantive rhetoric is at best only secondary in importance. In these exhortations, substance is often subordinated to style. Still, they must not be dismissed as "sound and fury, signifying nothing." Certain values, ideologies, social premises, etc., do show up rather consistently in this pulpit rhetoric, and these are worthy of analysis. These sermons may be characterized generally as "according to the Book," vigorously exhortative, intensely personal, very direct, and extremely traditional in the values they embody. The preachers who deliver them always name the sin and occasionally name the sinner. This chapter will examine what the preacher says, as opposed to how he says it.

According to the Book

"According to the Book" means that the messages central to these sermons are heavily Bible-centered. They are built around specific scriptural stories, New Testament admonitions that guide Christian behavior, articles of faith, and the traditional virtues and values stressed in the Ten Commandments and the Beatitudes. These Southern Appalachian preachers seldom wander far from specific scriptural moral, ethical, or doctrinal pronouncements, or take up any cause that is not directly Bible-based. If issues such as famine in Ethiopia; street people in Washington, D.C.; proliferation of nuclear arsenals; or America's treatment of the elderly are mentioned, they are usually discussed only as "signs of the times," indicators of a spiritual doomsday clock ticking away the minutes of man's existence. The focus, instead, is always on a simple tripartite message: the sinfulness of man, the saving grace of Christ, and the rewards (now and in the afterlife) of redemption. Larger social messages fade into the background, except as their causes constitute omens of Judgment Day or tests of faith for the individual "child of the cross." Local social issues are given some attention—beer, wine, and liquor sales; places of community debauchery; activities of area young people—but primarily as background factors affecting the individual believer's choices for behavior. By far the most important questions are the following: Do you believe? Do you practice your belief by church attendance, singing, praying, and testifying? And do you exemplify your belief through just and loving treatment of your family and church community?

These fellowships consider the Bible to be the best, and perhaps the only, moral document by which one can measure the goodness or badness of individual and group behavior. For Roscoe Greene and most of his fellow mountain preachers, the task of distinguishing between the godly act and the ungodly one is a fairly uncomplicated process. They ask: Is the act just and righteous (in accord with the Old Testament Golden Rule and the Ten Commandment principles)? And is the act in accord with the example of Christ and with his admonitions, particularly those voiced in the Sermon on the Mount? As one elderly Old Regular preacher stated, "I keep the Book on my knees. It's open, and the pages are worn. That's all I need." [1]

Indeed, the pages of Bibles carried by these ministers are worn. These books—especially those owned by Missionary Baptist preachers—show the effects of constant reading and underlining. Among Missionary Baptists, this heavily-used quality in one's personal Bible is a mark of pride, so much so that an exhorter or layperson would be hesitant to expose as her or his own a Bible showing little or no fraying.

One of my favorite Bibles belongs to "Sister Hazel," wife of Roscoe Greene. Its owner keeps it constantly present and would probably feel quite lost without it. Numerous markers separate its pages, and almost every one of these pages shows underlining, done with

1. From notes taken 13 May 1983, during a dinner-on-the-ground at Bethany Old Regular Baptist Church, Kingsport, Tenn.

different colors of ink. Slightly soiled and very limp and swollen from constant use, the volume is more than a symbol, certainly at least a sacred icon and perhaps a concrete extension of its owner.

One elderly member of the Silas Creek Union Baptist Church told me that she felt the biggest problem in the modern American home was the "Bible on the shelf," meaning of course that it should be down on a table or footstool, being read and studied. The woman also argued that it could not be just any version of the Bible; it had to be the King James version.[2]

Old Regulars, Regulars, and Primitives do not show the same attachment to personal Bibles that the Missionary Baptists do; or at least they do not to the same extent carry a Bible to church. Members of all these subdenominations have the "Holy Scriptures" in their homes, but Missionary fellowships' emphasis upon Sunday schools, and the place of Bible reading in these lessons, mandates that members of these fellowships keep their Bibles close at hand.

Without exception, our six Baptist subdenominations accept only the King James Bible. Fifty or sixty years ago these mountain church fellowships probably would not have been aware of any Bible other than the translation authorized by King James. Arthur Garfield Hays, one of the defense attorneys in the 1925 "Scopes Trial," reported that a great deal of confusion and consternation developed in Dayton, Tennessee—not a mountain town, but close enough—when Clarence Darrow attempted to introduce into evidence Bibles other than the King James version.[3] Many Tennesseans apparently were unaware that other translations existed.

That is usually not the case today, even in Southern Appalachia, because so many traditional churches have made arguments for the King James version their *cause celebre*. Indeed, several mountain Baptist associations have recently amended their articles of faith to accept only this "King James authorized" Bible translation.[4] As recently as 1978, for example, the Mountain District Primitive Baptist Association voted through the following resolution: "The second

2. From notes taken during homecoming meal, Silas Creek Union Baptist Church, 24 July 1983.

3. Arthur Garfield Hays, *Let Freedom Ring* (New York: Boni and Liveright, 1928), 52–53, 70–71.

4. Sardis Association of Old Regular Baptists, *Minutes* (1982), 51; Original Mates Creek Regular Primitive Baptist Association, *Minutes* (1976), 37.

Article of Faith be changed to read as follows: *We believe that the Scripture of the Old and New Testament, as translated in 1611 into the Kings James version of The Holy Bible, is the written word of God and the only rule of faith and practice.*[5]

This preference for the King James version is motivated not only by a liking for seventeenth-century linguistic style, but also by an uneasiness with the implications that other translations, notably the Revised Standard Version, seem to hold for some doctrines these fellowships consider vital. The dropping of key terms from certain passages appears to muddy traditional meanings. Primitives, for example, do not like what the translators of the Revised Standard Version did with Eph. 1:5 and 1:11–12. Both of these passages are used by this subdenomination to support its doctrines of predestination and election, but the Revised Standard Version replaces "predestinated" with a term which Primitives feel is much less precise:

Revised Standard Version	King James Version
He destined us in love to be his sons through Jesus Christ, according to the purpose of his will.	Having predestinated us unto the adoption of children by Jesus Christ to himself, according to the good pleasure of his will.
In him, according to the purpose of him who accomplishes all things according to the counsel of his will, we who first hoped in Christ have been destined and appointed to live for the praise of his glory.	In whom also we have obtained an inheritance, being predestinated according to the purpose of him who worketh all things after the counsel of his will: That we should be to the praise of his glory, who first trusted in Christ.

The groups that perhaps have felt most threatened by the Revised Standard Version are those mountain Holiness congregations in Tennessee and West Virginia who have persisted in the highly controversial practice of handling poisonous snakes as an act of religious faith. This study does not include these groups, because they are not Baptists and because their worship procedures have been examined by several other scholars.[6] Suffice it to say that the Revised

5. Mountain District Primitive Baptist Association, *Minutes* (1978), 3–4.
6. Steven M. Kane, "Holy Ghost People: The Snake Handlers of Southern Appalachia," *Appalachian Journal*, 1:3 (1974), 255–62; Marsha Maguire, "Confirming the Word: Snake-Handling Sects in Southern Appalachia," *Quarterly Journal of the Library of Congress*, 38:2 (1981), 166–71, 174–79; Eleanor Dickinson and Barbara

Standard Version omits as apocryphal the very passage which these fellowships use to justify not only snake-handling, but also "speaking in tongues," drinking poisonous liquids, and spiritual healing. The scripture in question is Mark 16:17–18, which the King James Bible records in this manner:

> And these signs shall follow them that believe; In my name shall they cast out devils; they shall speak with new tongues;
> They shall take up serpents; and if they drink any deadly thing, it shall not hurt them; they shall lay hands on the sick, and they shall recover.

The Revised Standard Version excludes not only these two verses, but all of Mark 16:9–20, which contains one of the most frequently quoted verses of the New Testament, Mark 16:16: "He that believeth and is baptized shall be saved; but he that believeth not shall be damned." Most of the Southern Appalachian preachers whom I know would be lost without this verse.

Their strong Bible-oriented faith tends to make these Appalachian churches impatient with and suspicious of more sophisticated, liberal, non-Bible-based, humanistic theology. Such was certainly the attitude of Arvel Hardy of Doe Ridge, North Carolina, when he said to his Missionary Baptist congregation:

> Brother, you'd better know where you stand,
> what you're following
> this day which you live.
> Because there's so many doctrines,
> so many corruptible things in this world,
> so many people changing the word of God
> and saying, "It's all right, brother, to do this."
> But, brother, sin's sin.
> Black's black and white's white;
> I don't care how you look at it
> or what you make of it.
> Brother, you can rub it down
> and smooth it out,
> but still underneath it's still black sin

Benziger, *Revival* (New York: Harper and Row, 1974), 127–43; *The Holy Ghost People*, a film (Contemporary Films/McGraw-Hill, 1968).

and corruptible sin,
sending men and women to a devil's hell.
Brothers, that's the way it is
and the only way it's gonna be.[7]

Vigorously Exhortative

Although the phrase "vigorously exhortative" refers to the fact
that these sermons are evangelistic in nature and exhort "sinners"
to salvation, readers should recall the varied beliefs of these Baptist subdenominations concerning evangelism. Primitive Baptists,
of course, do not evangelize at all, at least not if "evangelism" means
an effort to convert. Because of the elect doctrine, that is not seen as
a legitimate endeavor. All the other groups, however, include some
element of evangelism in the permissible purposes of a sermon. In
Old Regular belief, for example, the elect doctrine is tempered by
the claim that God elects only after we approach. People, therefore,
can and should be exhorted to make that approach. Of course, Free
Will and Missionary Baptists believe wholeheartedly in evangelistic
exhortation.

All of these churches hold that people are basically sinful and
must be redeemed. Thus there is an abundance of hell-fire-and-
damnation rhetoric to motivate this naturally depraved humanity to
seek salvation (or election). Indeed, these preachers seldom wander far from the basic tenet that hell awaits all who continue to
stray from the paths of righteousness. "I tell you tonight," pro-
claimed George Taylor to his Mountain View Missionary Baptist
congregation,

there's more fools
agoing to that place
where the worm dieth not,
where the fire is not quenched,
in a place of weeping
and wailing and gnashing of teeth. . . .
"If you ever die in your sin,"

7. Recorded 18 Nov. 1973, at station WMCT, Mountain City, Tenn. I am indebted
to Richard Humphrey for this tape.

Jesus said, but "where I am,
here you cannot come."[8]

The prevailing belief among the more evangelistic of these churches is that the moment of "salvation" from this eternity in a burning hell is one that should be clearly identifiable and permanently remembered. In other words, there should be no doubt in your mind about when you were saved. That state is not arrived at gradually or covertly, but explosively and overtly. As Brother Vance Triplett said, "If you don't know when it happened, it hasn't happened."[9] Consequently, many old mountaineers can tell you the day and the hour of their "salvations," even when the event occurred forty years ago.

During a homecoming at Proffit's Grove Baptist Church in the Meat Camp community of Watauga County, one elderly former pastor of that congregation, Carl Triplett, testified about dates and events pertaining to his being "saved." Those events had transpired in 1927, fifty-six years before.[10]

These believers contend, of course, that the battle with the Devil is not over once you have been saved; you have to be on guard constantly against temptations that Satan places in your path. Thus, a significant portion of exhortative pulpit rhetoric is directed at helping church members avoid these temptations. The next narrative not only illustrates this point, but also illustrates the improvisational nature of these sermons.

On November 18, 1973, Brother Bill Trivette, at that time pastor of the Calvary Baptist Church in Damascus, Virginia, began his Sunday morning radio show by calling upon every person in the WMCT studio to give her or his testimony. This practice is common among Southern Appalachian radio preachers, but the result that morning was that Trivette's program was devoted primarily to these brief, very emotional statements of personal conviction.

One young girl named Joyce gave her testimony, thanking her grandmother for having had such a strong influence upon her spiritual life but admitting that at her high school she had been expe-

---

8. Recorded 30 Apr. 1980, at Mountain View Baptist Church.

9. From notes taken 10 Oct. 1975, after a revival service at Bethany (Missionary) Baptist Church, Watauga County, N.C.

10. From interview notes taken 10 July 1983.

riencing some frightening temptations in the wake of behaviors of her "unsaved friends." She tearfully asked for strength in resisting these temptations.

After all the testimonies Trivette was left with only about five minutes for his sermon. Nevertheless, he quickly jumped in and rapidly built his tempo so that he was settled into his rhythmical pattern in practically no time at all. The message he developed was directed at the young high school girl, who was one of his singers.

> I'll tell you what to do
> when the Devil comes
> to you with a temptation.
> Instead of thinking
> of the thoughts of the world,
> and thinking after that manner,
> you might just begin
> and lift up your voice
> in song
> and in praise unto the Lord.
> The first thing you know, neighbor,
> your temptations are gone.
> And, neighbor, if you
> don't happen to be one
> that sings,
> I'll tell you what to do:
> neighbor, when the Devil comes to you
> with temptation,
> and wants you to make a pretense
> out of your life,
> and wants your life to be full of hypocrisy,
> I'll tell you what to do.
> Just humble yourself
> and call upon the Lord
> in sincere
> divine
> prayer.
> Begin to communicate
> with the Lord.
> And I tell you it won't be long
> until the Devil
> will begin to flee, neighbor.
> Because he's a coward,

and he can't stand
those
who talk to the Lord![11]

Intensely Personal

In speaking of these sermons as "intensely personal," I refer
to the preacher's immediate involvement in his message, the constant use of himself—"I am," "I believe," "I experienced"—as an
example or testimonial. This speaker never stands aloof from his
own sermon themes, but frequently interjects himself into their
applications. Seldom, for example, will he complete a message without supplying some kind of "witnessing," a confession that "I was
once a poor sinner myself" or an illustration that "there but for the
grace of God go I." Many preachers—recall the earlier Carl Triplett
example—are especially fond of relating the circumstances of their
own conversions or of alluding to the sinfulness of their own earlier
lives. Brother Gary Watson took the second of these courses when
he included the following passage in his address to the Mount Paran
congregation on August 11, 1979:

> Some of you have—
> have maybe lived the life—
> the life of a drunkard,
> the life that was reckless—
> never saw anything
> but trouble and sorrow out of it—
> and had Jesus come down
> and pick you up out of the filth of the world,
> the filth of sin,
> and establish a point,
> and set your feet on a new course.
> Brother Freddie, that's the reason today
> we ought to do this in reference of our lord and savior.
> Because back yonder a few years ago
> this little lad that you see here before you
> was doomed to eternal hell.
> But, oh, one day, Brother Ros,

11. Recorded 17 July 1983, at station WMCT, Mountain City, Tenn.

I'm so glad
I felt the holy spirit speaking to my heart and soul.
Brother, he came and told me
that I need not die and go there! [12]

Elder Harold Wilmoth pursued a similar course in this passage
delivered to his Saddle Mountain Regular Baptist congregation. The
Brother Glenn whom he addressed is Elder Glenn Killon.

So, men,
we have a choice this morning.
Therefore,
somewhere down through
the winding passway of life
there's going to be
a little voice that'll speak to us
there—just the same voice
there that John the Baptist,
that Brother Glenn
read about,
where he said there he came crying in the wilderness,
"Repent ye, for
the kingdom of heaven is at hand."
That was the voice of one crying in the wilderness.
So then that same voice
that they heard
over there
in the wilderness—
it's the same voice
that's crying today.
That's the same one,
Brother Glenn,
that spoke to you
when you was dead
in trespass
and sin.
You was a grown man
out in the world, and had committed sin,
no doubt. I've heard you tell it.

12. Recorded 11 Aug. 1979, at Mount Paran Baptist Church. When Watson delivered this sermon he was just starting out as a preacher. At the time of this writing,
he is pastor at Mountain View Baptist Church.

Oh, but the same voice
that spoke to you
spoke to me as a lad,
twelve years old.
Therefore, just a lad.
I'd never done very much wrong
in this world
here, but yet
I had sinned
in my body.
Therefore,
it was going to take—
and it did take—
the blood of the Lord Jesus Christ
to wash me
and to make me clean.
Therefore,
and to prepare me
[an unintelligible exclamation delivered in that elongated, upward
   sliding wail described in the last chapter]
so that that spirit
could come into
my heart and soul in life,
therefore,
and take up its abode
in me.[13]

While we have a sample of Elder Wilmoth's rhetoric before us,
note a couple of things about his delivery style. First, Wilmoth's
delivery sounds a great deal faster than it really is. If one counts the
words of this segment and divides that number by the time spent
delivering the passage, the rate, surprisingly, is only 118 words per
minute, considerably slower than Roscoe Greene's typical 200-plus
words per minute. What makes Wilmoth's speech sound so much
more rapid than it really is? First, with a mean of only 4.01 words
per line, he chops his rhetoric into much smaller units than perhaps
is average for these preachers. Second, he produces constant sound,
not only by inserting the "haah" at the close of each linear segment
but also by elongating many words through the use of that wavering,

13. Recorded 26 Aug. 1984, at Saddle Mountain Regular Baptist Church.

upward-sliding wail. And third, he allows no pauses to interrupt his flow, keeping some kind of sound going constantly. Moreover, his physical style makes him appear to be really pushing his limits. The result is the impression that he is traveling at that proverbial "mile a minute," while in reality he is just lumbering along.

Wilmoth also slows down the actual flow of his key words by constantly using "there" and "therefore" as fillers, giving himself time to form in his mind the next unit of thought. He does not, however, throw away these filler words by any type of undertoning. Instead he tends to give them some degree of emphasis, in part by frequently placing "therefore" on its own rhythmic line. The fillers thus become part of that constant flow of sound that communicates a sense of hurried and energetic urgency.

To illustrate the fact that these sermons tend to be intensely personal, examine one last sermon passage in which the preacher speaks of his own conversion. This particular preacher, Elder Shepherd Smith of the Union Baptist faith, is able to maintain an unusually high degree of poetic fluency in his style. And as is common with these Southern Appalachian preachers, he reports a direct, personal contact with the deity:

> I seen myself lost.
> I seen myself undone,
> without Christ Jesus, my lord.
> And, praise God, I'm glad for one thing.
> There was a man yonder,
> Brother Paul, seated at the right hand of the Father.
> And he seen my need.
> And he said, "That man there,"
> for to feed me the word.
> And his word was like a hammer
> that falls upon the stone
> and crushes the stone there.
> And that word fell upon my heart.
> And I came down then
> with a broken heart
> and a contrite spirit.
> And, thank God,
> after agonizing with God
> for a little while
> and a-begging for mercy,

> he had enough compassion on me
> to take the stony heart out
> and to put a heart of love
> in there! [14]

The preacher's credibility appears to hinge, in part, on these revelations of past or present struggles for salvation. To show that sin is universal, he must confess to its temptations in his own life. To demonstrate that redemption is an ever-present possibility, he must tell how its promises were revealed to him. To illustrate the joyous consequences of "salvation," he must proclaim its effects upon his own existence. No exhorter can be trusted who cannot point to the exact day and hour of his own spiritual rebirth, and no "child of redemption" should ever be ashamed of revealing the sins from which he has been freed.

It is also felt that the same directness with which you confess your own past sins should be applied in recounting the present sins of others. These preachers, therefore, occasionally are very outspoken in the pulpit, in interpersonal communications, and even in radio broadcasts.

One Sunday morning I was listening to "Gospel Time," a program produced by Brother Albert Tester of Sugar Grove, North Carolina, on WMCT. Tester was calling out a series of names, persons for whom the next hymn on his program was to be dedicated, when he came to the name of Mrs. Edna Morefield. He paused and then noted that during the week he had received a letter informing him that Mrs. Morefield had been "called to be with the Lord." Then he added the following:

> I'd like to pass on a prayer request to you people. The Mrs. Morefield whom God called home—her husband, Robert Morefield, is unsaved, up in years, and unprepared to meet God. Robert, if you're listening to me today—which I understand you do listen to me—God loves you, and God wants to save you. And all these years that has passed, you still have an opportunity today. Robert, will you give that heart and life to God today and let Him save you? Because then you can pass on over yonder to be with your wife in the presence of God. But if you refuse and go out to

14. Recorded at Baptist Chapel, Big Shelton Creek Road, Ashe County, N.C., 7 Aug. 1983. I am indebted to Debra Thompson for this tape.

meet God unprepared, you'll never see her again, because you'll have to go down to that awful lake of fire and brimstone.

Tester didn't stop here. He went on for another two minutes with this message, voiced over a very public medium, directed specifically and very personally at Brother Robert Morefield. And he returned to the issue later in his broadcast, again addressing Robert Morefield by name, this time offering to come to his house for prayer and testimony should that be desired.[15]

The episode illustrates a basic assumption of many Southern Appalachian preachers, that they have the right and the duty publicly to reprimand any and all of the spiritually errant. So Brother Albert Tester did not hesitate to remind Brother Robert Morefield that he was "not saved." To have failed to do so would have been to ignore his pastoral duties. "I'm not here trying to pick you apart, Amen, or to bawl you out," Roscoe Greene once declared to his Mount Paran congregation,

> I'm just trying to show you
> your responsibility. Amen!
> It's immaterial to me, beloved, as far as my part,
> whether people stand with me or not.
> That's up to you, Amen!
> It's my responsibility
> to preach the word.
> I don't worry about it either when I preach it.
> Hallelujah!
> I'll leave that with you and the Lord.
> It's up to you what you do with it.[16]

With such a premise in mind, the preacher feels secure in chiding his congregation about spiritual matters. He is, after all, only acting as the instrument of God. He merely points his congregation toward "known" truths. Furthermore, with God on his side, his reprimand is not personal, at least not personal in the sense that it is solely Roscoe Greene or Albert Tester issuing the rebuke. Instead, it is God using a Roscoe Greene or an Albert Tester as his instru-

---

15. Recorded 18 Nov. 1973, at station WMCT, Mountain City, Tenn. I am indebted to Richard Humphrey for this tape.

16. Recorded 12 Aug. 1978, at Mount Paran Baptist Church.

ment. Thus the preacher is able to maintain his own frail humanity, perhaps even his own sinfulness, while leveling some rather harsh indictments at his congregation. In addition, the congregation does not seem to take the criticism in a personal way. After all, according to their beliefs, the preacher has the right to remind them of God's demands.

Once when I visited the Scottsville (Missionary) Baptist Church in Ashe County, North Carolina, Reeves Jones, the preacher, knew in advance that I would be videotaping that particular service. Nevertheless, Jones chose the occasion to rebuke his congregation quite sharply for not giving sufficient financial support to their church. For example, Jones was literally shouting at the congregation when he spoke the following:

> You say, "Preacher, what are you saying?"
> I'm saying this tonight!
> If you don't have,
> God bless you, your all
> on the altar of God,
> did you know tonight,
> if you don't do your share tonight,
> did you know
> that God Almighty won't bless you? [17]

In spite of these harsh words, I saw no indication of sullenness or anger in the congregation's response. Indeed, they appeared to take the admonition as if it were spoken justly.

Something similar occurred in November, 1975, when Roscoe Greene preached his "invitation" sermon at Mount Paran. The church had lost its pastor, or sent him away, and had invited Greene to audition for the job by preaching a sermon. Greene himself apparently had some minor troubles with the church he was then pastoring, Bethany (Missionary) Baptist, and was seeking to move. Mount Paran seemed a good possibility, since as a young man Greene had been a member of this church.

One might think that on such an occasion, a tryout sermon, a preacher would "accentuate the positive." That, however, was not what Greene did. "I've been out here a time or two in prayer meetings," he charged, "when there wasn't a handful."

17. Recorded 7 Mar. 1976.

Not hardly enough, Amen,
that you could hold a conference.
I'm not bawling you out,
but I'm telling you, beloved,
somebody (shouted)
has took your eyes off the Lord,
and you're looking in the wrong direction.
There ain't a person in the church
that lives so far away.
On Wednesday or Thursday night
you ought to be here.
And if you love God
you will be here.
If you're looking in the right direction!
Don't you tell me
that you're expecting the Lord to come back
and then, beloved,
you don't have enough energy to get you out. . . .
If you keep your eyes upon the Lord,
and if you love Him,
you're going to be at the house of God! [18]

Mount Paran members apparently were not offended by Greene's
sharp attack, since they invited him to become their pastor.

Traditional Values

Sermons delivered from these Southern Appalachian pulpits are
filled with the advocacy of traditional values—home, God, country—
expressed with a high degree of absolutism. Indeed, charges Brother
Roland McClellan, relative to these basic values there should be no
room in the mind of the good Christian for uncertainty, indecision,
confusion, or vacillation. That good Christian must know who he
or she is and declare herself or himself accordingly. "I believe that
we're living in a day," says McClellan,

> that a lot of times God's people don't really realize
> who they are and what they are.
> Brother, I'm glad this morning to say

18. Recorded 8 Nov. 1975.

that I know who I am.
I know what I am.
I know what I preach.
And, brother,
I'll tell you when we come down
to know these things,
then God can really bless us.
But if our mind's confused
and we don't know anything about it,
we're in trouble! [19]

The trouble starts, argued Roscoe Greene, when the country at large forgets its religious traditions. "Don't you think, here in America," Greene declared,

that we've got to prove
to some of these heathen countries
that we've still got a God
in all America.
This country
was founded on the word of God,
and that's the reason why
she's stood the storm
like no other nation has ever
stood the storm.
I think we ought to come back
to this God that answers the fire.
I'm glad this morning
that I've got a little fire burning down here.
Amen!
When I come to this pulpit,
I thank God
I can feel the fire.
Amen!
I'm not ashamed of it.[20]

However, the degeneration of our nation's moral structure, this mountain pulpit rhetoric seems to suggest, is best measured by what

19. Recorded 31 July 1983, at South Side Free Will Baptist Church, Mountain City, Tenn.

20. Recorded 15 Sept. 1979, at Mount Paran Baptist Church.

happens in the home. Thus the family unit, particularly the roles of "Mom" and "Dad," receive much attention from these Southern Appalachian preachers.

Many of these mountain religious fellowships do not think too highly of the feminist movement or of the ideologies that under-girded the struggle for the Equal Right Amendment. In varying degrees, all of the six Baptist subdenominations place females in a subordinate position, both socially and in the official workings of the church.

The Old Regulars and the Primitives are perhaps the most extreme in this regard, with some of their fellowship holding adamantly to Pauline doctrines relating to women in the church and family. Consider, for example, what Paul had to say in 1 Cor. 14:34–35:

> Let your women keep silence in the churches; for it is not permitted unto them to speak; but they are commanded to be under obedience, as also saith the law.
> And if they will learn any thing, let them ask their husbands at home; for it is a shame for women to speak in the church.

In none of these churches do women actually remain silent in a literal sense. They sing, shout, pray, and often testify; but in the official business of Primitive and Old Regular fellowships they have no voice, and in none of these six subdenominations are they ordained to preach.

Paul also had fixed ideas about the place of the woman in the home. See Eph. 5:22–24:

> Wives, submit yourselves unto your own husbands, as unto the Lord.
> For the husband is the head of the wife, even as Christ is the head of the church; and he is the saviour of the body.
> Therefore, as the church is subject unto Christ, so let the wives be to their own husbands in every thing.

Of course Paul added, "Husbands, love your wives, even as Christ also loved the church . . ." But, as many Old Regular and Primitive males are quick to point out, he did not say, "Husbands, submit yourselves unto your wives."

Paul even made some comments about male and female hair-styles (1 Cor. 11:14–15):

>Doth not even nature itself teach you, that, if a man have long hair, it is a shame unto him?
>
>But if a woman have long hair, it is a glory to her; for her hair is given her for a covering.

As a young man in the 1960s, says Elder Bill Campbell of the Bull Creek Old Regular Church in Grundy, Virginia, he had allowed his hair to grow quite long, in the style of the "flower children" or "hippies" of that decade. But when he asked to become a member of the Old Regular church, he was told by the elder to whom the request was directed, "Yes, I'll baptize you, but you'll have to cut your hair first."[21]

Contrast Elder Campbell's situation with the 1983 action of the Sardis Association of Old Regulars to the effect that "if a Sister has cut her hair, she should be asked to let it grow out; if she fails to do so and cuts her hair again, she will be excluded."[22] As we have seen, dress restrictions are also placed upon women by some Old Regular fellowships.

Most of the Southern Appalachian churches I have visited are not quite this conservative concerning male-female relationships and male or female deportment or physical appearance, but traditional values pertaining to the sexes are still strongly held by all these fellowships.

During a revival at Bethany (Missionary) Baptist Church in the Rominger community of Watauga County, North Carolina, Brother Vance Triplett spoke on the theme, "When Men Go Down." His scripture was a passage in the first chapter of Ruth, recounting how Elimelech, the husband of Naomi, went down into the land of Moab. Springboarding from the phrase "when men go down," Triplett delivered a disjointed series of examples of how men "go down." They were, for the most part, homey stories illustrating violations of basic Ten Commandment virtues.

One story, however, stood out. It seems there was a man who, prior to his "going down," had been a solid mountain citizen, attentive to his wife and children and to his work as a farmer and part-time carpenter. His ruination, however, began when he left

---

21. From notes taken during a conversation between the author and Campbell, 10 June 1984, Maxie, Va.
22. Sardis Association of Old Regular Baptists, *Minutes* (1983), 9.

the farm and went to work for TRW, a manufacturer of electronic components, at its plant in Boone, North Carolina.

> They put this friend, Amen,
> in charge of a bunch of women, Amen,
> there at that TRW plant.
> I want you to know, Amen,
> when men give in to the flesh,
> they go down. Amen!
> They go down!
> That plant manager put him in charge, Amen,
> of this bunch of women.
> And he saw them every day.
> And he walked among them every day.
> And he smiled at them every day.
> And they smiled at him every day.
> And he went down.
> Amen, he went down,
> and under,
> and beneath,
> and below,
> and down!
> 'Til he forgot the spirit
> and gave in to the flesh.[23]

It must be noted immediately that there was in Triplett's demeanor no evidence of a conscious use of this passage for sexual titillation. He didn't smile, and his audience certainly did not respond with knowing chuckles. The "down, and under, and beneath, and below" ending seemed to be nothing more than a stylistic flourish.

For Triplett, the problem in this story was caused not by the man, but by the women; they were out of their proper element, the home. Triplett communicated this position clearly when, after he had finished the story, he leaned across the pulpit and said, "Now, mothers, you know we love you. Amen? You know we love you. But you know your place in this world. Amen, you know your place." Their place, suggested Triplett, is in the home, and when they move out of the home in any great numbers, society is thrown out of

---

23. Recorded 8 Oct. 1975; extant in manuscript form only.

kilter. Under such circumstances both men and women have to be on their guard against social disintegration.

I do not want to suggest that men escape the watchful eyes of these Southern Appalachian preachers. Males may be placed in command of both church and home, but they are sharply reminded occasionally of their responsibilities. One example occurred on the weekly broadcast of "The Morning Star Gospel Program" over radio station WATA in Boone, on June 19, 1977. It was Father's Day, and Brother T.J. Jackson was substituting for Roscoe Greene. At that time Jackson operated a gas station and automotive repair service in Boone and practiced his preaching only as an avocation. In Boone he is widely known for his inexpensive yet dependable automotive repairs and for his scrupulous business ethics. Therefore, his credibility is hardly to be doubted. Having been present in the studio, I can vouch that the sermon was both completely improvisational and apparently sincere.

On the morning in question Jackson used as his scriptural reference a brief question from 2 Kings 20:15: "What have they seen in thine house?" During the following segment, Jackson was speaking at an average of 224 words per minute. With some deletions as indicated, the passage went as follows:

And, dads, this morning listen to me,
as I speak unto you today . . .
As you walked down this past year,
since last Father's Day,
what have they seen in thy house?
Have they seen you walk upright before God?
Have they seen you on your face . . . before God?
Have they seen you sitting with the word of God stretched forth in your
    lap?
Have they seen you reading literature that's godly and something to
    feed your soul?
Or have they seen you pulling crooked deals? . . .
Oh listen to me, beloved, this morning.
If you're a-pulling crooked deals,
if you're a-smoking, and a-cursing, and a-damning, and a-running up
    and down the roads on Sunday,
and wasting God's precious time,
and you never spend any time in prayer,

and you never spend any time on the word of God,
listen to me, beloved, this morning. I cannot pat you on the back
and tell you that you're doing all right, friends,
when the word of God thus saith
that you're not doing right
and you must walk before God with a perfect heart
if you expect to get your people saved
and your chillun to walk in your footsteps.
Since I've been saved—I don't mean to brag on myself, friends,
but I want to drop a little testimony here
to some of you daddies out there in radioland—
Since I've been saved my chillun
has never seen me pull a crooked deal.
Down in my business dealings they saw me
give money back to people where they thought I had overcharged
    them,
when I took a loss myself.
But rather than have people think that I had done a crooked deed,
or gave them a crooked deal, I have give back the profit
that was rightfully mine,
to keep people from thinking I had done wrong.
My chillun has said, "Dad, you shouldn't do that."
But I said, "Yes, son.
I wouldn't want any people in this town
to think that I had rightfully wronged them."
I wouldn't wrong anybody.
I'd give them back the whole thing before
I would have someone step up and say Jackson has wronged me in any
    way.
Now listen to me, beloved, this morning.
In the nineteenth year that I've been saved, and converted, and walked
    before my chillun,
they've never seen me smoke a cigarette.
They've never heard me tell a smutty joke.
They've never seen me do one thing that they couldn't do themselves.
I thank God this morning
that though my chillun has watched my life down through the past
    nineteen years that I've been saved,
they can't put their finger in my face and say, "Dad,
I'm walking in your footsteps and you done thus and thus."[24]

24. Recorded 19 June 1977.

Jackson can be very pointed in his sermons. He is a man who does not hesitate to speak his mind on what he believes to be moral or religious issues. On another occasion I was in the WATA studios when Jackson was speaking. As it happened, Boone was then in, or about to be in, a community debate leading to a local option beer and wine referendum. This debate had, for the most part, turned into a town-gown split, with the Appalachian State University community supporting the sale of beer and wine while local fundamentalist churches rather solidly opposed such sales. Jackson viewed it as his duty, therefore, to speak against the referendum. Furthermore, since I, being a university professor, was the only person in the studio even indirectly connected with the opposition, he delivered his remarks, not in a hostile manner but firmly, straight at me:

> Beloved, we don't need this beer.
> We don't need this wine.
> We don't need the sadness they'll bring.
> He don't need the drunken daddies.
> We don't need the crying chillun.
> We don't need the highway wrecks.
> We don't need this money for the Devil's due.[25]

I considered Jackson a friend, and I think he felt the same way toward me, but this did not prevent his aiming this message in my direction.

One final traditional value that gets considerable attention both in sermons and in actions taken at association meetings is the desire for general peace and love in the local church community. These Southern Appalachian churches have relatively few members, and their worship methods are quite intimate. As these people are closely involved year after year with other humans in highly emotional services; as they are immersed in traditions of worship that require a high degree of tactile contact through embraces, kisses, and handshakes; and as they are constantly admonished to love their fellow communicants, they find it difficult to exist in the same fellowship with others they truly despise.

In larger, more formal churches that permit some distance between people, the average member doesn't feel that he or she has

25. Recorded 27 May 1979; extant in manuscript form only.

to love everyone else in the fellowship. Indeed, there is usually sufficient relational space to tolerate large numbers of subgroups, cliques, factions, etc. But in these small mountain churches, given the intimacy of their worship practices, true fellowship becomes highly important, discord may easily become magnified, and interpersonal problems can quickly result in church splits. These fellowships tend to be well versed in the writings of Paul, having received many of their important doctrines from his letters, and they know that one of his great concerns was the peace and harmony of the early churches. "Be perfect, be of good comfort, be of one mind, live in peace," he told the church at Corinth, "and the God of love and peace shall be with you" (2 Cor. 13:11).

To a significant degree, this concern for harmony in the local church has been motivated by the fact that in the past numerous Southern Appalachian Baptist churches have been prone to split over almost any bone of contention. Throughout the mountains there are pairs of churches, only short distances from each other, divided by some minor discord over doctrine, church governance, or worship practices. Consequently, associations are quick to act in trying to solve disputes and heal wounds festering at the local level.

An excellent example of such an association intervention was reported in the 1983 minutes of the Union Association of Old Regular Baptists. Pilgrim's Rest Church of Shelbiana, Kentucky, had been on the verge of splitting, and the association's moderator, Elder John C. Layne, hoping to heal the division, appointed a committee to meet with the discordant factions. The committee gathered at the troubled church on October 2, 1982, and later filed the following report:

> After a few words of introduction by Elder Frank O'Quinn and humble prayer by Elder James O'Quinn, they [the committee] proceeded to business in the following order:
>
> The Moderator called on the Clerk to read the Articles of Faith, The Rules of Decorum and the Constitution of the Union Association, which he did. Then the Moderator called for love and fellowship and found same prevailing.
>
> The Moderator seated the two factions of the church on opposite sides of the house, then ask[ed] for love and fellowship in the faction represented by the Moderator and Clerk which had been duly elected by the entire church before the abrupt breaking away of several members.

He, then, called for a move and second recanting the work pertaining to the differences among the brethren back to and including July. The move and second was made and passed. This cleared the way for a plea for peace and forgiveness among the offended and the offenders.

Elder Fon Bowling made an impressive plea to both factions of the Church to make acknowledgements for forgiveness of one another. It soon became evident that a spirit of humbleness prevailed among the entire brotherhood of this Church and Peace didn't seem so remote.

Elder Garland Mullins made an impressive and enlightening plea for peace and harmony at the close of which he called for a song and ask[ed] the church to show their love for one another by shaking hands, embracing and otherwise letting it be known how they felt toward each other. There was a wonderful display of humbleness and love as the song was sung.

The entire church was then seated together and love and fellowship was called for and found.

Elder Ruben Baker and Elder Cecil Burke embraced and forgave one another, and Bro. Virgil Addington and Brother Danna Robinette also forgave each other and the Church, being all seated together, forgave those who by move and second had broken away from the church. . . .[26]

Association actions usually deal with local church disputes only after they have threatened to split a fellowship, but sermons, on the other hand, are often aimed at ameliorating discord before it grows to such proportions, or before it even develops. Recall Roscoe Greene's sermon in which he told how, as a young man, he had fallen out with the folks who then composed the Mount Paran congregation. According to Greene's account, God convinced him that he wasn't just abandoning that group of church members but that he was abandoning *the Church*. By this anecdote Greene suggested that the church member ought to be careful about leaving one fellowship of believers just because of some minor dispute; he or she might be separating herself or himself from fellowship with God Himself.

Somewhat the same sentiment, but with a different twist, lay behind the appeal made by Brother Pete Tester during the 1980 revival at Boone Fork Baptist, discussed at the close of chapter 1. That appeal, the reader will recall, achieved what appeared to be an honest reconciliation between at least two couples, and perhaps

26. Union Association of Old Regular Baptists, *Minutes* (1983), 8.

kept that division from threatening the peace and harmony of the fellowship.

I once visited the Little River Primitive Baptist Church of Sparta, North Carolina, when the pulpit was being filled by a visiting elder whose name I never obtained. The elder in question had addressed a number of issues concerning church spirituality and cohesiveness when he hit on an issue that especially caught my attention—the question of whether a fellowship, or any member of that fellowship, should continue to think ill of any member for wrongs committed prior to her or his spiritual regeneration. "Many years ago," said the elder,

I come in possession
of a little pamphlet
of this association. . . .
In that *Minute*—
I gave it to a brother,
and I guess he's still got it.
In that *Minute*
the question was raised, . . .
"Should anything be brought up against
a member of the church
that was done
before they was regenerated,
or born again,
or had joined the church?"
And those old brethren
back in those days
got their heads together,
and they come back
with an answer—"No."
NO, NO![27]

By this method an elder told members of Little River Primitive Baptist Church that they should remain open to true changes in the human heart, that they should not hold grudges based on acts committed prior to these changes, and that they should be willing to forgive and forget. Don't generate discontent and ill will within the fellowship, implied the elder, by persisting in recalling the past

27. Recorded 17 June 1984.

wrongs of one who has sought to change. This is sound advice, regardless of whether the circumstances are religious in nature or not, but the fact that the advice was delivered in a religious context further illustrates the sensitivity of these preachers and congregations to harmonious unity.

A Concluding Thought

One attitude dominates the behavior and rhetoric of these Southern Appalachian preachers: the determination to be a *real* person, a down-to-earth, flawed person. The preacher must never rise very far above his congregation; instead, he must recognize and declare his commonness and thus his own vulnerability, perhaps even his own sinfulness. The interesting thing is that he can do all this while still directing rather harsh messages at his congregation, because of that idea that he is simply an instrument of God.

"I'm not a prophet. Neither am I a prophet's son," declared Vance Triplett in one of his revival sermons. "Thank God I'm just an old country boy, saved by the grace of God, doing everything I can while God lets me tell the truth."[28] And the "truth" Brother Triplett and his fellow mountain preachers relate tends to be a plebian truth, colored by religious fundamentalism, social and political conservatism, and distinct cultural values to which their congregations ascribe.

28. Recorded 10 Oct. 1975, at Bethany (Missionary) Baptist Church, Watauga County, N.C.

CHAPTER 4

Do As I Have Done

One attractive feature of Southern Appalachian Baptist churches is their tendency to preserve traditional services—footwashings, creek baptisms, homecomings, and the like. These "old-time-way" worship practices have held on in the mountains partly because of the general isolation that prevailed in the region until fairly recent times, and partly because of the practice of defining several of these traditional services—footwashing in particular—as church ordinances.

One Old Regular Baptist gentleman expressed his concern for tradition this way: "We don't ever change what Christ established."[1] His argument was that if the Bible says Christ washed feet and that He washed them immediately after the original communion service, then His followers ought to wash feet in exactly the same way. And if Christ was baptized by immersion in a natural body of water, then true Christians should be admitted into the faith in the same way, even if it means breaking ice away from the edge of a river or creek to achieve the immersion.

Brother W.E. Denny, a retired Missionary Baptist preacher of Crumpler, North Carolina, once spoke of several occasions when he had had to break ice on the edge of the North Fork of the New River to gain access to water sufficiently deep for immersion. He mentioned one such baptism that occurred when he was just getting over a case of the flu. He expected the icy adventure to aggravate the illness and put him back in bed, but found that after the event his remaining ailments quickly disappeared. Denny suggested that there had been a cause and effect relationship between his quick recovery and the spiritual work with which he had been involved.[2]

1. From notes taken during a conversation with Elder Fred Stiltner, Bull Creek Old Regular Baptist Church, 10 June, 1984.
2. Videotaped interview with W.E. Denny, Crumpler, N.C., 31 Jan. 1976. This tape is housed in the Appalachian Collection, Belk Library, Appalachian State Univ., Boone, N.C.

The next two chapters of this volume focus on some of these "old time ways." This chapter examines communions and footwashings, while the next looks at creek baptisms, memorial services, homecomings, and several other traditional modes of fellowship and worship. Consideration will be given not only to the mechanics of these services, but also to the roles they play in maintaining cohesiveness within these church communities.

Communions and Footwashings

I have been in some doubt as to what word to use in this chapter, "feetwashing" or "footwashing." The articles of faith that mandate this service are usually similar to this statement adopted by the Sardis Association of Old Regulars: "We believe that the Lord's Supper is the command of the Saviour, and that by the use of bread and the fruit of the vine; and feet washing should be kept up until His second coming by His believers."[3] But when I talk to the people themselves, I find that they generally say "footwashing." This latter term will be used during the remainder of this discussion.

Footwashing is regularly practiced by all Primitive, Regular, Old Regular, and Union Baptists throughout the Southern Appalachian region. In addition, most of the Southern Highlands' Free Will Baptists and quite a number of the area's Missionary Baptist fellowships maintain the tradition.

The ceremony always takes place in conjunction with the annual communion, and because the observance is such a special one it is generally well attended—far better, it seems, than the average service. June, July, and August are the favorite months for the joint event; a few churches opt for late spring or early fall dates. Associations—of Old Regular churches especially—make some effort to control the scheduling of these local ceremonies, since church members often travel to the footwashings of other fellowships in the alliance. A mountain church community would not hold its annual communion and footwashing on a late fall or winter date simply because weather conditions might result in very low

---

3. Sardis Association of Old Regular Baptists, *Minutes* (1983), 56.

attendance. Summer months in the Southern Highlands bring very full church calendars, including not only communions and foot-washings, but homecomings, memorial or decoration day services, union services (in Old Regular churches), revivals, and a great many baptisms.

The practice of footwashing derives from John's narrative of the closing moments of the Passover supper which Jesus had with his disciples just prior to events leading to his crucifixion (John 13:4–15). John's gospel is the only one of the four that reports this event. The King James version of the narrative goes like this:

> He [Jesus] riseth from supper, and laid aside his garments; and took a towel and girded himself.
>
> After that he poureth water into a basin, and began to wash the disciples' feet, and to wipe them with the towel wherewith he was girded.
>
> Then cometh he to Simon Peter: and Peter saith unto him, Lord dost thou wash my feet?
>
> Jesus answered and said unto him, What I do thou knowest not now; but thou shalt know hereafter.
>
> Peter saith unto him, Thou shalt never wash my feet. Jesus answered him, If I wash thee not, thou hast no part with me.
>
> Simon Peter saith unto him, Lord, not my feet only, but also my hands and my head.
>
> Jesus saith to him, He that is washed needeth not save to wash his feet, but is clean every whit: and ye are clean, but not all.
>
> For he knew who should betray him; therefore said he, Ye are not all clean.
>
> So after he had washed their feet, and had taken his garments, and was set down again, he said unto them, Know ye what I have done to you?
>
> Ye call me Master and Lord: and ye say well; for so I am.
>
> If I then, your Lord and Master, have washed your feet; ye also ought to wash one another's feet.
>
> For I have given you an example, that ye should do as I have done.

Most Southern Appalachian Baptist churches that practice foot-washing consider the service an ordinance and believe that the ceremony must be preserved and that all church members should participate. "We believe that Baptism, The Lord's Supper, and feet-washing," declare the articles of faith of Mountain View Baptist Church, "are ordinances instituted by Jesus Christ, and should be practiced by all true believers."[4] John 13:14 does contain what appears to be a clear admonition, at least to the disciples, to continue the practice. Therefore, as far as these Baptist sects are concerned, since contemporary church members are considered to be current extensions of the original disciples, any argument as to the mandatory nature of this service has been settled.

The footwashing service, however, is one of those practices that constitute the boundary between small, independent "missionary" Baptist churches and more "mainline" Baptist fellowships that end up joining the Southern Baptist Convention. The pattern seems to be that as a church moves toward becoming a full-fledged member of the local religious establishment, with its minister joining the area ministerial association, the traditional worship practice of footwashing, perhaps along with creek baptism, is dropped.

The following analysis of the communion and footwashing ceremony compares services witnessed at Silas Creek Union Baptist Church, Lansing, North Carolina; Bethany Old Regular Baptist Church, Kingsport, Tennessee; Mount Paran (Missionary) Baptist Church, Deep Gap, North Carolina; Little River Primitive Baptist Church, Sparta, North Carolina; and Saddle Mountain Regular Baptist Church, Ennice, North Carolina.[5] Although a basic pattern was common to all of these ceremonies, each had a distinctive format element or mood.

Footwashing at Silas Creek

On the Sunday I visited the Silas Creek church, activities began a little after ten o'clock in the morning and, including the dinner on the ground, did not end until past five in the afternoon. Approximately 250 members and visitors packed the small church, and the cumulative effect of the seven-hour event was both intense religious emotionality and warm social interaction.

4. "Articles of Faith," Mountain View (Missionary) Baptist Church, provided by Gaye Golds, Film Librarian, Belk Library, Appalachian State Univ., and a member of the Mountain View fellowship.

5. I attended the Silas Creek Union Baptist service 24 July 1984, the Mount Paran (Missionary) Baptist service 11 Aug. 1979, the Little River Primitive Baptist service 17 June 1984, and the Saddle Mountain Regular Baptist service 26 Aug. 1984. All of the observations that follow in this chapter have been drawn from notes on these visitations.

Union Baptist fellowships, like the Primitive, Regular, and Old Regular ones, hold services only once a month. But this does not mean that church members attend only one service a month; they are urged to visit other churches of the Mountain Union Association or of other associations with whom Mountain Union has correspondence. There are thirty such fellowships in a four-county (Ashe, Alleghany, Wilkes, and Grayson) area of northwest North Carolina and southwest Virginia; therefore, Union church members of the region circulate freely among the services of various congregations.

Union Baptist elders circulate, too. At any one service, especially the special services for communion and footwashing, there may be as many as ten or twelve elders, only two or three of whom hold membership in that particular church but all of whom are eager to preach if called upon. At the Silas Creek communion service, there were at least eight elders (I am not certain that I recognized all of them). Of these eight, four actually delivered sermons.

A graduate student who was assisting with this study, Debra Thompson, and I arrived at Silas Creek that morning just a little before ten. By 10:15 the small church was reasonably full, with a number of men still standing out front talking. Since it was a warm Sunday morning, all the church windows and doors were open. Numerous small children ran back and forth around the building. In many Southern Appalachian Baptist churches, particularly the Union and Old Regular fellowships, small children are given relatively free rein. They may pass in and out of the sanctuary at will, run and play around the church, fall asleep on pews, and even wander up front where "Grandpa," as one of the elders, might be sitting. The effect is warm, relaxing, and homey.

The attitude that seemed to prevail at Silas Creek concerning the worship format was also relaxed. In fact, there did not seem to be much in the way of a structured worship pattern. Almost everything appeared to be extemporaneous including all the sermons and the singing. The people simply gathered "to worship," and there was little apparent concern for exactly how that worship might transpire.

By approximately 10:20 a hush had settled over most of the people, as they prepared themselves inwardly for the service. Finally, one aging elder, unaccompanied by any musical instrument, began to sing "I Will Arise and Go to Jesus." This favorite Southern Appalachian spiritual captures in both its melody and its lyrics the flavor of an Elizabethan love ballad. On this occasion, led by this aging voice, it was particularly appealing.

> I will arise and go to Jesus.
> He will embrace me in his arms.
> In the arms of my dear saviour,
> Oh, there are ten thousand charms.

By the second line, a dozen or so voices had joined that of the elder, and by the third or fourth lines the entire congregation was singing softly and slowly. Silas Creek's rendition of the old hymn assumed a quiet intensity that established a foundation for the slow development of religious fervor that would continue to grow until it peaked in the communion and footwashing ceremony. Several hymns were sung, with a pause following each song as the congregation waited for the next selection to be announced by Elder Earl Sexton, who was moderating the devotion. As the service progressed and intensified, the hymns were no longer announced. Instead, someone would simply lead out with the first line of the hymn, and the congregation would follow.

None of these first hymns was lined. Although lining is practiced in all singing in Old Regular fellowships, in most Union Baptist services a voice will simply lead out with the opening line, and the congregation will join in by the second or third line. Furthermore, the hymns sung by Union Baptists are usually more modern than those rendered by Old Regular and Primitive fellowships; Union Baptist hymns show a heavy influence from the Stamps-Baxter gospel sounds that predominate in small rural Baptist churches throughout the South.

After some twenty or thirty minutes of congregational singing, one elder stepped forward to preach. Apparently the moderator had selected him to be the first speaker, but I never established that that was the case. Each of the four sermons that morning lasted about thirty or forty minutes, so there were approximately two or two and a half hours of preaching, with another hymn or two between sermons. No integrating theme of any kind linked the messages; the only factors tying the sermons together were their delivery style, their evangelical tone, and their totally extemporized nature.

After each sermon there was a round of handshaking and some embracing among the various elders, deacons, and brothers. As in most of these mountain churches, the males worshipers were very tactile throughout the service. Within the confines of their churches, these Appalachian males observe a touching code that is considerably warmer than the one they follow in their secular lives.

At about 1:00 P.M., the preaching and singing part of the service ended, and the communion and footwashing ceremony began. Elder Danny Miller, who had delivered the last of the four sermons, was in charge at the beginning of the communion service. He led off by lining an old hymn titled "That Doleful Night." This was the first and only hymn to be lined, and its use seemed to be a definite attempt to establish the traditional character of this part of the service. Miller read one couplet of the hymn at a time, then the congregation sang that couplet.

(Read)   That doleful night before His death
        The Lamb for sinners slain
(Congregational reprise)
(Read)   Did almost with His latest breath
        This solemn feast ordain.
(Congregational reprise)
(Read)   To keep the feast, Lord, we are met,
        And to remember Thee.
(Congregational reprise)
(Read)   Help each poor trembler to repeat,
        "The Saviour died for me."
(Congregational reprise)
(Read)   Thy sufferings, Lord, each sacred sign,
        To our remembrance bring,
(Congregational reprise)
(Read)   We eat the bread and drink the wine,
        But think on nobler things.
(Congregational reprise)
(Read)   Oh, tune our tongues and put in frame
        Each heart that pants for Thee,
(Congregational reprise)
(Read)   To sing hosannas to the Lamb,
        The Lamb that died for me.
(Congegational reprise)

Following this hymn there was a lengthy prayer, and then the communion service itself began, a rather quiet and solemn service compared to the strong emotional display that was soon to be un-leashed during the footwashing.

It may come as a bit of a shock to realize that many of these Southern Appalachian Baptist fellowships use actual wine in their enactments of the Last Supper. I had always supposed that the tra-ditional Baptist attitude toward alcoholic beverages would preclude the use of real wine. But in this Union Baptist service a somewhat cloudy home-fermented substance was poured from three large Log Cabin Syrup bottles into several common cups.

The bread also was homemade, a heavy, unleavened loaf broken into thumbnail-size bits for serving. Deacons of the church handled this serving with an unrushed solemnity, taking the bread and wine to the people as they sat in their pews.

Participation in the communion was open only to members of Silas Creek Union Baptist, members from other churches in the Mountain Union Association, and members of churches in other as-sociations with which Mountain Union has correspondence. There was no singing in the background while the bread and wine were served, and all was fairly still and quiet, except for the soft sobbing of a few women.

After all participants had been served and the materials of the communion had been cleared, the fellowship moved directly to the footwashing part of the service. Several metal basins, pitchers of water, and white towels were brought to a table in front of the pulpit. The procedure was a simple one. If you wished to wash a fellow worshiper's feet, you moved to the front of the church, took one of the towels and tied it ceremoniously around your waist, poured water into a basin from one of the pitchers, and moved out into the congregation where that brother or sister was sitting. You knelt before that individual, removed her or his shoes, and then dipped each foot separately into the basin, while cupping your free hand into the water and gently pouring water over the top of the foot. As each foot was finished, you then took the free end of the towel and dried that foot.

The ceremony was unhurried, gentle, and very loving, the essence of the event being a reverent humility demonstrated through service to a fellow communicant. Frequently both participants were crying throughout the event. This was especially but not exclusively the case with the women.

When a washing was completed, the participants—whether male or female—stood and embraced, and usually both wept as they hugged each other warmly. This embrace was the culmination of a deeply felt communal experience, and it, too, was not rushed.

After each washing, the washer in question took her or his basin and tossed the water out the back door of the church. The basin was then delivered to another participant, often the individual whose feet had just been bathed, and the process started over again in reciprocity or with another pairing.

The choices of whose feet, or how many pairs of feet, to wash were personal ones. Basin holders moved to other individuals in the church not in accordance with any formalized pattern of selection, but motivated by some particular need they were experiencing to commune with a member of the family, a close neighbor or friend, or even someone with whom relationship had become strained. There were, nevertheless, no instances in which a male washed a female's feet or vice versa.

The general emotion of this ceremony was extremely high. Almost everyone seemed to be crying, shouting, or singing. It was a joyous sound that complimented the affectionate embracing seen throughout the church. One woman tearfully kept shouting, "Jesus, sweet Jesus!" A male worshiper led a handful of singers in a hymn about Calvary, "His Place on a Lonely Dark Hill." And some of the elders and deacons simply wandered back and forth shaking hands with each other and often embracing.

Two women, both apparently in their late thirties or early forties, epitomized this entire service for me. The first of these women came to the front of the church to secure a basin and fill it with water. Her movements seemed slow, undecided, and troubled. When she turned back toward the congregation she hesitated a moment and then headed directly toward a second woman near the rear of the church. This second woman was noticeably agitated by the prospect of what was obviously about to happen. As the first knelt before the second and began to remove a shoe, their emotions burst forth with a force that suggested release from months—perhaps years— of interpersonal tension. I do not know what problem had existed between these two, but I felt that I was watching the purgation of a malevolent spirit or a deeply embedded pain. During the remainder of the service the two were never separated. They clung to each other as if fearing a return to some state of interpersonal torment which they both had hated.

Nor did the service allow me to escape without a challenge to my role as objective observer. I had just finished adjusting my tape recorder, when I discovered an elderly gentleman standing in front of me with towel and basin. "Can I wash your feet?" he said.

For a moment I was really without words, but then I managed to mumble something like, "No thank you. I really appreciate it, but . . ."

Still he persisted: "I really wouldn't mind."

But I had already declined and stuck to that decision. "I have to watch the recorder," I said, recognizing at the moment of speaking the lameness of my excuse. And the elderly gentleman turned and moved to a communicant sitting nearby.

On our way home that afternoon, after a traditional "dinner on the ground" feast served from tables supported by sawhorses, I couldn't help feeling somewhat disappointed in myself, particularly when my graduate assistant remarked, "I got my feet washed today." Would it have been all that discomfiting to have my feet washed by that kindly gentleman?

I also tried to imagine myself washing his feet, or anybody's feet, or the feet of any of those few professors at my university whom I considered professional adversaries. I kept recalling an encounter session I had gone through back in the early 1970s when such sessions were in vogue, an affair in which all participants were supposed to "open up" and then learn to trust and empathize with each other. It occurred to me that a "good ol' fashion" footwashing might have been as effective, if not more so.

Footwashing at the
Bethany Old Regular Church

The Bethany Old Regular Church is a concrete block structure, veneered on the front with brick, that sits on a small hill a few hundred yards off Bloomingdale Road in Kingsport, Tennessee. Although the fellowship requested, on both my visits there, no recording or photographing of the proceedings, most of the members seemed flattered by my interest in their worship service and eager to explain any aspect of the service to me. Elder Foster Mullins, assistant moderator of the Bethany Old Regular Church, my original contact with this church, was especially supportive.

The Bethany fellowship meets the Sunday after every second Saturday of the month, and their May meeting is their communion, footwashing, and dinner-on-the-ground meeting. Although this event is not specifically labeled a homecoming, it appears to serve that purpose, and attendance swells accordingly. The first time I visited a Bethany service, ten months earlier, there had been only about twenty people in attendance, but on this May Sunday over one hundred worshipers crowded into the small church.

Visitors had come for this occasion from churches in Virginia, Kentucky, and West Virginia. The dozen or so elders present represented churches in two associations, the Union Association and the Sardis Association. Like Union Baptists, Old Regular Baptists are accustomed to frequenting each other's churches.

The service began at 9:30 A.M. As Old Regulars do not believe in Sunday schools, the main worship service was all there was, and it began early. The service itself was relatively unstructured. In charge was the church moderator, an elected official who presides over all church business meetings and directs all worship services; it is he who selects who is to preach and who is to lead singing or prayers.

Ordinarily the moderator selects three elders to preach, but tries to involve as many of the others as he can in the prayers or singing. This generally presents no problem, since on regular meeting Sundays there may be only three or four elders present, including the moderator. But on special occasions, such as this one, there may be a dozen or more elders in attendance. Selection of the three preaching elders, therefore, involves some delicate interpersonal factors. The selected elders seem sensitive to this problem and frequently begin their sermons by complaining that there are others present more qualified to preach than they.

When I arrived that morning, about ten minutes late, the congregation was already singing, the hymn being lined by one of the visiting elders. It soon became obvious that there was no great shame in arriving late, as people kept entering the church for at least an hour after I did. Each time a visiting elder arrived he would make the rounds of the congregation, shaking hands with all and frequently embracing other elders, deacons, or brothers. A good portion of this congregation was made up of visitors, people who perhaps see each other only two or three times a year and may have traveled a hundred miles or more to attend this event.

Before the moderator called upon the first preacher, several hymns were lined by different elders. This hymn lining can be remarkably effective if the elder in question has a clear and melodious voice. In an Old Regular church the liner sings out one line or a couplet, using a highly compressed, chanted melody. This method contrasts with that employed by Elder Danny Miller at the Silas Creek service; Miller did not sing the lined verses, he simply read them.

At Bethany Old Regular, lining becomes singing or chanting, with the congregation then taking the compressed melody offered by the elder and stretching it out. The effect is that one set of rapidly-paced, lyrical, and spirited sounds is followed by another set that is slow, elongated, and wailing.

By far the most effective liner that morning was a young elder, Bill Campbell. When Campbell lined a hymn, he did so with obvious relish for the task, giving each linear segment a special exuberance and passion. In comparison, the other liners sounded passive.

Campbell, with a full beard and a dark suit, looked very much like an Amish farmer; however, he caught my attention primarily because, at age thirty-two, he was one of the younger elders of the Union Association of Old Regular Baptists. He is a bit of an anomaly in this Baptist sect, since Old Regulars tend to be an aging group. One gets the impression that the average age of elders in this church is between fifty-five and sixty-five. And there is a noticeable absence, within these congregations, of a strong base of young worshipers, the deacons and elders of the future. One reason for this is that Old Regulars have disavowed infant baptism and even discourage baptism at any very young age. According to Darvin Marshall, these fellowships do occasionally baptize a young person in her or his early teens, but this is the exception. Although Campbell himself was not baptized into the Old Regular fellowship until 1979, he is already an ordained elder whose home church is Bull Creek Old Regular in Maxie, Virginia. He is quite popular within the Union Association as preacher and liner.

At approximately 10:15, the moderator called for the first sermon. In Old Regular services this initial message is labeled the "introductory sermon," and its main functions are to get the service going, to establish a spirited mood, and to settle the congregation into formal worship. Up to this point in the Bethany service, the church members and visitors had been involved largely in social greetings and other informalities, but now the atmosphere changed sharply as the morning's activities moved into a much more emotional stage.

Usually this opening sermon is the shortest of the morning, and it is always closed by a "sing down," as another elder lines a hymn and the congregation falls in behind. During this "sing down," all members and visitors rise and go through another round of handshaking and embracing, but now there will be some crying and often some shouting and praising, as the Old Regular worshipers take on the mood of emotional fervor that predominates during the remainder of the service.

During this first sermon, Elder Jesse Viers employed a delivery mode similar to the fourth style described in chapter 2, including the hand cupped over the ear. When the second elder began lining while Viers was still preaching, the act seemed puzzling. It seemed rather rude just to cut Viers off that way. Cratis Williams used to speak of this practice, apparently common in the Kentucky churches of his childhood, as a tactful way of closing out a sermon that was becoming too long. But Viers had spoken less than thirty minutes, and I knew Old Regulars often preached much longer than that, even when there were several sermons in a service.

In fact, I learned later that opening sermons are always sung down as an integral part of the Old Regular service. At this interim a number of things are going on at the same time—a hymn is being lined and sung, the introductory sermon is continuing in competition, the congregation is shaking hands and embracing, and a number of "shouters" or "praisers" are making their contributions to the lively scene.

Viers was followed by Edwin May, a visiting elder who was also moderator of the Sardis Association. Just as a moderator of a local church is the highest officer in that fellowship, the moderator of an association is the highest officer in that larger body.

At the close of May's sermon, Elder Bill Campbell lined another hymn and then became the third and final speaker. It was during Campbell's song and sermon that congregational responses reached a peak of intensity. One woman punctuated the sentiments of the hymn with shouts of "Oh, sweet Jesus! Bless him, dear Jesus!" Several elders, deacons, and brothers expressed approval of the sermon by crying out, "That's right," "Bless him, Lord," and "Stay with him, Lord!"

The most emotional responses occurred when Campbell spoke of his mother. It was Mother's Day, and Campbell mentioned the years of pain he had brought his own mother during a period in his life when he was frequently in trouble. After telling how he telephoned her on several occasions to ask for money or, even worse, for help with the authorities, he closed by describing his call to inform her that he had been baptized. At this point two women were standing, crying audibly, with their arms stretched toward the ceiling.

Campbell's delivery style contributed greatly to the general emotional fervor. He was constantly in motion, moving from the pulpit to various elders behind and to the left of him, shaking each elder's hand as he stood in front of them preaching. Three times he stepped out in front of the pulpit and walked directly into the main congregational area, inciting a wave of emotional responses wherever he went. But the most dramatic congregational reactions occurred when Campbell moved to the section of pews reserved for female members. This occurred while he was talking about his mother. In addition to the two ladies already mentioned, who were standing, all the occupants of these pews, mainly older women, were crying and/or shouting.

After this third sermon the church moderator again took charge and announced a brief intermission to set up for the communion and footwashing. Most of the men left the church at this time for fellowship outside, while the women stayed to talk or to set the communion table. Two deacons arranged the utensils and towels for footwashing.

In about fifteen minutes a hymn signaled the resumption of the service, and the men closed out their conversations and slowly returned to the interior of the church. It was now about 12:30 or 1:00 P.M.

A communion table, covered by a linen cloth, had been placed directly behind the pulpit. Several long white towels, pitchers, and basins had been arranged on the right and left wing ledges of the pulpit.

Deacons Prepare the Basins for Footwashing at Little Martha Old
Regular Baptist Church, Leemaster, Buchanan County, Virginia.

The moderator first called two deaconesses to "prepare" the communion table, which simply meant that they removed the linen
cover to reveal the bread, wine, and requisite serving utensils. Then
the deacons were asked to prepare the bread and wine for distribution. This consisted of breaking a flat pancake-like loaf of home-
baked unleavened bread into bite-size pieces, arranging the bread
on several serving trays, and pouring the wine into four common
cups.

The moderator then carefully explained just who could participate in this service: church members, members of other churches in

the Union Association of Old Regulars, and members of churches in other associations with which that association had correspondence.

Once again the communion service itself was extremely sedate and dignified. Those emotional displays I did see were kept quiet and controlled. The servers engaged in no talk as they took the trays of bread and the common cups out to the participants, and all movements were taken with slow solemnity.

When communion was completed, the congregation moved directly into the footwashing service, and, as with the Union Baptists, this was the point at which emotional displays grew in frequency, volume, and intensity. Throughout this part of the service there was considerable crying, shouting, singing, praying, and even preaching.

After her feet were washed, one woman moved about the church crying, clapping her hands, and shouting, "Oh, sweet Jesus! Bless his holy name! Someday I'm going home! Oh, God, I'm coming home! Oh, children, get ready if you want to see that blessed mother!" At one point, Elder Foster Mullins, overcome with emotion, stood preaching to the brother whose feet he had just washed. I overheard another brother shouting, "We'll just take wings and fly away. And I'll see Abraham, and I'll see Jacob!" One worshiper hugged and kissed a foot he had just washed, and another sang softly as his own feet were being bathed.

At the beginning it was the men who took the lead in the service by being the first to move forward for towels and basins. The women seemed to hold back until several male pairs had already begun the ceremony. Again, no male washed a female's feet or vice versa. In fact, this gender separation has held in every mountain footwashing service I have witnessed, with the exception of the ceremony at Saddle Mountain Regular Baptist, to be described shortly. No formal, structured method of gender separation is established at Bethany Old Regular during footwashings, but the men do informally restrict their activities to the right side of the church (the congregation's right), while the women restrict theirs to the left.

This footwashing service at Bethany Old Regular was one of the most intense, energetic, tearful, and yet joyful of all the Southern Appalachian services I have observed. These Old Regulars were extremely happy during their service. Most of these celebrants were elderly, and their rhetoric centered on "going home." They cried, shouted, and clapped their hands "for joy" at this prospect.

The Children at Mount Paran.

Footwashing at Mount Paran

A Missionary Baptist fellowship that is large enough to have a pastor exclusively its own, Mount Paran meets not just once a month or twice a month, but every Sunday. The Sabbath schedule there begins with Sunday school, consisting of one class for adults and two classes for children and young people, and then progresses to a fairly traditional eleven o'clock service, considerably more structured than the worship procedures at Silas Creek and Bethany Old Regular.

This eleven o'clock service usually begins with some special singing from the children and young people. Children are very noticeable in this fellowship—well-scrubbed, combed, freshly-dressed children who have been taught to sing or recite. They obviously are the pride of the church and of their families, and every effort is made to show them off. On Sunday they are paraded before the congregation to sing little hymns that they have learned, I assume, in their Sunday school classes. An impressive number of young girls of the membership have been taught to play the piano, and an equally impressive number of young boys play the guitar.

Music is always a rich and vital part of worship services at Mount Paran. In contrast to the lined or *a cappella* singing of Primitive, Union, Old Regular, and Regular Baptists, Mount Paran music is enriched by various instrumental accompaniments—on the piano and guitar, especially, and sometimes on other instruments such as the accordion, banjo, and mandolin.

This is the home church of "Doc" Watson, a bluegrass and traditional music performer who has been very successful in the highly competitive world of country music. "Doc," a blind but skillful and versatile instrumentalist and singer, was "discovered" during the heyday of folk music festivals in the 1960s, and by now, in addition to recording numerous albums, has traveled throughout the United States, Europe, and Japan introducing outsiders to the rich musical traditions of Southern Appalachia.

Perhaps in part because of "Doc," the Mount Paran membership is filled with individuals and groups who "pick and sing," and who are eager to share their musical talents with the congregation. In turn, the children and young people appear to have inherited this eagerness.

While the children at Silas Creek were allowed to play rather freely in and outside the church during services, at Mount Paran the children are a little more regimented and are kept inside, sitting with their parents or grandparents. Nevertheless, they are given more behavioral freedom than probably would be allowed a child in a typical mainline Protestant church, and there is still a naturalness about their actions. They are present, not tucked away in a downstairs nursery, but in a reasonably quiet way they are still behaving like children.

Anyway, at the beginning of this eleven o'clock worship service—really as a transitional feature that forms a bridge between Sunday

Roscoe Greene Begins the Communion and Footwashing Service
at Mount Paran (Missionary) Baptist Church.

school and the main worship ceremony—two or three children or
youth groups are asked to sing. After that the congregation sings
several hymns. A novel feature of this congregational hymn-singing
segment of the proceedings is that Roscoe Greene asks the worshipers if any of them want to be "the singers" that morning. The
result is that a string of people, young and old, moves to the head
of the church to form the choir, standing in an elongated cluster

behind and beside the pulpit, singing the same way the rest of the congregation sings, but, by their presence at the front, constituting "the singers."

At some point in these early proceedings Greene asks his congregation to pray. But instead of staying in their pews, bowing their heads, and being led in prayer by one spokesperson, the Mount Paran congregation is accustomed to a much different type of invocation. First, a sizeable number of the people move directly to the head of the church and kneel around the pulpit or in front of the forward pews. Next, when the prayer begins, everyone is heard to make his or her own private supplication, aloud and with considerable vocal force, but blending their own pleas with the pleas of others and coordinating their variations in pitch, volume, and pace with those set by the group. Individual supplicants play off the constant fluctuations in the larger group's passion. The result is an orchestrated sound that rises, falls, and vibrates in unison, while all the individual prayers remain separate in content.

A fellow student of Southern Appalachian religious practices, Richard Humphrey, has labeled this type of prayer a "concert prayer." The name seems a good one: the people certainly act in concert, and the general sound they produce is a kind of concert.

The people seem to feel that this method of praying produces a message that is more likely to be heard than the traditional one voice leading a silent mass. There is a passion, power, and plurality in the "concert" that the solo voice cannot achieve.

On communion and footwashing Sunday at Mount Paran, Roscoe Greene will invariably read from that part of John's gospel that tells of the first communion and footwashing, and remind the congregation that its articles of faith consider both ceremonies to be ordinances. The faithful are in turn urged to participate. Even so, it is my observation that not all members do participate, especially in the footwashing; a few quietly slip from the church just before the event. It may be that a small minority of Mount Paran members believes that the footwashing service is a ceremonial remnant of the past that should be discarded.

Two aspects of the communion part of the service deserve comment. First, as in the two previously discussed churches, this is the most solemn and dignified part of the ceremony. Second, Mount Paran also uses real wine during this rite. In fact, one member of

Footwashing at Mount Paran—the Women's Side.

the fellowship, Willard Watson, for years has supplied this wine, a homemade plum wine of which he is very proud. In a purely technical sense, of course, this plum wine fails to conform to the biblical precedent, as it is made not from a "fruit of the vine" but from a fruit of the limb.

The Mount Paran communion service is a beautiful and deeply-felt ceremony, with all participants demonstrating true involvement with the symbolic events. Plum wine, or muscadine wine, or grape juice—it is unlikely that any such options would make a significant difference for the Mount Paran participants in this solemn rite.

At the close of the communion ceremony there is a brief pause in the proceedings as the bread and wine are cleared away and the

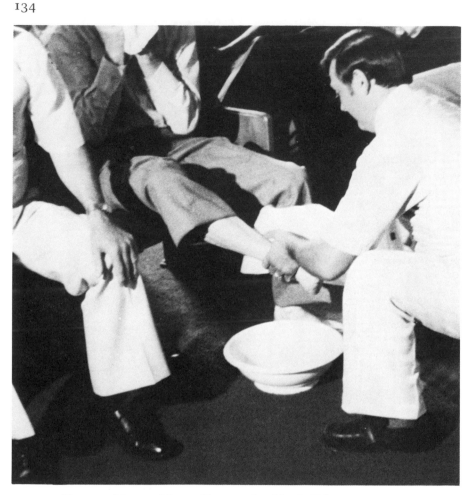

Footwashing at Mount Paran—the Men's Side.

implements of the footwashing service are arranged on a small table in front of the pulpit. It is at this time that a small number of people, most of them young adults, may leave the church. However, the vast majority of the members remains to participate in the footwashing.

During this interim, also, the pews to the immediate right of the pulpit (the preacher's right as he faces the congregation) are rearranged to create a more enclosed area, an inverted horseshoe.

It is within this area that the women participate in the ceremony, with no man entering the enclosure. The result of this reshaping of the physical space is that the women restrict themselves to only this region of the church for their footwashings, while the men tend to use all the rest of the space for their activities, especially the ends of pews where it is easier to access the feet of a fellow communicant. As at Silas Creek and Bethany, no male or female crosses the gender line to wash the feet of an opposite-sex friend or loved one.

The footwashing service at Mount Paran is somewhat more reserved than those described above. There is still an intense emotionalism, an abundance of embracing and crying, particularly among the women; but there is none of the shouting and testifying, and less of that general movement throughout the church as individuals seek to communicate their joys of the moment. What one still sees, however, are those touching scenes of warm, loving interpersonal interaction, precipitated by the enormous sensitivity of the footwashing act.

Communion and Footwashing at Little River Primitive Baptist

The most reserved and formal of all the Southern Appalachian communions and footwashings I have observed was a service at the Little River Primitive Baptist Church in Sparta, North Carolina. Although great depth of feeling was demonstrated throughout the ceremony, the precise procedures appeared more set and ritualized than those of the other three services examined thus far. The footwashings at Silas Creek and Bethany, for example, seemed more spontaneous and improvisational than the solemn formality of the rite at Little River Primitive.

As the congregation arrived that June morning, the older men took seats in the first two or three pews down front on the preacher's right, while the older women sat down front on the preacher's left. After about the fourth row from the front, however, this strict separation of the sexes broke down, with couples sometimes sitting together on either the right or the left. Later, during the communion and footwashing, this mixed seating pattern changed, as we will see.

About 175 people attended that morning, with the average age of the worshipers in the early sixties. There were two young families with small children and three other couples who appeared to be in their late thirties or early forties. The remainder of the congregation could be classified as elderly. The pastor, Elder Walter Evans, is probably in his early to middle seventies. His physique and demeanor show remnants of an earlier strength and dynamism, but today his voice is going, and that diminishes the power of his preaching.

The hymns that morning—sung from the old Goble *Primitive Baptist Hymn Book*—were not lined, as I had expected, but were nevertheless rendered in that slow, elongated, almost plaintive sound earlier characterized as being the method of singing in Old Regular fellowships. And the preaching, delivered by a visiting elder, was not nearly as colorful in style as some of the rhythmical delivery patterns described in chapter 2. Indeed, the overall impression was one of reserved and controlled passion—not cold, but restrained by a more conservative decorum.

After the morning's sermon there was a brief intermission to allow the deacons to set up the furniture, supplies, and implements for the communion and footwashing. A small table was brought into the sanctuary and placed directly in front of the pulpit. Then one chair was set at each end of this table, facing the congregation, and five chairs were arranged in front of the table, facing the pulpit. The end chairs were for the two officiating elders, and the five forward chairs were for deacons.

On the table was placed a large decanter of wine and two goblets sitting on saucers. In addition, there was a covered platter containing the unleavened bread and two serving dishes. Behind the table, flanking the pulpit on both sides, were two small lecterns that had been draped with the towels to be used during the footwashing, and on the floor beside each lectern was a stack of basins and a pitcher of water.

When all these items had been arranged and the congregation had returned to the sanctuary, Elder Walter Evans announced that all who were to participate in communion should move to the first three or four rows of the church and that the men should sit on his right and the women on his left.

The congregation had thinned considerably during the intermission, at least by half and perhaps by as much as two-thirds. In consequence, all those who remained for the service could easily sit in those first three or four rows. I was the only individual who remained behind that line. By now five deacons were sitting in the chairs facing the table, and the two presiding elders were sitting in the two chairs facing the congregation. All had become very quiet and still.

Speaking rather softly, Elder Evans opened the communion and footwashing service by saying a few words about the biblical justification for the ceremony. Then Evans formally blessed the bread and wine and led the congregation in prayer. Following this, two deacons rose from the table and moved to the pitchers and basins. One deacon obtained a pitcher of water, and the other obtained a basin. The first then poured water in this basin so that the two elders could wash their hands before breaking the bread.

The two elders, having washed, then uncovered the flat circular loaf of unleavened bread and began to break it into small bits that were placed on the two serving platters. While this was being done, Elder Evans, speaking very softly and slowly, commented on the spiritual significance of the bread. At the end of this process the two serving platters were handed to two deacons, who then proceeded to distribute the broken bread to the congregation, one deacon taking the male side and the other the female side. When this was completed, the five deacons then ceremoniously served each other. At no point in the process did anyone serve himself. If, for example, a deacon had just taken a piece of the broken bread from a platter held by a second deacon, then the role immediately would be reversed, with the served deacon now doing the serving. All this was done with absolute solemnity.

When all communicants had participated in this first part of the service, then the remaining bread was covered, and the second elder took charge of the wine segment of the ceremony. After commenting briefly on the significance of the wine, he read a short scripture and led the congregation in another prayer. Following this he poured wine from the decanter into the two goblets and immediately handed them to two deacons who had not served the bread. One of these goblets of wine was first served to the other three deacons and then passed to the men's side of the congregation. The second goblet was used in serving the ladies. At all times each server held a saucer beneath his glass to prevent spilling. When these two deacons returned to the table, they handed their goblets to the fifth deacon, who then served them prior to pouring the remaining wine back into the decanter.

At this point all five deacons participated in clearing the bread, wine, and various serving vessels from the table prior to arranging on it the two stacks of basins and the two pitchers of water. When this was completed, the second elder now took charge again and spoke for a short time on the importance of the footwashing ceremony, stressing that it was an ordinance of the church and that it had been "commanded" by Christ. He then invited all remaining members of the congregation to participate, which they did.

In contrast to the footwashing services at Silas Creek and Bethany, this part of the ceremony at Little River Primitive remained quiet and controlled. A few of the women did cry softly as they washed each other's feet, but no individual roamed about the church singing, preaching, or testifying.

Participants tended to pair off and wash each other's feet, and few people were involved with more than one of these reciprocal exchanges. The result was that this part of the service did not last nearly as long as it did at either Silas Creek or Bethany. The basic procedures, however, were essentially the same as at the other two churches. A person would come forward, obtain a towel, tie it ceremoniously around her or his waist, fill a basin with a small amount of water, approach a fellow communicant, wash and dry the feet, embrace that communicant when the rite was finished, and then discharge the used water out a side door. Usually the individual whose feet had just been washed then took the basin and started the process all over again.

The towels used appeared to be linen and were about six feet in length—much longer than the ones I had previously seen used. This allowed the material to be draped around the loins with enough excess to hang down near the floor. This in turn permitted a ceremonial flourish in the use of the material, both in the initial draping and in the drying maneuvers.

Interestingly, when a woman's feet were washed she would not remove her stockings. Her stockinged foot would be lowered only slightly into the water, and the woman performing the ritual would then scoop water in her cupped hand and spill it over the foot. That would be all the washing involved, and the foot immediately would be dried. The procedure was very much the same as that used by the women at Mount Paran, and was much more symbolic than real, especially in comparison with the more vigorous bathing of feet at Bethany, where most of the women did not wear stockings for this service.

Although this ceremony was less demonstrative than others I have watched, it never seemed superficial or unsupported by fervent emotions. These Primitive Baptists feel deeply about the communion and footwashing service, but their overall worship style keeps them from being overtly emotional about the whole affair. Even the preaching at Little River Primitive is more subdued in style than that at other Southern Appalachian churches.

Communion and Footwashing at Saddle Mountain Regular Baptist

The reader will recall that Saddle Mountain Regular Baptist Church is something of a maverick fellowship, in having adopted a doctrine of open communion. This liberality has also carried over to the footwashing service. This is the only Southern Appalachian Baptist fellowship I have observed that allows, or at least engages in, mixed-gender participation in the footwashing ceremony. Even at Saddle Mountain Regular, however, these gender crossovers are exceptions to the general practice and most frequently involve a husband and wife pair or some other pairing within a family unit. More broadly, there is little or no partitioning of the sexes in this church. Some of the older women and a few of the older men do form gender clusters, but a majority of the membership chooses to sit in mixed-gender family units.

The communion and footwashing I attended at Saddle Mountain Regular occurred on my third visit to this church. I was introduced to it first on Sunday, July 24, 1984, when Joel Poteat, a colleague at Appalachian State, and I were photographing several churches just off Highway 18, south of Sparta, in Alleghany County, North Carolina. At the Liberty (Missionary) Baptist Church we met a woman who was placing fresh flowers on a grave in the church's cemetery. In conversation I told the lady of my work on Southern Appalachian

Baptist churches, and she suggested that I might want to visit Saddle Mountain Regular Baptist and Saddle Mountain Union Baptist, two churches that stand side by side just off the Blue Ridge Parkway northeast of Sparta near the Virginia line. Joel and I drove east of Sparta on Highway 21 until we intersected the parkway, then traveled north until we sighted the churches.

When we drove up in front of Saddle Mountain Regular Baptist, it was obvious that something big was going on. Cars crowded the driveway leading to the church, the building itself was packed with people, and numerous individuals stood out on a small stoop connected to the front of the church. My first thought was that a funeral was in progress, but then I noticed that there was no hearse anywhere in sight. Besides, it was about 11:30 on a Sunday morning, and therefore it seemed reasonable that this was a crowd for a regular worship service. When we approached the church, Joel and I discovered that this was a special service in honor of Elder Glenn Killon, who was at that time celebrating his fifty-second year of service to this fellowship. The event had attracted hundreds of church members and visitors.

Because of the preaching I heard going on inside, I resolved to return to this church as soon as possible. Three weeks later I did return, but on a Sunday when the Saddle Mountain fellowship only had Sunday school. Nevertheless, I met Elder Glenn Killon and received an invitation to return on the following Sunday, when the church had scheduled its annual communion and footwashing, a dinner on the ground, and a creek baptism.

That turned out to be the Sunday I finally got my feet washed. The fellowship was well into the footwashing part of the service that morning, and I had moved to the back of the church to take some pictures. I had just snapped a shot when I looked toward the front of the church and saw Elder Killon coming directly toward me, basin in hand. On this occasion I had plenty of time to consider what I would do, and before Killon reached me I determined that I would have my feet washed. Because all of the pews at the rear of the church were filled and I could find no place to sit for the ceremony, we had to return toward the pulpit. So there I sat, at the front of the church in a ladder-back chair that Killon himself used when he sat behind the pulpit, feeling very awkward, as this aging elder knelt before me, crying as he washed my feet. It was the severest test of "scholarly objectivity" I had faced.

In both procedure and mood, the communion service at Saddle Mountain Regular Baptist was very similar to the one at Silas Creek Union Baptist. Once again this part of the service began with a lined hymn. In this case, Elder Harold Wilmoth did the lining, calling out one couplet at a time, but not in the compressed singing style used by Old Regulars:

(Read)   Here at the table, Lord we meet
                To feed on food divine.
(Congregational reprise)
(Read)   Thy body in the bread we eat;
                Thy precious blood the wine.
(Congregational reprise)
(Read)   He that prepares the rich repast
                Himself comes down and dines,
(Congregational reprise)
(Read)   And then invites us thus to feast
                Upon the sacrifice.
(Congregational reprise)
(Read)   The bitter torments he endured
                Upon the shameful cross
(Congregational reprise)
(Read)   For us his welcome gifts procured
                These heart-reviving joys.
(Congregational reprise)
(Read)   His body torn with rudest hands
                Becomes the finest bread.
(Congregational reprise)
(Read)   And with the blessings he commands
                Our noblest hopes are fed.
(Congregational reprise)
(Read)   His blood then from each open vein
                In purple torrents ran,
(Congregational reprise)
(Read)   And filled this cup with generous wine
                That cheers both God and man.
(Congregational reprise)
(Read)   Sure there was never love so brave,
                Dear Saviour so divine.

(Congregational reprise)
(Read)   Well, Thou may claim this heart of mine
              That owes so much to Thine.
(Congregational reprise)

After the lined hymn, Elder Wilmoth remained in charge as a small table in front of the pulpit was first covered with a linen cloth. Then two round perforated trays containing the individual tumblers traditional for use in most Protestant communion services and a plate containing an unbroken cake of unleavened bread were arranged on the table. Wilmoth then called Elder Killon down to help him break the bread, but before they proceeded with this task, Wilmoth led the congregation in a prayer.

As he and Killon slowly broke the heavy bread into bite-size pieces, Wilmoth spoke softly about the significance of the communion service, observing in particular that he and Killon did not have power to change the respective substances into the real body and blood of Christ, and that the bread and wine thus had to be accepted merely as symbols. This thought contrasts markedly with the transubstantiation doctrine of Roman Catholic and Eastern Orthodox churches concerning the consecration of the eucharistic elements.

When the bread had been broken and placed on two serving trays, deacons were called forward for the actual distribution. Two deacons handled this part of the ceremony, moving with slow and dignified pace through the congregation. As in other communion services, all this was done in relative silence and with immense solemnity.

When the deacons had returned to the table, they faced the congregation as Wilmoth asked if all who wanted to be served had indeed been served. Completely absent from this procedure was an announcement—conspicuously present in the communion services at Silas Creek, Bethany Old Regular, and Little River Primitive—concerning who could participate. At Saddle Mountain Baptist their "Lord's Supper" is open to all "Christian" individuals who choose to join the service, and no questions are asked about the individuals' particular beliefs.

Following the serving of the bread, Elder Killon took charge for the wine part of the ceremony. Again there was a prayer, words about the significance of the service, and a disclaimer of any power to change the actual nature of the wine. Then the deacons were called to distribute the tumblers. All became extremely quiet, except for the clinking sounds of emptied glasses being returned to stainless steel trays. Nothing was rushed, and each participant lifted her or his tumbler with studied gravity.

Once again the deacons returned to the table, and after serving each other faced the congregation as Killon asked if anyone had been omitted. It was then that he turned to me. I was seated near the left forward wall in the last of a section of pews that faced inward toward the right side of the pulpit, having been guided to this seat because of its accessibility to an electrical outlet for my tape recorder. But the pew had provided me a position somewhat outside the mainstream of activity.

Elder Killon, however, wasn't about to allow my peripheral stance. When he asked if any had been omitted, he turned directly toward me. Then he instructed the deacons to serve me, noting aloud that his congregation opened their communion service to anyone who had been baptized into any branch of the Christian faith.

One of the deacons had to retrieve a tray of bread, since that part of the communion fare had already been cleared from the table and placed in a small camping cooler that had been used to bring the eucharistic elements into the church. Two deacons then approached me, one holding the bread and the other the wine.

This was an awkward moment for me. There were brief seconds during which I did not know if I should accept the offered sacrament or not. However, before the deacons reached me I decided that it would be best for all concerned, if I participated in this ceremony. These people were offering me a form of both spiritual and humanistic fellowship I could not reject.

Once the bread and wine were cleared and the basins, pitchers, and towels had been brought to the table, I sensed an immediate shift in the mood of the congregation. The communion had been marked by the usual quiet, controlled, reverent decorum. In this particular instance there had been no noticeable emotionalism at all.

Now, however, the mood quickly changed to one of tearful but joyous celebration. The spirit was suddenly very upbeat, emotional, joyous, celebratory. There was absolutely no holding back, as the first wave of footwashers moved to the table to obtain basins and

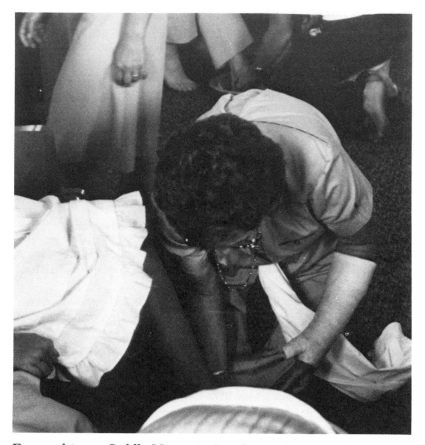

Footwashing at Saddle Mountain Regular Baptist Church, Ennice, Alleghany County, North Carolina.

towels. In addition, there was an immediate flood of emotion as this first wave selected fellow communicants for the foot-bathing rites.

Shoes, socks, and some stockings were placed to the side of basins as bare feet were lowered into clear water—ashen feet, contrasting sharply with ruddier hands and faces; aged feet, swollen veins often standing out sharply against pallid skin; infirm feet, showing the effects of crippling disorders; young feet, healthy and ready for years more walking and washing.

As these feet were lowered into these enamelware or stainless steel basins, the stimulating chill of the water seemed to unleash the subsequent emotional responses. Some individuals whose feet were being bathed slumped back in their pews, threw their heads back, covered their faces, and cried. Others leaned forward, hugging the head of the person doing the washing, and again wept. Still others simply placed a hand on the head or shoulder of the bather and whispered softly such phrases as "Bless her; bless her, dear Jesus." Finally, there were those who sat quietly for the ceremony but embraced their fellow communicants warmly after the event.

Women were more openly emotional than men, but it was not unusual to see tear-stained male faces, and to witness men in firm embraces following a footwashing exchange. In this service washing crossed gender lines, usually but not exclusively between members of an immediate family. Several women chose to wash the feet of the two elders.

One special feature of this church's footwashing ceremony was that the individual exchanges did not necessarily involve just two persons. I saw as many as three people washing one individual's feet, and on one occasion several worshipers clustered closely around a single pair of communicants, drawing emotional fervor from the interpersonal and spiritual drama being performed in their midst. In fact, at times one washing episode would command the attention of most of the congregation, with members crying, clapping their hands, or "praising" as they witnessed the performance.

Such was the case when the wife and daughter of Elder Wilmoth washed his feet. The two women were already crying when together they moved to the table for a basin and towel. Then as they approached Wilmoth, who at that moment was sitting at the front of the church, he also began to weep. When the wife and daughter knelt before him to begin the rite, he leaned forward to embrace both of them at the same time, precipitating an even more intense response from the congregation, particularly from several women, than had already been elicited. Three or four women simply rose from their pews to move closer to the action, then stood with hands partially covering their faces, crying. It was a scene of climactic pathos, and it is difficult for me to imagine one of greater emotionality.

This footwashing part of the service at Saddle Mountain Regular

Baptist lasted longer than any such ceremony I have witnessed, consuming at least forty-five minutes and perhaps even an hour, during which there were several peaks of religious enthusiasm. Twice the service appeared to be ending, as the individual exchanges seemed to taper off. Then a new burst of passion would revitalize the scene, as some individual would almost rush to the table for a basin, as if having finally determined to wash a particular person's feet.

As in the incident of the two women at Silas Creek, on several occasions I felt I was watching acts of interpersonal reconciliation or renewal. There were moments of impassioned breakthrough, when the holding back was finally over; and there were scenes of abject contrition and humility, as individual bathers bent low over feet that had toes tensely curled. The reward afterwards, however, was always a genuinely warm embrace.

The overall service was so filled with fervor that it seemed to drain all emotion from the participants. Thus at the close of the ceremony the congregation appeared thoroughly spent, lethargic, but also relaxed and open, ready to resume whatever struggles might lie ahead. I was convinced that what I had witnessed was in part a purgation, an annual draining off of bad interpersonal humors, a reestablishment of congregational cohesiveness, a reaffirmation of a sense of community. It seemed very fitting, therefore, that all of this should be followed immediately by the traditional dinner on the ground, another form of communion.

CHAPTER 5

Old Time Ways

The Flower Service at Mount Paran

Not long after I became acquainted with Roscoe Greene I was visiting Greene's radio program, and after the broadcast "Preacher Ros" suggested that I follow him to Mount Paran to see their "Flower Service," a service he said was a very special one. This ceremony needs to be distinguished from the "Decoration Day" service, in which fresh flowers are placed on graves in the church's cemetery, with appropriate songs, prayers, and remarks memorializing the dead.

On the second Sunday in September, members of the Mount Paran Church arrive for morning services carrying large clusters of fall flowers. As the worshipers enter the church, they place these bouquets on a table directly in front of the pulpit. There the display remains throughout Sunday school and the morning preaching service, giving the sanctuary a very festive appearance.

These bouquets are not the formal, professionally-produced products of floral shops. Rather, they are collections of homey fall flowers—marigolds, dahlias, zinnias, daisies, chrysanthemums, asters, and the like, cut from flower beds cultivated at least in part for this specific occasion. Furthermore, the flowers are brought not only by the women of the church, but also by the men and children. Indeed, frequently a child may be seen carrying a bunch of flowers that are very small and thus consonant with the youngster's size. The more attentive mothers see that their children, particularly the girls, carry bouquets coordinated in color with the particular child's attire.

Roscoe Greene's sermon that morning will concern the general theme, "Get right with thy neighbor." In fact, he may employ as the scriptural base for his sermon the two verses from Matthew that constitute the biblical mandate for this service:

> Therefore if thou bring thy gift to the altar, and there rememberest
> that thy brother hath aught against thee;
> Leave there thy gift before the altar, and go thy way; first be reconciled
> to thy brother, and then come and offer thy gift.
>
> (Matt. 5:23–24)

That morning the preacher's words emphasize such aspects of interpersonal healing as forgiveness, reparation, and reconciliation; and at the close of the sermon he calls each church member to retrieve her or his flowers, to seek out any brother or sister with whom interpersonal conflict exists, and to redress the grievance. This is to be done through an exchange of flowers. But the minister actually charges that no-one be overlooked in these amenities, lest some need for reconciliation be forgotten or ignored. Therefore, each church member goes to every other church member, offers a flower, is given one in return, and engages in such embraces and tearful supplications as are necessary to seal the bargain of renewed brotherhood or sisterhood.

The three occasions I have witnessed the Mount Paran Flower Service, I have been strongly impressed by the general emotional intensity of the event. As in the footwashing services, there is a tremendous amount of crying and warm physical contact. The minimal physical interaction is a handshake or an arm around a shoulder, but it is not unusual to see a pair of church members, generally but not always women, clinging to each other for several minutes or more as they complete the requisite rejuvenation of spiritual fellowship.

Once the exchange of flowers begins, the service loses all formal structure, as members mill about in search of individuals with whom they have not yet interacted. After five or ten minutes of this, someone will begin to sing, with perhaps only one voice heard for a few moments, then joined by others. The music adds to the emotionality of the event, and soon most people are singing between the various interpersonal exchanges.

There is no formal stopping place for a flower service, and the exchanges and interactions go on as long as they need to. Mount Paran is a small church, however, and usually within thirty or forty minutes a member will have had a chance to make contact with every other member. At that time people will slowly begin to leave the church, clutching clusters of flowers different from the ones they brought. Other people will linger, absorbing as much of this rich fellowship as they can.

Although there is always a gender separation in the footwashing rituals at Mount Paran, in the flower service no such rule obtains; males and females exchange flowers and embrace freely. There is, however, a tendency for the warmer pairings to occur along gender and age lines, with grandmothers hugging grandmothers, and the like. Interestingly, the teenagers of this church seem to have some problems with this service. Remember that Mount Paran is a Missionary Baptist church and as such has a fairly strong program to insure youth involvement—early baptism, Sunday school, singing groups, etc. Thus, at any typical service a dozen or so youngsters of junior high and high school age are present. Nevertheless, the young men between roughly thirteen and twenty disappear during the flower services. Teenage girls generally are there, however.

This is not a service practiced in any large area of the Southern Appalachian mountains. So far I have visited only two churches— Mount Paran and another Missionary Baptist church in the same area, Mountain View—where the ceremony is a regular part of the annual church calendar. The older members of both these churches do not remember a time when their respective congregations did not have an annual flower service, but none of them seems able to give me any specifics about the service's origins.

When I witness a flower service, however, I am inevitably reminded of an old gospel song that I have heard as recorded by the Stanley Brothers, a bluegrass duo from southwest Virginia. The lyrics of the first two verses go like this:

Wonderful things of folks are said
After they've passed away.
Roses adorn the narrow bed
Over their sleeping place.

Give me the roses while I live,
Trying to cheer me on.
Useless are flowers that you give
After the soul is gone.

Praises are heard not by the dead;
Roses they never can see.

Let us not wait 'til souls are fled
Generous friends to be.

Give me the roses while I live,
   Trying to cheer me on.
Useless are flowers that you give
   After the soul is gone.[1]

I do not know if there is any formal connection between these old gospel lyrics and the flower services at Mount Paran and at Mountain View, but there certainly is a philosophical relationship. While the scriptural justification for this ceremony calls for forgiveness, reparation, and reconciliation, the flower exchange also allows each church member to say to every other church member, "You are of value; you are cherished; you should hold in there and struggle; there's eternal solace forthcoming; that's when it will all be made worthwhile; I love you."

Most of the flower exchange conversations fall into this second category of sentiments, rather than asking, "Will you forgive me?" Although the scriptural justification for the service calls for forgiveness, reparation, and reconciliation, the auxiliary objectives of encouragement, conciliation, praise, and loving support appear to have become dominant in actual practice. Undoubtedly there are times when the need for reconciliation becomes paramount and when communicants use the ceremony for that purpose, but members of Mount Paran and Mountain View do not wait for this need to surface before engaging fellow worshipers in flower exchanges.

As for people everywhere, the flower is a potent symbol for Southern Appalachian worshipers. They seem constantly to be aware of the numerous native blossoms that festoon the mountains from early spring to late fall, especially the blooms of dogwood, wild azalea, mountain laurel, and rhododendron. Preachers invariably refer to such annual displays of color as analogous to spiritual rebirth and "the flowering of the soul," but they also are fond of lauding the flower as a gift, first from God to humanity and then from one person to another. The gift is treated as an expression of condolence, support, praise, or love.

Elder Walter Evans employed the flower symbol when he spoke

---

1. "The Stanley Brothers of Virginia," vol. 4 (Floyd, Va.: Country Records, 1976).

to the Union Primitive Baptist Church of Sparta, North Carolina, on June 3, 1984. That morning Evans's theme was very much in line with the sentiments of the old gospel lyrics quoted above. He urged his flock to give each other roses before they died, but the roses he spoke of were metaphors for praises and kindly deeds. Evans recalled a conversation he once had with an old elder whom he had known for years. One Sunday after the man had preached a powerful sermon, Evans went to him and told the old gentleman, "Nobody's preaching has had as much good influence on me as has yours. I wanted to pin that rose on you before you die. Wear it with pride." [2]

At the close of Evans's service that morning I asked him if he was familiar with the hymn "Give Me the Roses While I Live." He said he was, but when I asked him if he knew anything about the flower services I had witnessed in Deep Gap, North Carolina, he had to say that he knew nothing of this tradition.

Over the years at Mount Paran there may have been a slow fusion of two symbolic meanings of the flower—the flower as sacrificial gift for reconciliation and the flower as statement of praise and love. The mandate in Matt. 5:23–24 calls the believer to leave her or his "gift before the altar" while seeking to become reconciled to estranged brothers or sisters. Indeed, in the Mount Paran service the flowers initially are placed on a table before the pulpit, and in these traditional churches that pulpit is frequently called the altar. The retired Missionary Baptist minister, Rev. W.E. Denny, remarked that in his early ministerial days the pulpit was *always* called the altar.

Nevertheless, Mount Paran worshipers do not leave their gifts "before the altar," or at least they do not leave them there while they are making reconciliation. Instead, they are instructed to pick them up and to distribute them to their brothers and sisters of the church. Thus the flower gift, which first symbolized a gift to God, becomes to the individual brother or sister a gift of either reconciliation or loving support. No part of the ceremony seems to stand for the final command of Matt. 5:24: " . . . first be reconciled with thy brother, *and then come and offer thy gift.*"

2. From Notes taken 3 June 1984, at Union Primitive Baptist Church, Sparta, N.C.

In a small church that practices both this service and the foot-washing ceremony, it must become very difficult to maintain really lasting antipathies toward fellow communicants. Under such pressures toward unity, estranged parties would have to become reconciled or join separate churches.

The Annual Memorial Service at Bull Creek Old Regular

As mentioned above, I had met Elder Bill Campbell of the Bull Creek Old Regular fellowship at the Bethany Old Regular Church in Kingsport, Tennessee. After that I had looked for an opportunity to visit the Bull Creek fellowship. Bull Creek Old Regular Baptist is located some ten or twelve miles northwest of Grundy, Virginia. To visit this fellowship, one travels from Grundy on Highway 460 toward Pikeville, Kentucky, then turn left on Route 609 and proceed approximately three miles up a narrow valley to where the church sits on the right. The house of worship is a rather plain red brick structure, appearing to be about thirty years old. Meetings are held on Sunday following the second Saturday of the month, and visitors are welcome, so long as they "come in the proper spirit."

Elder Bill Campbell had told me that the service would begin at 9:30 A.M. But when I arrived at approximately 9:20, the church was crowded with some 300 to 350 worshipers who had already begun to sing, shout, and clap, led by the lining of Campbell and one other relatively young elder. At Bethany church, this second Elder, whose name I had not learned, had told me very firmly that audiotaping the Bull Creek service would not be acceptable.

When I stepped inside the church, Campbell came forward to meet me with a handshake and an embrace. Being made the immediate focus of attention in this way made me somewhat uneasy, but I noticed that Campbell's actions appeared to render me acceptable to those who witnessed the scene. The congregation was engaged in a song at that moment, but several people were just milling about the sanctuary, greeting old friends or visitors from other churches. The atmosphere was rife with anticipation for a fervent service, and two elderly women were already shouting.

I managed to obtain a seat in the pew fourth from the rear of the church and settled in for what was to become a four-hour event. In past visits to such churches I had been able to find a spot of relative isolation and avoid being surrounded by the impassioned displays that followed. On this morning, however, there was no way for me to maintain the desired distance, and I was really jammed in among the crowd.

Bull Creek had its beginning in 1891 as a Primitive Baptist fellowship but broke away from this tradition in 1895 in a doctrinal squabble over predestination. Bull Creek has been a member of the Union Association of Old Regulars since 1897.[3]

The church's inside walls were of dark-toned tongue-and-groove knotty pine. Hanging on the wall immediately behind the pulpit were twenty-five or thirty framed photographs of past elders of the fellowship, including two that dated back to the 1890s, when the church was founded. The old photographs gave a sense of longstanding tradition to this otherwise fairly contemporary structure. As we have seen, Old Regular congregations routinely display photographs of past leaders, particular former moderators of fellowships, in their churches, and I have received the definite impression that current Old Regular leaders look forward with warm anticipation to this form of immortalization.

At Bull Creek the benches to the left of the pulpit (the preacher's left) were occupied by women, while the benches to the right were filled by men—an arrangement just opposite of that at Bethany Old Regular. Two pews immediately behind the pulpit were filled by the local and visiting elders. All of these benches, along with the pulpit, sat on a raised level of the floor. In front of this were approximately fifteen rows of pews, divided by a center aisle. Here sat nonmembers and visitors from other churches.

By 10:00 A.M., all these pews were completely filled. The elders and a few other men wore coats, but most of the males either had worn no coats to begin with or had hung them on one of the coat-racks that extended along the full length of both side walls. A handful of older men were dressed in new-looking overalls or clean, heavily starched khaki or denim work clothes. Women wore their best dresses, which ranged from very traditional cotton prints to the

---

3. Rufus Perrigan, comp., *History of Regular Baptists* (Haysi, Va.: Privately published by Rufus Perrigan, 1961), 225.

most stylish attire. In general, the crowd was well dressed, given the heat, and tastefully groomed. In addition, the few children who were in the congregation exemplified the care these parents traditionally give their offspring.

It was warm that morning, and getting warmer as the congregation swelled to at least four hundred, with forty or more individuals (mostly older men, teenage boys, and young children) remaining outside. Windows had been opened as wide as possible, and five ceiling fans whirled at maximum speed. In addition, cardboard fans had been passed to every individual in the congregation. The fan I received had been provided by the Virginia Division of Forestry, Department of Conservation and Economic Development, and it contained on its face a picture of Smokey the Bear talking to various animals. On its back were messages about forest fires and conservation, supported by numerous Bible verses treating themes of nature and its preservation. Some state bureaucrat had discovered an interesting way to communicate with this group of Virginians.

A five-gallon yellow water cooler that sat on a wide ledge of the stand provided another method of dealing with the heat. Throughout the service, during singing or sermons, individuals periodically moved to the front of the church and poured cups of water, generally shaking hands with several fellow worshipers when going to and from the cooler. This activity beautifully illustrates the informality of the typical Old Regular worship service, during which people walk in and out of the church at will, small children sometimes play just outside the open windows, and individuals move freely about the church during the singing or preaching.

Only about a third of the congregation that morning seemed to be affiliated with the Bull Creek fellowship. The rest of the crowd were visitors from other churches in the Union Association of Old Regulars, with at least a few people from fellowships in the Sardis Association. For example, one woman turned out to be the daughter of Elder Edwin May, moderator of the Sardis group of churches. Her home fellowship was the Bent Branch congregation of Meta, Kentucky. Like many other visitors that morning, she had come to Bull Creek for this service because it was a special one, promising considerable religious fervor.

To judge by the license plates of cars parked along the road in front of the church, the congregation represented churches in Kentucky, Tennessee, Virginia, West Virginia, and even Ohio. There were the usual efforts to become reaquainted with fellow Old Regulars not seen for a year or two, and a great deal of handshaking went on throughout the service, especially during the early part of the morning.

The three annual services that traditionally draw the largest number of visitors to any Old Regular church are the communion and footwashing service, the union service, and the memorial service. Dates of these events are published in the association's minutes, and Old Regulars frequently plan long in advance which churches they will visit during a summer. In fact, it is not unusual for families to structure vacations around key church events, particularly events in a distant fellowship in the association.

The Bull Creek memorial service on June 10, 1984, had been set almost a year before when the following announcement was published in the 1983 minutes of the Union Association: "BULL CREEK CHURCH— Second Saturday and Sunday [in June] will be a memorial of all the deceased members. Ministers requested to attend are Elders Fred M. Stiltner, James O'Quinn, Freeland Yates, Arnold Clevenger, Frank O'Quinn, Frank Newsome, and John C. Layne."[4]

Seven elders were requested to attend this particular service, including John Layne, the moderator of the entire Union Association. Calling seven elders (nine, including the moderator and assistant moderator of the local church) is not atypical for such an event. At least three elders are needed to preach, one to act as moderator, one or two to line the hymns, and, for this service, one to read the names of the deceased. Calling seven also allows some leeway in case one or more of the requested elders cannot attend.

The lineup of elders seldom stays exactly as stated in the association minutes, since illness or other factors invariably thwart the plans of individual ministers. Originally Bill Campbell was not called for this particular service; yet he ended up officiating during much of the morning, lining some of the hymns, and reading the names.

The service that day consisted of numerous songs, four prayers, three sermons, and the central event, the reading of the names

4. Union Association of Old Regular Baptists, *Minutes* (1983), 13.

of every deceased individual who had ever been either a formal member or a faithful attender of the church. The remainder of this discussion focuses on the calling out of names, since that is the main purpose of this ceremony.

As Bull Creek Church was founded in 1891, when Elder Bill Campbell stood to call out the names of the fellowship's deceased, he had ninety-three years of dying to memorialize. It took him over an hour and a half to get through his lists.

After a name was called, Campbell might pause briefly and make some special comment on the individual. This tendency was particularly marked for three groups of persons: (1) those who had played important roles in the early church, (2) elders, and (3) church members who had died in recent years. In cases of such special mention, Campbell's remarks ranged from a brief sentence such as "Brother So-and-So really liked to wash feet," to rather complete narratives. These remarks frequently engendered fervent verbal or nonverbal reactions from the congregation—shouted exclamations, tears, hollers, and hand clappings.

Some families waited for their loved one's name to be called and then responded, not with cheers or anything like that, but with prayerful supplications such as "Keep him near you, Lord." A congregational interjection seemed also to cause Campbell to pause on the respective name when he might not otherwise have done so.

It was a particularly emotional moment when Campbell read out the name of Billy Ray Harrison, a man who had been buried only the day before. Another high point occurred when Campbell read the name of a recently deceased member who had passed away right in church. The young elder pointed to the spot where it had happened, and he could not pass up the opportunity to tell his congregation that this also could happen to them at any moment, that they were mortal, and that they should always have their lives in preparation.

Although the reading of a long list of names might have been expected to put the congregation to sleep, Bull Creek's memorial service was only slightly less emotional than the footwashings at Bethany Old Regular and at Saddle Mountain Regular Baptist.

Three periods in the morning's activities were particularly poignant. The first of these occurred when Campbell called out the name of a church member who had died three or four months earlier. After reading the name, Campbell paused to report that he had visited the gentleman in the local hospital just prior to his death. The ailing man had wanted to talk about the state of his soul, not because he was in doubt as to his "salvation" but because he was extremely confident of his redemption and wanted his family to know of that confidence.

On hearing Elder Campbell's account of the conversation, two women in the congregation—one apparently the late member's wife and the other his daughter—threw themselves into each other's arms, crying, shouting, and embracing with body-circling hugs that went from shoulders, to upper waist, back to shoulders, and then to neck in such quick succession that the two appeared to be grasping frantically for a moment of joy for which they had an insatiable appetite. They were soon joined by two or three other women who alternately embraced first one and then the other of the pair, crying all the time. The scene was a draining one even to watch, filled as it was with indelible pathos.

The other two moments of high passion occurred after Campbell had completed the lengthy reading of names. At the close of the initial sermon of the morning, one elderly woman began to shout, infecting others with her passion. Indeed, when emotions such as this were unleashed they tended to sweep through the congregation, striking exuberant responses primarily from the women, but also inflaming the emotions of men.

The final moment of intense fervor transpired during the last hymn of the morning. This was a more general response, seeming to come from almost every member of the congregation. Men and women milled throughout the sanctuary, shaking hands, embracing, and joyously weeping, all while Campbell lined the hymn and another elder exhorted the congregation with final words about "the glories of God."

It was about 1:30 P.M. when the service closed. The last remarks were made by several visiting elders who one by one invited the people to attend ceremonies at their respective churches, particularly for communions and memorials. Old Regulars call this process "announcing appointments." The congregation then retired outside, where women of the church had arranged an abundance of food along both sides of a twenty-five-foot expanse of tables.

Homecomings and Dinners-on-the-Ground

Neither homecomings nor dinners-on-the-ground are indigenous to or exclusively found in Southern Appalachia. These events are not even exclusive to the South. Many of us, perhaps as children, attended such events, and the sponsoring churches may have been Advent Christian, Baptist, Church of Christ, Methodist, Presbyterian, or any of a wide range of denominations. Probably, however, the congregation was relatively small, rural, and traditional.

As the name implies, a homecoming invites people to return home to their original church—the church that baptized them, where Mother and Dad were members. This church figures prominently in many cherished memories—of Sunday school, summer Bible school, revivals, singing, first romances played out amid youth group activities, and the first stirrings of a spiritual self. Homecomings are for reacquainting, revitalizing, refocusing, and perhaps reconstructing. They are times for talking, singing, praying, eating, and visiting graves. They are nostalgic, spiritual, and social, reflecting most aspects of the human need for love and belonging.

Homecomings vary sharply from church to church. Nevertheless, there are a handful of traditional features, some emphasized by one fellowship and some by another. The following remarks about homecomings, excluding the dinners-on-the-ground that follow services, apply primarily to the Missionary Baptist churches. As far as the other subdenominations go, either I have not witnessed enough of their homecomings to be sufficiently knowledgeable, or the homecoming service *per se* is not a part of their tradition. The latter is the case, for example, with the Old Regulars, for whom communion, memorial, and union services serve much the same purpose as a homecoming.

It is not unusual for people to drive hundreds of miles to attend a Southern Appalachian Baptist homecoming. The retired couple who sold their mountain farm and moved to Florida, the family who migrated to the Upper Midwest during World War II when labor was needed in war-related industries, folks who simply moved to another end of the county, preachers who once served the church, young people who got married in the church and now bring their own children to see "Grandma" and "Grandpa," and former members who moved their membership to follow a preacher or slid up a notch or two in the social heirarchy of church affiliations—all of these individuals join with the current members to celebrate the ongoing history of a particular church. Add to all of these the numerous visitors from neighboring fellowships, and a church whose regular congregation numbers only around a hundred may find its attendance swelling to three hundred or four hundred on this one day.

For such a crowd there must be a special service, with special preaching and special singing. The preaching may be provided by one or more former ministers of the church, or at least by some highly-sought-after exhorter. Generally the main purpose of the morning's sermon is not so much to evangelize as to celebrate and praise, to speak glowingly of the past and to unify all within a single enduring tradition. This is a time to speak of the good men and women still struggling to build and sustain a church, and a time to say, "Welcome home, all you who have wandered."

The special singing will probably be provided by a mixture of in-house groups and visiting singers—single individuals, duets, quartets, etc. At a more affluent, more "establishment," somewhat less "mountain" church, a professional gospel-singing group may have been booked for the event.

For example, Proffit's Grove Baptist Church, in Watauga County, North Carolina, is a former Missionary Baptist church that left some of its earlier traditions behind as it prospered. For its 1983 homecoming, this fellowship scheduled a gospel group from Valdese, North Carolina, "The Shuffler Family." As is generally the case in such situations, these singers became the afternoon entertainment, performing in the church for a couple of hours after the homecoming meal. The singing family had arrived in a large recreational vehicle which bore on its sides, in elaborate script, the name of the group. Inside rode the five singers and all their instruments and electronic gear. Such conveyances flourish on the highways of the South, ferrying performers from one church event to another. The groups do not always just sing; they may also testify and generally "carry the word."

Smaller, more "mountain" churches, however, cannot afford such professionals, even if their congregations' tastes do gravitate toward the artistry of these touring gospel groups, with their stylized and polished Nashville sound. Instead, these smaller fellowships rely

Fellowship Meal after a Service at Tivis Chapel (Old Regular) Baptist
Church, Haysi, Buchanan County, Virginia.

heavily upon groups and individuals from other churches similar
to their own, songsters eager to perform at homecomings, revivals,
and sings. Mount Paran, for example, has at least half a dozen duos,
quartets, etc., who generously perform for other area churches. On
one occasion I traveled with the Mount Paran singers as they jour-
neyed to perform at a service in Alleghany County. We rode in a
fifteen-passenger Dodge van purchased by the church in the mid-
1970s for this and other purposes. En route the group discussed
the summer to come, filled with short trips—to a revival here, a
homecoming there, a singing elsewhere.

Perhaps the most memorable aspect of the typical homecoming is the big dinner-on-the-ground held after the morning service.
For such feasts many fellowships have built, beside or behind the
church, an open-sided shed twenty-five or thirty feet long, under

which are placed long tables or four-by-eight-foot sheets of plywood resting on sawhorses. On these surfaces churchwomen then spread tablecloths or white butcher paper, unless the table tops are left bare. Here wonderful collections of food are placed. Every family brings several dishes—pies, cakes, casseroles, breads, salads (particularly potato salad), deviled eggs, endless choices of vegetables, fried chicken, country-cured ham, meat balls, chicken-fried steak, ham or sausage biscuits, and barbecued pork or beef.

Usually there is a system to the arrangement of all this food: paper plates, napkins, plastic utensils, and styrofoam cups at the head of the table, vegetable and meat dishes next, then salads, and finally desserts and drinks. But occasionally there is no plan at all, with foods placed wherever open spots are found.

The latter picture of a jumbled, bountiful cornucopia gives rise not only to pleasing mottled aesthetics, but also to a special pattern of initial reconnoitering. People move thoughtfully around the expanse of tables, checking out the complete spread before beginning, to avoid filling their plates with foods that ultimately would have been their second or third choices. The children are particularly amusing, as they scurry from dish to dish, suspiciously eyed by parents who do not want them to take only desserts.

Morning services frequently continue until long after 1:00 P.M. By then everyone, but especially the children, are very hungry. The good, plentiful food tastes even better consumed in the pleasant Appalachian setting, often under a large silver or red maple or beside a mountain stream that later in the afternoon will be used as a baptismal pool.

Fellowship meals at Sandy Ridge Old Regular Church are eaten in an old two-room schoolhouse that has been turned into a community center. There I discovered on the table a large platter of fried chicken livers and confessed to the woman behind me that this was one of my favorite foods—only to find that she herself had prepared the dish. When I returned the next year for the Sandy Ridge union service, this lady was quick to point me toward the fried chicken livers.

At Silas Creek Union Baptist I had already filled my plate when I came upon a pecan pie, for me the ultimate in gustatory indulgence. I passed over this treat but must have said something about my

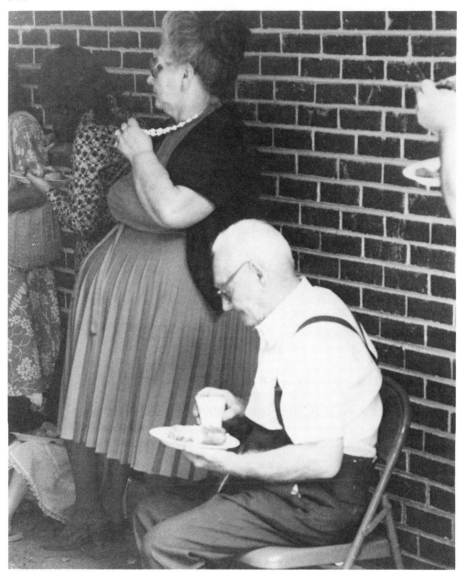

Eating Dinner-on-the-Ground at Bull Creek Old Regular Baptist, Maxie, Buchanan County, Virginia. Photograph: Joel Poteat.

weakness for this particular dessert, since halfway through my meal I was faced by a grinning youngster holding a slice of the pie out toward me.

On the table at Saddle Mountain Regular Baptist, I counted four banana cream pies, all of which I sampled. At Mount Paran, Willard Watson insisted that I try his barbecued pork, long after I could not comfortably "try" any additional dish. At Bull Creek I sat for almost an hour with a delicious plate of food that I never finished, because I was engaged in an fascinating conversation with Elder Fred Stiltner, the eldest elder in the fellowship.

The welcome is invariably hardy, the scenery always beautiful, the air cool, the fellowship warm, and the culinary fare highly satisfying. One could do worse than be a follower after Southern Appalachian religious traditions.

The Union Service in Old Regular Baptist Churches

Earlier we examined a problem once prevalent in the Old Regular associations, the doctrinal splits that occurred as a result of the fact that individual churches were isolated from each other for prolonged periods of time. In the late 1800s, mountain roads, where they existed, were hardly more than trails—narrow, winding, difficult to maintain, and generally slow and treacherous. Winter travel was virtually impossible except on horseback, and spring travelers frequently found creeks swollen and impassable. Indeed, during long months entire communities were shut off from the rest of mountain civilization. It was difficult for individuals to make it to their home churches once a month—so difficult that many churches did not have much in the way of winter services. And visits to other churches in an association were fairly rare.

With isolation came independence. Elders of local fellowships were forced to deal with issues without the guidance of other association leaders. Questions frequently arose concerning both doctrine and worship procedures, and the local elder or elders felt obliged to provide answers. But the answers these locals gave were often wrong, at least as measured by association orthodoxy. Thus problems of heresy sprang up, and the longer and more intense the states of isolation, the greater the dangers of such heresy.

The union service was designed as one answer to this problem. Once a year three or more elders from other churches in the association would be invited to a service for the purpose of preaching. As originally conceived, the procedure would allow local congregations and their elders to hear how Old Regular doctrine was preached in sister churches. As a result, heresies would be more easily avoided. In the early days of this practice, the elders who would be "called" would be ones from the more distant churches in the association, and it was not uncommon for the home-based preachers and the visiting preachers to question each other on doctrine in order to guarantee "unity."

Although today much of the original impetus behind the union service apparently has been lost, the service still stands as one of the four important events on the Old Regular spring-to-fall church calendar (the other three being the communion and memorial services and the annual association meeting). Like the memorial and communion services, the union service usually attracts a number of visitors, giving that morning's events a little more importance and excitement than usual. But there will probably be no trace of the old objective, to sniff out deviant doctrines or practices. In fact, the "called" elders will have been chosen primarily because these are preachers the church membership likes to hear.

The calling of these elders to speak at certain churches is an action organized during an annual association meeting. In the Union Association the same thing is done for the memorial meetings. The Sardis Association, however, combines the communion and union services and thus calls elders for these combined meetings and for the memorial services. In both associations, the dates of services and lists of called elders are published in the minutes. The master schedules of these union, communion, and memorial meetings begin in April and end in October, with September left off the Union Association calendar because it is the association's annual meeting month. September is also the annual meeting month for the Sardis Association, but these fellowships simply keep the second weekend of this month clear.

Before and after this seven-month timespan, Southern Appalachian weather could result in cancellations. Furthermore, since clustering these events in a much shorter time wouldn't be conducive to visitations or afford the most effective use of available ministers, associations try to spread the events out fairly evenly. Nevertheless, there are not too many of these special services in either April or October. Individual fellowships wanting to change the dates of any key services seek the approval of the association via "requests" advanced at the annual meeting. There are not a great number of these changes, however, since the association calendar becomes very traditional.

I have attended only one Old Regular union service, held at Sandy Ridge in June, 1984. The form of the service did not seem significantly different from a regular Sandy Ridge service I had witnessed the year before.

Creek Baptisms

All of our six Baptist subdenominations baptize in natural settings, usually in mountain creeks or rivers but occasionally in the shallow waters of lakes. By far the most frequently used body of water is the creek, first, because there are plenty of these small streams in the mountains; and second, because churches are often built close to, or right beside, a creek. Where the newly saved would be immersed was always a consideration when locations were originally chosen for these churches, and it was considered ideal if the members could step outside their house of worship and move directly to the baptismal site.

One slight problem existed, however: these mountain streams often were far too shallow for baptisms. The cold water ran swiftly over beds of polished rocks, creating stream levels only ankle to calf deep, and the preacher needed water up to his thighs or hips for a good immersion. This necessitated finding a spot either where eddying currents had created a natural bowl in the creek bottom or where a small dam could be built to back up the water. It also would be helpful for the access to the spot to be gentle in slope and for the creek bottom to be level, smooth, and covered with sand or small pebbles.

This search has led to widely varying ways of using these baptismal streams. The Mount Paran church sits beside a shallow creek that is only about four feet wide. The water runs under a culvert where the creek crosses Wildcat Road, and on the morning before a baptism someone places a cap over the church side of the culvert and backs up the creek to a depth of about three feet, ensuring a water level sufficient for a good immersion.

At one time elders of the Bull Creek fellowship were able to baptize only a few feet from their church, in the stream for which the church was named. That, however, is no longer possible; coal-mining operations in the hollow above the church have polluted the creek so badly that health officials have warned the church against continued use of the stream. Now the elders baptize in a river several miles from the church.

The folks at Saddle Mountain Regular Baptist use for their baptisms a stream that also runs very near their church. But to find a spot deep enough for immersions, they have to move up the creek about a quarter of a mile to a point where this stream crosses a mountain meadow currently used to pasture cattle. At one spot in this meadow the creek makes a slight bend and in the process pools out sufficiently to allow hip-deep water to accumulate. On a Sunday in August, 1984, when I witnessed a baptism in this setting, someone had thoughtfully mowed a path through the high grass and thistle down to the water's edge.

My plan that August morning had been to attend a communion and footwashing at Saddle Mountain (the service described in the last chapter). I didn't know that a baptism was also scheduled to take place before the regular service.

Highway 21 crosses the Blue Ridge Parkway just southeast of Sparta, North Carolina. The traveler driving several miles northeast on the Parkway from this juncture will sight two churches just off the road on the right, standing no more than fifty yards from each other. The first of these buildings, a white wood-framed structure, is the Saddle Mountain Regular Baptist Church; and the second, a very plain red brick structure, is the Saddle Mountain Union Baptist Church.

Years ago these two fellowships were one, but a doctrinal dispute arose and the congregation split. One segment remained in the Regular Baptist fold, while the other affiliated with the Union Baptists. The land, however, was jointly owned, so the new fellowship built its church on the same plot of ground. Today the buildings stand so close to each other that if they held services at the same time, they could hear each other's singing. But they conduct their preaching services on different Sundays of the month.

On the August Sunday in question, I was nearing the Parkway turnoff to the church when I noticed a group of "church dressed" people gathering out in the middle of a meadow. As I pulled up in front of the church, I quickly saw that although there were a few cars around, no-one was in sight. Turning my car around, I drove up a dirt road that ran parallel to the Parkway between two cornfields. After only a short distance, I noticed an open gate leading into the pasture where the people were gathering. Several cars were parked just inside the gate. When I heard an old hymn, I knew that I was indeed headed toward a baptism.

The group had gathered by a creek that was perhaps eight to ten feet wide at that slight gooseneck bend mentioned earlier. With his back to the water, Elder Glenn Killon stood leading the cluster of some twenty people in a hymn. Standing near him was a young girl of about sixteen, attired in a high-necked, lace-trimmed white dress, and behind her waited an older woman with a large bath towel draped across her folded arms. The girl's face was already wet with tears.

Killon led the group in three hymns before being joined by Elder Harold Wilmoth, who delivered a prayer. Killon then read from the first chapter of Mark the account of Jesus's baptism by John the Baptist, ending with these verses:

> And it came to pass in those days, that Jesus came from Nazareth of Galilee, and was baptized of John in Jordan.
> And straightway coming up out of the water, he saw the heavens opened, and the Spirit like a dove descending upon him.
>
> Mark 1:9–10

Killon then offered a second prayer before he and Wilmoth led the girl down into the thigh-deep water. The use of two ministers for this service is not just a purely ceremonial factor; according to some preachers, it is also mandated by safety needs. The actual moment of immersion is frequently a highly emotional one for the individual being baptized, and some persons swoon or begin thrashing about in uncontrolled joy. Two ministers may be needed to hold the enthusiast when this happens.

Early Morning Baptism at Saddle Mountain Regular Baptist Church.

When the three principals reached the deepest spot in the stream, the girl turned to face the waiting group with her hands overlapped across her breast. Wilmoth and Killon stood on opposite sides of her, each holding one of her upper arms with his left hand. This positioning placed Wilmoth with his face toward the crowd and Killon with his back toward them. At this point both elders raised their right arms toward the sky as Killon called out, "We baptize this our sister in the name of the Father, the Son, and the Holy Spirit." Then quickly Wilmoth placed his right hand over the girl's lower face, apparently pinching her nostrils closed as he did so, while Killon placed his right hand behind the girl's head. Together they plunged her backwards into a total immersion and immediately brought her up.

The girl was crying now and trembling from the water's coldness, and the two elders led her back to the bank, where the woman waited to fold the towel around the girl's shoulders. This newly consecrated sister quickly received the hugs of several who stood close by, as the crowd broke into a final hymn. Killon closed the ceremony with a short prayer, and the group wandered back toward their cars and then on to the church, later to begin their regular service and their annual communion and footwashing.

Creek baptisms often are held separate from any other service, but perhaps just as frequently they are staged before or after a main worship ceremony or as part of the day-long series of events at a homecoming. This means that the ministers involved have to arrange some way to change clothes. It seemed obvious, in the case of Wilmoth and Killon, that the pants they wore to wade into the baptismal stream were not the best items in their wardrobes; they probably have certain articles of clothing that they reserve for these events. Nevertheless, they still must change before taking charge of the main service of the day.

At Mount Paran, Roscoe Greene has solved this problem with a method that might offend some purists: he and his assisting minister both wear waist-high fisherman waders when they go into the water. They can quickly slip out of this gear and proceed directly to the church for the next event. In 1980 I witnessed a baptism of three new converts to the Mount Paran membership, and Greene and Gary Watson, the assisting minister, were both wearing their waders. When "Preacher Ros" came out of the water that day, he said to someone standing close at hand, "These things started to leak, and I thought I was going to sink out there." During the church "sing" that afternoon, Greene stood in one soggy shoe.

CHAPTER 6

Turn Your Radio On

Driving through the mountains of Southern Appalachia on a Sunday morning with the car radio on, one is almost certain to be introduced to broadcasts with titles such as "Gospel Echoes," "The Old Fashioned Gospel Time," "The Morning Star Gospel Program," "The Holy Ghost Broadcast," "Words of Grace," "The Bread of Life Program," "The Voices of Zion Broadcast," and "Gospel Airwaves." A program of this sort features fifteen or thirty minutes of locally-produced sacred music, prayers, testimonials, dedications, announcements, and preaching, all thrown together within a format that sounds decidedly unstructured and unrehearsed.

The program's personnel typically consists of a preacher, some singers and musicians, perhaps a guest or two who wishes to testify, and someone (if the preacher does not handle this task) to read announcements, make dedications, and acknowledge correspondence. The sponsoring organization might be Calvary Baptist Church of Damascus, Virginia; Shoun's Mission Church of Shoun's Mill, Tennessee; Rainbow Chapel of Sugar Grove, North Carolina; or The Full Gospel Fellowship of Creston, North Carolina.

The broadcast would originate from one of a large number of small stations scattered throughout the Southern Appalachian ranges—stations such as WATA, Boone, North Carolina; WKSK, West Jefferson, North Carolina; WMCT, Mountain City, Tennessee; WLSD, Big Stone Gap, Virginia; WSCB, St. Paul-Castlewood, Virginia, or WNRG, Grundy, Virginia. Most of these small Appalachian stations allocate sizeable blocks of their Sunday schedules to locally-produced religious broadcasts. WMCT or WNRG, for example, goes on the air at 6:00 A.M. on Sunday mornings with recorded gospel music and stays with religious programming (except for news, public service announcements, and sometimes a NASCAR race) until deep in the afternoon, a large portion of this time being devoted to live broadcasts. Other stations such as WATA, however, may broadcast only one or two locally-produced religious programs.

This chapter moves away from our six subdenominations of Baptists to examine a phenomenon involving a number of Protestant mountain denominations. The fellowships in question are not Old Regular or Primitive Baptists, and probably not Regular Baptists, since these subdenominations do not believe in overt evangelism, much less by radio. Instead, the fellowships sponsoring these broadcasts are usually Missionary Baptists, Free Will Baptists, Union Baptists, Holiness, Church of God, or other independent religious groups. At times a broadcast is not sponsored by any particular church, but is produced instead by one preacher who has assembled an independent group of singers, musicians, and supporters, and raises the necessary funds for the show through "free will offerings." The type of program discussed here is not a broadcast of a regular Sunday morning worship service. Rather it is specially produced in a studio and involves prayers, singing, preaching, and other religious activities.

If one sits in the studio while a typical program of this sort is being produced, one notices several things. First, the actual physical plant of the station is probably quite modest in size, just large enough to contain a couple of studios, an office or two, and a room for the transmitting equipment. Ten or twelve people, with requisite musical instruments, are crammed into a production studio approximately twelve to fifteen feet square. The furnishings of the room are plain but functional and may include a small table or podium, one or two microphones, a half-dozen folding chairs, and perhaps a piano. Otherwise, the setting of soundproof glass and acoustical paneling is fairly barren.

Adjoining this space will be an equally small studio packed with records, tapes, turntables, tape decks, the central production console, storage cabinets, and other miscellaneous furnishings and equipment. On Sunday morning the person seated at the console, serving as disc jockey and announcer, is apt to be a young man or woman of high school or college age, speaking in the idiom of the region and controlling the broadcast with a loose informality.

These are not "fast lane" stations, and the general discourse that is heard between gospel music selections, or between the various

Station WMCT, Mountain City, Tennessee.

thirty-minute religious broadcasts, is slow, provincial, and often not very grammatical. This intervening discourse contains a heavy dose of local public service announcements and advertisements, comments on the weather and other topical subjects, and "call-in" commentary. All of these elements add to the general rusticity of the programming.

During the week this kind of station schedules a daily morning devotional led by various ministers in the community and broadcasts a daily "Obituary Column of the Air." At 11:00 A.M. on Sunday it always carries the main worship service of one of the "downtown" churches. Before the airing of this service, however, the station probably broadcasts two or three shorter shows like the ones under examination in this chapter.

As a general rule, the people who gather for one of these locally-produced religious broadcasts are older than average, although there may be some youthful faces among the singers and some children or grandchildren who are allowed to play quietly in the studio while the program is in progress. The typical participant, however, is around sixty or older, minimally educated, traditional and evangelistic in

religious indoctrination, Appalachian in speech and culture, lower-
to lower-middle-class in socioeconomic status, and, in terms of
her or his personal commitment to the religious cause, strongly
motivated to "spread the word."

The number of participants varies depending on the nature of
the program and the size of the studio, but ten to fifteen is typical:
the preacher; perhaps his wife to make announcements; a pianist,
guitarist, or accordionist; three or four singers; and a half-dozen
or so friends, supporters, spouses, etc., who line the walls, join
the singing, and provide frequent "Amens," "Praise Gods," "Bless
him, Lords," and other audience responses. This latter auxiliary
group provides the "friends and neighbors" atmosphere that so often
characterizes these broadcasts. Indeed, the friends and supporters
present at any given broadcast may be part of a larger cadre of
program followers who drop by occasionally to lend their spirit to
the show.

The relaxed nature of the productions allows people to wander in
at almost any moment. Regular supporters, in particular, feel free
to drop in while a show is in progress. When they do so, they are
invariably greeted by those standing close by, and their entrance
may be acknowledged on the air. Furthermore, under certain circumstances a latecomer may be asked immediately if he or she has
any testimonial to give. Such practices endow these friends and supporters with a sense of importance and cultivate a body of followers
who feed on these experiences, so that the programs frequently
seem to become Sunday morning get-togethers of old friends and
neighbors. It may be that the broadcasts are listened to as much for
this "old friends and acquaintances" ambiance as for their purely
religious content. When a show such as "The Morning Star Gospel Program" has been on the air for thirty-five years, this familiar
folksy atmosphere is an extremely powerful attraction.

Another very strong factor, however, is the emotional level of
these broadcasts and the emotional ties between the participants.
Since these groups in some cases have been together for decades
and have shared much of the joy and grief of life, and since their
religious practices are by their very nature imbued with a heavy
emotionality, there are moments when these small studios reverber-
ate with cries and tears of grief or happiness. Deaths are endured,
offsprings or other family members "saved," major illnesses suf-

fered, and marriages and births celebrated, and all are shared on the program with friends of long standing.

The significance of all this intimate pathos is increased when one remembers that while all these tears and expressions of pain and joy are being shed in a small room with a group of close friends, the happiness or grief also is being broadcast over the very public airwaves. From anguished prayer requests, occupants of Southern Appalachian homes learn that some "brother" has a son whom he considers "fallen away," that a certain "sister's" husband lingers painfully near death in a local hospital, that a particular church community is experiencing internal discord, that a young singer suffers temptations when among "unsaved" high school friends, that an elderly widower yearns for death because he misses his wife of fifty years, or that one "sinner" has become very disturbed over the uncertain state of his "soul."

One of the most emotional of these area radio shows is "The Prayer Band Program," aired each Sunday morning over WBEJ in Elizabethton, Tennessee, and featuring Brother Charles Hill, Jr. This broadcast seldom ends before at least one participant has burst into tears. Hill himself is what one might call a "crying" preacher, heavily dependent on overt emotionality for sermon impact. He has a soft, kindly voice that communicates great concern for others, and he revels in talking about the "joys of salvation." His favorite illustration is a tearful account of his own "redemption" some thirty years ago, an event which he describes as having set him free from an extremely sinful existence. When he moves into this frequently repeated narrative, he sobs profusely, proclaiming over and over again, "Thank you, Jesus! Thank you, Father!" Other members of the group then add their tearful rejoicing to his, with cries such as "Bless him, Lord!"

In addition to this general emotionalism, another broad characteristic of these broadcasts is their improvisational nature. The programs appear to be only minimally planned and are never totally rehearsed. The basic tenet of the Southern Appalachian preacher, that he should never prepare his remarks and that he should remain open to divine on-the-spot inspiration, seems to prevail for most aspects of these productions. Singers, musicians, and other personnel make their contributions in accord with the same philosophy.

Improvisation guides the entire production—the issues of what songs are to be sung and to whom they will be dedicated, who will lead various prayers or perhaps give testimonies, and even who will preach. Roscoe Greene once was asked if he always knew who would do the preaching on his show. He said that he didn't, that he liked to give other preachers a chance to speak if they wanted to, but that he had to be a little careful in this practice because sometimes a spur-of-the-moment speaker would say something that would get the program and the station into trouble. When Greene was asked to elaborate on this point, he admitted that occasionally, during moments of exuberance, these preachers would attack individuals and other church groups or denominations. "I've been fairly liberal with preachers, you know," said Greene, "and some of them broke the rules of the station. You can't get on the radio and personate [sic] people and call them names. You just can't do it. . . . You see, this fairness doctrine, if you personate a fellow, they could force the station to give them the same amount of time to answer me back. . . . Well, that's really not the gospel nohow."[1]

Still, as Greene said, he is rather liberal with other preachers, and on several occasions, at other stations as well as at WATA, I have witnessed a visiting brother enter a studio and immediately be asked if there were any words he wished to say "for the Lord."

Although I myself have generally been able to avoid such involvements, even I have been asked to speak. I had been sitting in on several religious program broadcasts at WMCT, and one morning I found myself witnessing a production of "The Back to the Gospel Hour," featuring Brother Dwight Adams. About midway through his show, Adams decided to ask everyone in the studio to give a testimonial. He quickly made it clear that this included me and the graduate student Debra Thompson. I smiled and lightly shook my head, a technique that had worked a couple of times in the past, but Brother Adams was not to be denied. He insisted that I step to the mike and say whatever I wanted to say. I saw no way out of the situation except to offend him or to do as he requested. As I moved to the mike I heard several of the singers say, "Bless him, Lord." Frankly I needed a little blessing; I wanted to say something that would be acceptable to the group, but I didn't want to voice any implicitly dishonest emotions, attitudes, or theological beliefs. "I'm impressed

1. Interview with Roscoe Greene, recorded 31 Aug. 1983.

by the beautiful devotion that I've seen here this morning, that is the result of the faith these folks have," I said haltingly. "There's nothing wrong with that." It was not a very clear statement, but it seemed to satisfy Adams and the others, to judge by their "Amens."

Encouraged by his success with me, the preacher then turned to Debra. "Come on, sister. Say something," he said. "Just a word or two, however you feel."

"I feel good to be here," she asserted. "I feel very welcome, and I really appreciate all the good music and the good preaching." Again there were several "Amens," and Adams moved on to the other persons in the studio, each of whom unhesitatingly took her or his moment at the mike. Adams even asked the young man on the board in the control room to testify, suggesting by the confident manner in which he made the petition that this was a common procedure. However, the fellow was away from the board at that moment and apparently did not hear the request.[2]

This episode illustrates not only the improvisational nature of these broadcasts but also the level of each participant's personal involvement with the program. In addition to performing her or his specialized role as singer, musician, etc., each individual stands ready to join in the exhortation. All agree that the responsibility of "saving souls" is a shared one. Here, then, is the central purpose of these broadcasts—to evangelize. These people do not come to a radio station every Sunday just to find an environment in which to practice their religion; they can do that in the relative seclusion of their home churches. Instead, they are there to "spread the word," to convert. In such a task they could not be joined by their Primitive or Old Regular brethren.

The Morning Star Gospel Program

In 1971, soon after I moved to Boone, North Carolina, I first heard "The Morning Star Gospel Program." Currently in its thirty-fifth year as part of the regular Sunday morning programming of WATA in Boone, the broadcast is such a tradition that many elderly people of the area would not think of beginning their Sunday reli-

2. Recorded 17 July 1983, at station WMCT, Mountain City, Tenn.

gious activities without first tuning in at 9:00 A.M. to hear "Preacher Ros" and the Morning Star Trio. There are people in Boone and Watauga County who can run down the list of personnel changes that have occurred among the show's principals since "The Morning Star Gospel Program" first came on the air.

I once went on Roscoe's broadcast to ask people who had listened to the program for years to call and tell me what role the broadcast had played in their lives. One lady told me about a winter in the mid-1960s when the snow was so deep that she and her husband could not get out of their hollow. But she remembered turning on the radio that Sunday morning and hearing Sister Dollie, Sister Hazel, and Brother Ros talk about how they had made it to the station.

One gentleman in a rest home said that Greene's program was about the only "churching" he got "nowdays." Another gentleman told me that he listened to the show because of the singing, that this was a way he could hear "the old songs." A lady said she listened to the broadcast because she was afraid that someday Preacher Ros and Sister Dollie would not be on the air anymore. She worried about what that would say concerning the old ways she liked.

When I first heard the broadcast, I was fascinated by Greene's preaching. I called WATA to determine how I could reach him, and a secretary suggested that the quickest and surest way to make contact with Greene was to drop by the station one Sunday morning at 9:00 A.M. It was two weeks, however, before I made it to the WATA studios.

At that time T.J. Jackson operated a Texaco service station at "greasy corner" in Boone, and I was one of his customers. The Sunday after I had spoken with the WATA secretary, I was listening to the program and heard "Preacher Ros" announce that Jackson would deliver the short sermon that always closed the broadcast. That was the first time I realized that the man who had been servicing my car was also a lay preacher. During the following week I made a point of speaking with Jackson, asking him if he thought the "Morning Star" group would mind my visiting their broadcast. He asked me to meet him there the next Sunday and promised to give me an introduction.

In 1973 radio station WATA occupied the second floor of the Watauga Savings and Loan Association building on King Street, Boone's main "downtown" thoroughfare. When the station first went on the air in the early 1950s, it was located above the bus station on Depot Street. Sister Dollie recalls liking that original facility better than either of the two they have been in since, because it was so large. Brother Ros remembers having as many as forty visitors standing around listening to the broadcasts in the old studio. Roscoe and Dollie speak of these early years of the show as possibly the best years—the time when the group's following was largest and the Morning Star Trio in top form.

WATA is a small station trying hard to serve a diverse listening clientele: an educated but largely youthful market connected with the local university; an older but also well-educated group of individuals who have come to these mountains as retirees, mostly from Florida; a family-oriented tourist industry tied to the numerous campgrounds and other vacation attractions along the Blue Ridge Parkway; patrons of a winter ski resort; and the indigenous Watauga County community, including those mountain folks who have felt increasingly dispossessed by all these "immigrants." One way in which WATA has accommodated itself to the tastes of this "local" market has been to devote its Sunday morning programming to country gospel music and to locally-produced religious broadcasts. Of the latter, "The Morning Star Gospel Program" is the only one that has lasted year after year.

"Preacher Ros" and his group perform several services for that segment of the Boone and Watauga County population that regularly follows the program. They make church announcements for a half-dozen or so congregations; report the present condition of incapacitated supporters of the show (particularly those in hospitals); pass along prayer requests; occasionally note the condition of local roads during periods of snow, rain, or heavy fog; and generally inspire, instruct, and entertain.

Of the original four persons who started the broadcast, Sister Dollie Shirley is the only one remaining. Her father, Brother Bob Smith, and a preacher, Brother Otis Cook, were the actual originators of the show. Dollie, her father, and Brother Stewart Hamby constituted the first Morning Star Trio, handling all of the musical aspects of the production, while Cook took care of the preaching. Two of Hamby's children—his son Silvester and his daughter Nona—are, at the time of this writing, teamed with Dollie as the trio.

Sister Dollie Holds Songbook for the Morning Star Trio on the
Morning Star Gospel Program, WATA, Boone, North Carolina.

In the 1950s the Morning Star Trio was in demand in a several-
county area for singing at revivals, homecomings, and the like. Dollie recalls that in the spring and summer the group was on the road
almost every night but Monday, the evening that they rehearsed
their music. During those years the trio used no instrumental accompaniment, employing only a pitch pipe to get them started.

Preacher Otis Cook stayed with "The Morning Star Gospel Program" only a short time, about three months to be exact. Thus
Roscoe Greene joined the broadcast during that first year and has

been with the production ever since. His wife, Sister Hazel, later came into the group to make all of the weekly announcements.

There were times in those early years, however, when Roscoe Greene could not be on the show, and apparently in some cases these circumstances developed quite unexpectedly. On these occasions Dollie and her father would run by Perkinsville, just east of Boone, and get Brother Raymond Hendrix to substitute for Preacher Ros. On at least one morning, the time involved in all this running got very tight. When Brother Smith reached the Hendrix place he found the minister milking his cow. Since it was only a short time before the broadcast was to begin, Hendrix told Smith that he and Dollie should go on into town and start the program with the singing and announcements and that he would get there as quickly as possible. So Dollie and her father rushed into town and got the show under way. In the meantime Brother Hendrix had his wife finish the milking while he hurried to get ready. Apparently Preacher Hendrix arrived just in time to deliver a short message for the morning.[3]

Sister Dollie has missed only six broadcasts in thirty-five years. That's a record of persistence anyone could be proud of, particularly considering the winter weather in the mountains of northwestern North Carolina.

The show first started as a fifteen-minute broadcast, and then Roscoe expanded it to thirty minutes. In the program's current format, this time is divided into three roughly equal parts, with ten minutes of singing; ten minutes of prayer, announcements, and special requests; and ten minutes of preaching. But it is hard to predict how the time sequencing will develop on any given Sunday. Occasionally Roscoe has only three or four minutes for his message.

There is a basic pattern for the broadcast, but the entire production takes on such an improvisational, spur-of-the-moment quality that it is impossible to predict the precise form it might assume on a given day. It is a relaxed, folksy half hour of what Greene calls "taking joy in the Lord"; in addition to its religious character, it possesses a significant social dimension.

The first morning that I ventured up to the WATA studios to meet

3. From recorded interview of Sister Dollie Shirley, conducted 3 Sept. 1983 by Debra Thompson, included in tapes housed in Appalachian Collection, Belk Library, Appalachian State Univ., Boone, N.C.

Roscoe Greene and his group, I arrived at about ten minutes before the hour. There was no-one in the studio where I had been told the broadcast would take place. In fact, the only person at the station at all was the young male high school student who was the Sunday morning disc jockey. He was at that moment in the middle of a gospel music program, and he stared at me through the soundproof glass that separated us, as if to ask what I wanted. I waited until he had a record on the turntable and then stuck my head into his area to ask if this was the right spot to visit "The Morning Star Gospel Program." He told me that it was but that the people probably would not start arriving until about five minutes before the show.

The young man was right. At almost exactly five minutes before the hour two elderly couples wandered into the studio and began to carry on a conversation. I soon found out, however, that Preacher Ros was not in this group. He and Sister Hazel did not arrive until about two minutes before the broadcast began. Between the arrival of the two couples and the entrance of the Greenes, several other "Morning Star Gospel Program" principals, including Sister Dollie and the other members of the Morning Star Trio, made their entrances into the studio. T.J. Jackson did not show up until after the show had begun.

The format followed that morning was the one that has become traditional. First, the listener heard an announcer lead into the show with the following: "It's time now for the Morning Star Gospel Program, sponsored and conducted by the Reverend Roscoe Greene. This program is on the air every Sunday morning at nine o'clock, with hymns sung by the Morning Star Trio." Then on the tail of this last line the trio began the program with a rendition of "Must Jesus Bear the Cross Alone?"

> Must Jesus bear the cross alone,
> And all the world go free?
> No, there's a cross for everyone,
> And there's a cross for me.
>
> The consecrated cross I'll bear,
> Till death shall set me free,
> And then go home my crown to wear,
> For there's a crown for me.

As the trio closed out this opening hymn, Roscoe came in with an "Amen," and then began to speak as a piano continued playing softly in the background:

> Thank you, singers. Good morning to our radio audience. It's a real joy to be able to visit back with the Morning Star broadcast, and as we usually say, it's a real joy to have you join in with us to worship together. You know, the Lord's been good to us this last week, and we ought to really thank the Lord and we ought to really praise His name for His goodness. There's a lot a things that could have happened this past week, and of course in a lot of families it has happened; but, you know, through the grace of God we're here this morning that we might be able to exalt the great name of the Lord Jesus. So we trust that whatever you might be doing, that you'll just stop long enough now as we go to the cross. We've got many objects, many requests, that we'd like for you to share with us as we go to the rich throne of God's grace. And we'll ask the singers now to take us to the cross.[4]

Now the trio picked up the cue by singing the old hymn, "Kneel at the Cross": "Kneel at the cross. Christ will meet you there. Somebody waits for you. . . ." But throughout this hymn and the ones to follow, Greene kept up a rather steady stream of audible exclamations such as "Bless them, Lord," "Amen," "That's right, brother," and "That's right, sister."

When this second song ended Roscoe came back in, again with the piano playing softly behind him. "You know, my friends, it's one of the greatest privileges that Christians have just to kneel at the cross, knowing that Jesus waits for us there."

There were two mikes in the studio, one at the table where Greene sat, and the other, a standing mike, placed close to the piano and used by the singers and by Sister Hazel for the announcements. Preacher Ros sat leaning closely over his mike, his Bible in his left hand and his right hand cupped lightly under his right ear. During these opening moments of the broadcast he spoke softly, almost intimately, and directly into the mike, his eyes gazing down at the table and partially closed. He seemed thoroughly to enjoy moments such as these.

The woman at the piano had a small daughter in the studio with her, and this child sat on the floor looking up at Roscoe, studying

4. Recorded 19 Aug. 1973, at station WATA, Boone, N.C.

his face closely, her lips moving silently in unison with his. Later in the program, the little girl became restless and started rocking the standing mike back and forth. This was during Preacher Ros's sermon, so the mother picked her up and placed her on her lap. There the child remained during the rest of the broadcast, even when the mother was playing the piano for the closing hymn.

Following the second hymn, Greene moved into the segment of the program during which he always mentions people who are in the hospital, in a rest home, or at home ill, and asks listeners to pray for them. During these moments he may also provide some details about how a particular person is getting along. If you listen to the program several weeks in a row, you will hear many of the names repeated, as Roscoe lets his infirm supporters know they are remembered constantly. A couple of years ago Sister Dollie's husband was in the hospital for some time before he died, and through Brother Ros and Sister Dollie's comments the regular listener could keep up with the man's condition.

Naming the "sick and shut-ins" precedes the first prayer of the broadcast. To lead this prayer Greene called on one of the visitors who were standing around the walls of the studio. But when the individual began his prayer, Roscoe also prayed, and so did everyone else in the studio, each delivering her or his own private supplications. It was another example of the "concert prayer."

Following this prayer two or three songs were sung by the trio, each hymn preceded by a series of dedications. Sister Hazel read names of individuals for whom a particular song would be dedicated, but the singers also added names with the result that each hymn was dedicated to at least four or five persons.

After the two or three main hymns of the morning, Sister Hazel again returned to the mike to give the morning announcements of regular services of several supporting churches and additional information concerning revivals, homecomings, or singings. Then Roscoe preached his five-to-ten-minute sermonette and, watching the studio clock, took the message right up to within thirty seconds of the end of the show. His closing remarks went something like this: "I see our time is about up. Let's have a little fellowshipping as we go off the air." This became the cue for the trio again to sing "Must Jesus Bear the Cross Alone?" When the singing began, everyone milled around the studio shaking hands with or hugging the other broadcast participants and visitors. At the appropriate moment the announcer came in with, "You've been listening to the Morning Star Gospel Program, sponsored and conducted by the Reverend Roscoe Greene. All mail to this program may be addressed to the Reverend Roscoe Greene, in care of WATA, Boone, or to Route 3, Box 245, Lenoir, North Carolina. It's 9:30 at WATA in Boone."

Concluding Thoughts

Sooner or later the "Morning Star Gospel Program" tradition will end. Preacher Ros or Sister Dollie will pass from the scene, and no-one will have enough tenacity and/or vested interest to keep the broadcast going. Furthermore, time will finally overwhelm the lifestyles and many of the values that the show represents, while advancements in communications technology and programming policies will render similar productions obsolete. Old-timers will then speak of "The Morning Star Gospel Program" as the "good old days" and bemoan the fact that no-one ever sings the old songs or preaches in the old style.

CHAPTER 7

Passing Over Yonder

> There is a home just over yonder
> that is shining bright and fair
> in that city of the Saviour.
> There will be no troubles there.
>
> —Obituary for Faye Ramey McCormick, *Minutes*,
> Little River Regular Baptist Association, 1964

Since older people tend to dominate within these churches, their attitudes, values, and needs also tend to dominate in those normal struggles to establish the ideologies, theological themes, and general interests of the various church communities. The one topic that stands out most strongly in all the preaching, praying, and singing of these churches is a vision of absolute "eternal glory," that joyous time when God's elect will be united around the "great white throne" that believers hold was promised in Rev. 20:11. The first gate to that land of glory is opened by death.

> Let death dissolve my body now,
>   And bear my spirit home.
> Why do my days move on so slow,
>   Nor my salvation come?
>
> God has laid up in heav'n for me
>   A crown which can not fade;
> The righteous Judge, at that great day
>   Shall place it on my head.
>
> Jesus the Lord, shall guard me safe
>   From ev'ry ill design;
> And to His heav'nly kingdom take
>   This feeble soul of mine.[1]

---

1. D.H. Goble, comp., *Primitive Baptist Hymn Book* (Greenfield, Ind.: Goble Printing Co., 1887), 140.

This old Primitive Baptist hymn captures a plaintive call commonly heard in the services of these mountain churches: "Let death come. I await the promised eternity of joy and peace. This earthly existence drags on, and I yearn to join my loved ones who have preceded me into that glory."

> There is a land of pure delight,
>   Where saints immortal reign,
> Infinite day excludes the night,
>   And pleasures banish pain.[2]

The pain alluded to here is often that which comes from being "left behind" when loved ones have "gone on ahead," of spending endless hours in an empty house, a sterile hospital, or a loveless nursing home, remembering departed parents, a late spouse, even deceased children. An elderly member of the Scotsville (Missionary) Baptist fellowship in Ashe County, North Carolina, once came up to me at the close of a revival service. The old gentleman wanted to know what I was all about, but he also wanted to tell me what he was all about. One of the things he wanted to tell me was that he was looking forward to the end of his earthly existence. "My wife is there," he said. "My mother and dad are there. Two of my five children are already there, bless their memory. Lots of old friends I knew are there. Why should I want to be here?"

During a footwashing at the Bethany Old Regular Church of Kingsport, Tennessee, one woman moved about the sanctuary crying and shouting joyously, "Oh, Sweet Jesus! Bless his holy name. I'm coming home, Sweet Jesus. I'm coming home! Oh, Children, get ready if you want to see your blessed mother. She's going home."

> Shortly this prison of my clay
>   Must be dissolved and fall,
> Then, O my soul, with joy obey
>   Thy heav'nly Father's call. . . .
>
> We walk by faith of joys to come;
>   Faith lives upon His word.
> And while the body is our home
>   We're absent from the Lord.

2. Ibid., 138.

Old Regular Outdoor Memorial Service, Mary Lou Cemetery, State
Line Road, Buchanan County, Virginia.

> 'Tis pleasant to believe Thy grace,
>   But we had rather see;
> We would be absent from the flesh,
>   And present, Lord, with Thee.[3]

This chapter looks at the images of life, death, resurrection, and
eternity projected in the beliefs and practices of these Southern
Appalachian Baptists, especially in funeral services and in the obitu-

3. Ibid., 136.

aries published in minutes of annual association meetings. In all their preaching, singing, praying, and eulogizing of the dead, these people struggle with three basic questions: What are the true meanings of life? What are the consequences of death? And what is the nature of eternity?

Obituaries

When Old Regular, Regular, Primitive, Union, Freewill, and some Missionary Baptist associations print the minutes of their annual sessions, they always include obituaries of members who died during the previous year. This honor is not reserved for leaders of the association or of affiliated churches. Rather, any member—and sometimes a nonmember—may have her or his obituary printed in these pages. Some person in the family, or one of the elders, need only compose the document and submit it in time for publication. Usually the cost of printing is borne by the association, with perhaps a small charge made to those families wanting to include a picture of the deceased.

Having a loved one's obituary published in the association's minutes constitutes a final tribute and farewell that is too important to be overlooked, and Old Regular families in particular seem quite diligent in this duty to the deceased. Once published, the document is preserved as one of the more important memorials of the "departed." It will be read and reread in months and years to come; therefore considerable care is taken in its composition. Frequently special poetry is written:

> Sad and sudden the shock severe,
> We never thought your death so near,
> Only those who have lost can tell
> The pain of parting without farewell.
>
> Our hearts still ache with sadness,
> Our eyes shed many a tear,
> God alone knows how we miss you
> At the end of the sad year.
> —Written for Connie Andy Simcox by Verna Ramey[4]

4. Little River Regular Baptist Association, *Minutes* (1964), 21. I am quoting all

The cover of Life's Book is closed
For the one we loved so well,
But the loving deeds of by-gone days
Are what the pages tell.

When evening shades are falling
And we are all alone,
In our hearts there is a longing
For you to be at home.
    —Written for Charity Combs Scott by Elder Millard F. Pruitt[5]

A precious one from us is gone,
A voice we loved is still,
A place is vacant in our home
That never can be filled.

When all our paths on earth we trod,
We'll meet him at the gate
For he is not dead, just gone before
To meet his long lost friends.
We, too, will meet when we cross o'er
Where pleasures never end.
    —Written for Carl J. Higgins, author unstated[6]

The Pearly gates are open,
For our grandmother to walk through;
Her pain and suffering is over,
She done all she could do.
We will all miss her greatly,
Now that the Lord has took her away,
But she deserves her reward that's waiting,
That is something we can all truly say.
There will be no pain and suffering,
In that heavenly place,
I can see her now with God,
With her lovely, smiling face.

---

of these obituaries precisely as published, with the exception of my corrections of
obvious typographical errors.
    5. Ibid. (1970), 19.
    6. Ibid. (1972), 14.

Don't weep for me, Children, she would say,
Just prepare to meet me in heaven someday.
　—Written for Bessie Pruitt Caudill by Elder Millard Pruitt and
　Tammy Caudill[7]

My Legacy
I have no wish for greatness, I've gained no wealth nor fame,
But it's always been my heart's desire to honor Jesus' name.
I know I've not been perfect; we humans cannot be,
But maybe God will use the little good He sees in me.
I would not have my loved ones grieve when my race down here is run,
But struggle on to gain the prize paid by God's Own Son.
I'm glad I've known and loved each one I've met along this way,
And, by God's grace, we'll meet again in Heaven some sweet day!
　—Written for John Talmadge Reeves by Pat McMillan[8]

Occasionally an individual writes her or his own obituary for publication later, with some member of the family updating the document at the actual time of death and adding whatever sentiments seem appropriate. Such was the case for Alice Belcher, who wrote the following statement about herself on July 24, 1980. Mrs. Belcher was in her eighties at the time, and her writing shows not only her age but her limited education.

Alice Belcher
I will now try with the help of my good Lord to write my obituary. I was borned February 10, 1899. At Lookout, Ky. I was the daughter of the late Dave Mercer and Alfire Castle Mercer.

I was married Bowes Belcher, June 8, 1920. To this union was borned six children. One boy and five girls. The boy and one girl were still borned, leaving four girls. Vivan died in 1970, Mrs. Geraldine Compton of Fofpit [Wolfpit], Ky., Mrs. Etta Garney of Wooster, Ohio, Mrs. Phyllis Pigg of Hellier, Ky. I have eight grand children, eleven great grand children. One sister Mrs. Viola Hall of Manchestor, Ky. I love them all very much. I wount all my Brothern and Sisters to pray for them all.

I joined the Old Regular Baptist Church at the Little Hattie Church in May 3, 1950. I was baptised by Elder Jim Green and Fon Bowling. I all ways love to go to church. I love all my brothers and sisters.

7. Ibid. (1982), 16.
8. Mountain District Primitive Baptist Association, *Minutes* (1982), 12.

I fell and broke my hip and did not get to go. I prayed to the good Lord to let me get so I could go. I could not get off the porch with out help. I set at home by my self so many long days. I hope this life will soon be over. I wont have to suffer and set alone.

Cheldren remember the good council Mother gave you. Be good to each other. Read the bible. It will not tell you anything wrong. I hate to leave my family, but God is able to take care of them, if they will only listen.

Have mine and Daddy picture put in minutes. My husband has been gone for sixteen long years. I miss him so much.

Written by Sister Alice Belcher, Wife and Mother.

By God's help, I love you all.

Mother passed from this life February 4, 1984. At the age of 84 years, 11 months and 25 days old. Mother was a devoted mother and a loving grand mother. A dedicated Sister in the Church for over 33 years.

She has fourteen great grand children now. Daddy passed from this life October 4, 1964. We miss them so very much. But we know they are to-gether up in heaven [where] there will be no more sorrow, truble or pain to bare.

If we take mothers advice, by the grace of God we will meet them in Heaven some sweet day.

With all our love, Her Doughters. Phyllis, Etta, Geraldine.[9]

In most instances it appears that loved ones have relegated to the more literate family members responsibility for penning the farewell document. Writing skills, however, do vary sharply among these obituaries.

Small associations, such as the Senter District Primitive Baptists and the Little River Regular Baptist, devote only a few pages to these statements; but the Union Baptist Association and the Sardis Association of Old Regulars run twenty to twenty-five pages of memorials, while the Union Association of Old Regular Baptist regularly publishes fifty or more pages of obituaries. Old Regular obituaries tend to be much longer than those included in the minutes of other subdenominations, showing the importance of these statements to this particular group.

These final tributes, written by husbands, wives, children, or other loved ones "left to mourn," serve not only as farewells to the

---

9. Union Association of Old Regular Baptists, *Minutes* (1984), 45.

deceased but also as opportunities for these writers to summarize their conclusions about life, to reaffirm basic beliefs, and to call other family members to repentance and change, should these loved ones not be following accepted life patterns. For the most part, the statements are uncomplicated, straightforward, fervent defenses of the "earthly life" contributions of the respective brother or sister, augmented by calls to the living to remember and to emulate. Frequently the eulogies make pointed reference to individuals who must change their lifestyles "if they are to follow the deceased into heaven." Occasionally the statement becomes an apologia for the dead, as if to say, "This individual was a person of goodness and worth; God should take note of the stars in her or his crown and open wide the gate."

Despite some variation among the subdenominations, a basic format seems to be followed in these obituaries. First comes the traditional opening statement, a general comment by the writer about the personal pain involved in writing the document, along with a suggestion that the eulogist feels inadequate to the task at hand, unable to compose an appropriate memorial statement without first calling upon God for inspiration and guidance.

> It is with much sadness and by the love and help of God that I write an obituary of our beloved Brother Bill Adkins.[10]

> Trusting to be guided by God's holy hand, I will try to write the obituary of my dear and precious father, Willie Stanley.[11]

> It is with sad and aching hearts that we try to write the obituary of our dear beloved mother, Darcus T. Coleman.[12]

Next, there is a succinct review of the departed person's life, with particular emphasis upon the family left behind. An accounting of the deceased's descendants is usually provided, and pride seems to be taken in the extensiveness of the list of children, grandchildren, and great-grandchildren.

10. Ibid. (1981), 45.
11. Sardis Association of Old Regular Baptists, *Minutes* (1982), 28.
12. Original Mates Creek Regular Primitive Baptist Association, *Minutes* (1980), 26.

[Elbert (Ebb) Fuller] died suddenly on October 27, 1978 about 10:00 A.M., making his stay on earth 76 years, 9 months and 26 days. He was married to Eura Blankenship on March 30, 1921. To this union were born 13 children. Twin sons Clyde and Claude preceded him in death. He leaves to mourn his loss his loving wife, Eura Fuller, 7 sons, Donald of Harman, Herby of Davenport, Foster of Vansant, Tom, Perry, Jerry, and Buck of Haysi; 4 daughters, Sarah Deel, Betty Jean Deel, and Susan Fuller of Haysi; and Roxie Hobbs of Galveston, Indiana; 1 sister Carrie Yates of Harman, 52 grandchildren, 23 great grandchildren and a host of friends and neighbors.[13]

Sister Fannie [Hale] was the daughter of the late Johnny Elliot Taylor and Sophia (Maynard) Taylor. She was born September 1, 1895, and departed this life October 14, 1982, making her stay here on earth, God's footstool, 87 years, 1 month and 13 days. Sister Fannie was united in marriage to the late Brother Alonzo Hale in 1914. To this union was born four children, namely: Brother W.H. Hale of Williamson, W. Va.; Brother John B. Hale of Wilkersville, Ohio; Sister Sophia Williamson, who preceded her in death in 1978; and Joseph Hale who died at the age of 6 years.

Sister Fannie leaves her two sons; her eleven grandchildren; her fourteen great-grandchildren; two sisters, Georgia N. Hale and Virgie Pinson Maynard; a host of relatives and friends; and the entire membership of the Pilgrim's Home Church to mourn her passing. She also had 3 sisters and 3 brothers who preceded her in death, namely: Anna Pack, Bam Stepp, Angie Maynard, Tom Taylor, Jordan Taylor and John D. Taylor.[14]

John Preston Irwin was born October 13, 1880, and passed from this mortal life August 14, 1972, making his pilgrim journey here 91 years, 10 months and 22 days. He was married to Olevia Rose Wagoner May 22, 1907. He leaves to mourn his passing his wife, Olevia Irwin; two sons, Joe Irwin, State Road, N.C.; John Irwin, Sparta, N.C.; six daughters, Mrs. Rose Joines, Mrs. Matilda Joines, Mrs. Minnie Wagoner, Mrs. Alice Cranford, all of Sparta, N.C.; Mrs. Lona Osborne, State Road, N.C.; Mrs. Audra Skinner, Jackson, Mississippi; one sister, Mrs. Lundy Nichols; 27 grandchildren, 33 great-grandchildren and a great number of friends. . . .[15]

13. Union Association of Old Regular Baptists, *Minutes* (1979), 64–65.
14. Sardis Association of Old Regular Baptists, *Minutes* (1983), 35.
15. Little River Regular Baptist Association, *Minutes* (172), 15.

[Edith Mae Perry] was born January 1, 1900, and departed this life April 23, 1981. Her life here on earth was 81 years, 4 months and 23 days. She was the daughter of Andrew Jackson and Nancy Vanover Hale.

She was married to Darrell Perry January 31, 1930. They had 6 children. She had 3 children by a previous marriage, 21 grandchildren, 9 great-grandchildren and 1 great great grandchild.

She was a member of the Mill Creek Freewill Baptist Church. She was loved by everyone who knew her, and missed so much by her family. . . .[16]

At this point in the usual progression of these obituaries, statements are made about how important the individual was to family, friends, neighbors, and church and how much the deceased will be missed. An argument is generally made that the family's loss is "heaven's gain":

[Gladys Pruitt Evans] was a devoted wife and mother, ever faithful to her husband, children, and church, and will be greatly missed by all her family and all who knew her. . . . But God saw fit to remove her from our midst to await the resurrection morn. As we behold the setting sun, may we say, "Lord, Thy will be done, for here on earth, there is no other that can take the place of mother."[17]

All us children can say that Papa [Elbert (Ebb) Fuller] was the best example we could follow for our lives. We have lost something so Precious that can never be replaced here on earth. We all hope the Good Lord will strengthen us and help us take care of our dear mother. Papa and Mommy were so good to each other that all Mommy has to worry about is the loss of Papa which will be hard. . . . I had a good papa here on earth. Jesus took him to heaven. He knew what he was worth.[18]

Sister Fannie [Hale] was a pillar in the Church for the 61 years that God blessed her to spend in the Church. She baked the bread to be served in our Communion meetings from the time I first can remember until these last few years when her health wouldn't permit her to continue. She seemed always present when her name was called. Her warm felt, kind and sweet spoken words of counsel would be good for each of us as we journey through this lane of life.[19]

16. John-Thomas Association of Freewill Baptists, *Minutes* (1981), 28.
17. Little River Regular Baptist Association, *Minutes* (1964), 18.
18. Union Association of Old Regular Baptists, *Minutes* (1979), 64.
19. Sardis Association of Old Regular Baptists, *Minutes* (1983), 35.

At times the writer of an obituary will break into one of these eulogistic passages and address some thoughts directly to the deceased. These tend to be moments of intense pathos:

> Papaw [Elder Jay Johnson] I miss you and loved you. You were a good friend and a wonderful father-in-law and the grandest of grandfathers. Thank God some of your children gave you roses while you lived. I pray that the others will seek Jesus before it is too late.
>
> The teachings you gave us, the many talks around the kitchen table, the old songs of Zion you sang for us is greatly missed but we feel our loss is Heavens gain.[20]

> Mother [Jettie Hackney Swiney], there is an empty place in our home, it's not the same without you. My husband Paul and daughter Becky we miss you very much, the home is so lonesome mother but we hope our loss is Heavens gain, and mother we will never forget you; we will always think of you and miss you. It's not the same without you.[21]

> Dearest daddy [Arvil Toliver Shumate], how we miss you
> No human tongue can tell.
> But someday we shall meet you
> And never say farewell.[22]

Near the end of an obituary there is usually a statement to the effect that the departed has merited redemption and the rewards of heaven. This passage serves as a final note of assurance to loved ones that all is well with the deceased's soul. Often some brief narrative is given to illustrate the departed's own awareness of imminent death and subsequent passage to "glory."

> So many times we have heard Mom [Dollie Bartley Ratliff] tell of her experience as she would cast her eyes toward Canaan's Land. She led a good Christian life, and her influence will continue to give faith and hope to the ones who knew and loved her. Mom's life here on earth and her honesty and thoughtfulness will long be a glorious record worthy enough for anyone to follow. The night before her passing, even while enduring severe pain and suffering, Mom continued to quote verses of scripture from the Bible. She seemed to know that the death angel was near and sincerely believed in God's mercy and goodness. . . . [Mom is]

20. Union Association of Old Regular Baptists, *Minutes* (1980), 27.
21. Ibid. (1982), 30.
22. Union Baptist Association, *Minutes* (1983), 34.

resting in Ratliff Family Cemetery awaiting the coming of Christ, and to
go home with Him to live forevermore in that country where sorrow and
trouble are unknown.[23]

[Maude E. Ferguson] professed a hope in Christ at the age of 16 years,
and united with Little Bethel Church. How many times have we seen
her rejoice in her Savior's love when she would hear the Gospel in its
power and purity and point a feeble trembling hand toward that home
that awaits the soul of all God's children.[24]

He [Walter Hardin Higgins] told the writer he professed a hope in
his youth and joined the church and was baptized but got led off with
the wrong crowd, and failed to live as he should, but in his suffering he
told me he had got forgiveness of all he had done, and there was nothing
in his way, and he was waiting for the call. . . . We will say to all, don't
grieve. He has paid the debt we all owe.[25]

Some associations allow the publication of obituaries for individuals who never joined one of the member churches. This is the case,
for example, with the Union Association of Old Regulars, the Little
River Regular Baptist Association, and the Union Baptist Association. It is not the case for the Sardis Association of Old Regulars.

Occasionally a regular member of one of the churches has a
deceased friend or loved one who was never church affiliated or
never baptized. The member in question might be motivated by a
desire (1) to give the deceased the best sendoff possible under the
circumstances, (2) to assuage the fears of other friends or loved ones
by assuring them that the deceased really merited eternal glory,
and/or (3) to put forth a defense for the deceased, just in case some
power in heaven might need additional evidence of the departed
individual's good works or good intentions.

[Joseph Harrison May] never united with the church but was a strong
believer in the Primitive Baptist Doctrine and was willing to help the
church in any way he could. . . . We feel sure that our loss is Heaven's
gain.[26]

23. Union Association of Old Regular Baptists, *Minutes* (1980), 58.
24. Little River Regular Baptist Association, *Minutes* (1970), 14.
25. Ibid. (1971), 14.
26. Original Mates Creek Regular Primitive Baptist Association, *Minutes* (1976),
26.

[Leslie Compton] was a sick man having trouble breathing all the time. He joined the Bethlehem Regular Baptist Church on March 27, 1982, but was never able to be baptized. He told the brothers and sisters the night he joined the church, that he had prayed all he knew how and felt the good Lord had forgiven him. He said he wanted to be baptized if he ever got able but said if he didn't get to the water he felt he would be alright anyhow.[27]

He [Hibbert Elkins] never joined any church, but was a firm believer in the Old Regular Baptist. He worked many hard days to help build the Georges Fork Church house. He had a great love for humanity. Always met you with a smile and a handshake.[28]

Commonly obituaries close by turning the discussion away from the deceased and directing an urgent admonition toward remaining members of the family, particularly the children. Traditionally this admonition calls upon those "left behind" to straighten out their own lives, if need be, so that they will be able to reap the same eternal reward claimed for the one who has passed on. These gentle—or not so gentle—reproofs and warnings are occasionally directed at specific people, with names given. It would be a mistake, however, to conclude that every time a name is mentioned in such a passage it means the writer of the obituary strongly believes that that person is headed for perdition. This style of closing has become so common that obituary writers attach these admonitions even when they believe that the rest of the family is in reasonably good spiritual condition.

I would like to say to the rest of the children, if you ever want to see Mommie again. You will have to fall out with sin and be born again in Christ our Lord and take the same road Mommie took.[29]

I want to say to Bob and Louise and all the other children if you get to where I feel Mother is you must repent and be born again. To do that when Jesus Christ reveals himself to you, you must believe in him and obey his spirit. . . . He'll deliver your soul from a dead state to a lively hope in the Lord Jesus Christ. . . . My hope is that you will repent and

27. Union Association of Old Regular Baptists, *Minutes* (1982), 49.
28. Ibid. (1980), 38.
29. Union Association of Old Regular Baptists, *Minutes* (1982), 29.

be born again and we'll all live together in a land where there is no more dying, but peace and love, joy and rejoicing.[30]

Children, be ready, when the master calls for you for that call will surely come at a time you least expect. Mother cannot come to you anymore, but you can go to see her in that restful home in heaven.[31]

So now to the family, I want to say that we have lost a great dad and grandfather. He cannot come back to us but we can go to him. You that have not made peace with God, if you ever expect to go to Heaven and be with Dad and Mom, you will have to make preparations on this side of the grave. . . . So, while we have life and opportunity, let's get ready to live in that place where there is no more pain and live with God forever.[32]

Reflections on Life

By studying these obituaries, one can obtain an understanding of how these Southern Appalachian people view the normal vicissitudes of life. Do they generally consider their lives pleasurable or painful? How do they summarize the basic meanings of life and the fundamental standards by which a life is judged? Indeed, how do they rate life relative to death and the promised afterlife? Do they, for instance, view their earthly periods of struggle solely as passages to be endured, with little to be accomplished other than preparation for that eternity of joy? If not, what is it that one should accomplish in one's life on earth?

Obituary writers see the pleasures of life as centered in the family, community, and church, with the establishment of warm or loving interpersonal relations taking priority over such other accomplishments as the building of careers, the amassing of estates, or the creation of institutions. When "good" things of life are mentioned, they are viewed as being found (1) in the family setting; (2) in relationships with friends and neighbors; (3) in the traditional activities of the church—singing, shouting, praying, preaching, fellowshipping, and ministering; and (4) in the personal conviction of

30. Ibid. (1984), 31.
31. Little River Regular Baptist Association, *Minutes* (1964), 20.
32. Sardis Association of Old Regular Baptists, *Minutes* (1982), 41.

spiritual salvation. The "bad" things of life are hard, monotonous work; the travails of poverty; the sufferings of ill health; the pain of losing loved ones (particularly children and spouses); worries over unconverted loved ones; struggles for personal salvation; the loneliness of old age; and the slow movement of time when one is ready to "pass over yonder."

Fairly precise images of what is "good" emerge in the virtues and accomplishments lauded in these obituaries. We can see, for example, prototypes of the ideal "Mom" and "Dad." In general, "Mom" is lauded for the wonderful nurturing she gave her children, the memories she left them and the spiritual guidance she provided; the loyal devotion she accorded her husband; for the abundance of friends she had who subsequently mourned her death and the service she gave her brothers and sisters in the church; for her faithfulness in church attendance and the "joy" of her singing, shouting, and other forms of religious expression. "Dad" is lauded for his years of hard work and diligence as the family provider; for love of children and dedication to his wife; for ability to endure hardships; for firm and righteous counsel; for generosity to family and friends; for faithful service to the church; and for his personal religious testimony. We see all these virtues heralded in the following obituary passages from the 1981 minutes of the Union Association of Old Regulars:

> Our memories of Mother [Emilie Tuttle Slone] is so sweet. I loved to go to church with her. She loved to sing and Shout the praises of God. . . . Her house was ever open to her friends and her neighbors. Her hands was always ready to help in time of trouble, Sickness or need. She loved for her brothers and Sisters in the church to come and talk about the Goodness of God and Sing and Pray in her home. She loved preparing food for them to eat no one left her house hungry.[33]

> Daddy [Theodore "Ted" R. Coleman] loved to go to the Church, he would get up so early and get ready and start out walking to Church. He also would take candy and chewing gum with him. He loved to give it to the young people as well as the elderly. He loved to talk with people and enjoyed cheering them up when visiting the hospitals and the nursing homes. . . . Daddy leaves a host of friends and young people and Brothers

33. Union Association of Old Regular Baptists, *Minutes* (1981), 31.

and Sisters in the Church who will miss him. He was the dearest person in the world to us.[34]

Mother and Poppy [John and Margaret Raines] will be remembered by all who know them for what they were, hard working, honest, praying, God Fearing people. . . . The old home doesn't seem like home without Mom and Poppy sitting on the porch. No-one could tell a story like Poppy and no-one understood like Mommy. All her children were tender and beloved in her sight. She wouldn't leave home for anything if she was expecting any of the children to visit. . . . Some of the children would travel hundreds of miles to be with them whenever they could, if only for a weekend. . . . The family gatherings won't be the same now, with vacant seats at the long table where mother had prepared hundreds of meals for the family, friends and the church.[35]

She [Flossie Henson] lived a life filled with sorrows, troubles, and hard work, rearing a large family, which she was so devoted to. The love of her God, her church, her family, her Sisters and Brothers and loved ones gave her courage and strength to carry on.[36]

Grandpa [Billie Hall] was the most unselfish and humble man I have ever known. In all my life, I never heard him raise his voice or say a bad word against anyone. He cared about people and in return, they cared about him. He was kind, gentle and giving.[37]

Mother [Mima Bartley Childers] would sit and talk to us children and tell us how we ought to live and to be good children. When we were growing up she would read the Bible and sing the old songs of Zion. They were a comfort to her and made her happy. Sometimes I can still hear those old songs she loved so much.[38]

This dearly beloved old lady [Pricey Fuller Dixon] was a faithful member of the Old Regular Baptist Church, having been baptised way back in the early 1920s. She was a praying, hymn singing, shouting, old time black bonnet wearing member of this body of Christ, faithful to the end.[39]

34. Ibid., 26.
35. Ibid., 44.
36. Ibid., 48.
37. Ibid., 52.
38. Ibid., 57.
39. Ibid., 58.

Through his long illness he [Paul Bartley] bore his pain as he had lived his life, with a smile for all and a desire to have his friends and family near him.[40]

Little or nothing is said in these obituaries about careers, accumulations of property and other "worldly" possessions, positions of power over other men, artistic or academic prowess, service to the body politic, or even military accomplishments, perhaps because these forms of achievement are not considered to be of ultimate value, and perhaps because these individuals have not commonly excelled in most of these fields.

Work is sometimes mentioned, but usually not in any detail. A father may be praised for having worked hard all his life at some trade to provide for his family, and frequently a man is identified as a retired miner, farmer, mechanic, poultry raiser, etc. Often a life's work is mentioned only in reference to hardships endured: a mother is praised for years of struggle to raise eight children, five of whom survived; a father is lauded for thirty-one years of service to the furniture industry; a son's early death is attributed to a coal-mine accident that broke his back. The dominant image of labor painted in these obituaries is certainly not a negative one, however. In fact, labor is frequently mentioned as a dignifying factor, and there are occasional glimpses of lives that appear to have been particularly fulfilled by labor:

> Bob [Robert Walter Williams] had resided at this farm for about 50 years and worked very hard, he and his wife, to raise their children, and continued to work after the children left home, raising a garden and canning and freezing so we and our families could have fresh vegetables and country meat when we visited the farm to see Grandpa and Grandma, and they insisted everybody take some back to the city. He achieved self satisfaction and pleasure from his long weary hours on the farm, something very few of us accomplish.

> Dad was a team driver by trade, I suppose the men in his profession called him a Mule Skinner, that was many years ago when logging and lumber was the largest industry around Virginia and Kentucky, and when coal mining became the primary industry, he worked several years at Harmon Mines on the tipple and then retired from public works to live out his remaining years swapping and bartering and farming which

40. Ibid., 65.

he truly enjoyed, because it required running around the country in his pick up truck and meeting and talking to the people. Most everybody around in that country knew him. Daddy loved to listen to the old time singing in the Old Regular Baptist Church, and he liked the preaching, but he had his preferences of preachers.

He died from a heart attack, while cutting briers on his farm in the late afternoon and we truly believe he would have wanted to go this way.[41]

The overall perspective on life presented in these obituaries is a strongly positive one, but that perspective is also considerably romanticized. There are the allusions to hard work and personal sufferings, but the broader vision of "earthly" existence is one of perseverance, happiness, and love. The real hardships of life seem forgotten when these final summations are recorded, and deceased individuals are depicted as having made it through this temporal life with courage, fortitude, and joy, while providing inspiration, strength, and loving counsel to those fellow travelers of lesser talent, experience, or grit.

Life, then, is viewed as pleasurable if lived well, with particular emphasis upon one's personal duty to family and church. Furthermore, it is a clear sign that an individual has indeed lived well when a multitude of loved ones and friends remains behind to speak highly of her or him and to mourn her or his passing.

Has your life been an inspiration to all your family, friends, neighbors, and fellow church members? Have you suffered bravely, prayed fervently, sung joyously, loved generously, and struggled diligently? If you have, then people will remember your example and themselves be strengthened by it. When your name is called out in future memorial services, there will be good things to mention about your life. The elder will stand before the church, read your name aloud, and then stop and say: "He loved to sing the old songs of Zion"; "She thrilled us with her joyous shouting"; "He always had a kind word for each Brother and Sister"; "She suffered her hardships bravely"; "He was a favorite with children and young people"; "She maintained a warm, loving home and kept it open to her neighbors and church brethren"; "He was poor in earthly goods, but rich in spirit"; "She was such a witness to her children and grandchildren";

41. Ibid. (1982), 57.

"He served as moderator of our church for twenty years"; "She always baked the communion bread"; "They always filled their seats in church."

Reflections on Death

God saw the road was getting rough,
the hill too hard to climb.
He gently closed her loving eyes,
and whispered peace be thine.

—Obituary for Emma Johnson Rice, *Minutes*,
Little River Regular Baptist Association, 1964

One ironic characteristic of these obituaries is that they generally communicate the idea that while life, though often troubled, is basically good, death is even better. In one way or another, these farewell statements proclaim the passing of the loved one to be a positive good, not of course for those left behind, but for the individual who "departed this world." Death has removed the deceased from an existence painful physically, emotionally, or psychologically. Death is allowing the deceased a reunion with loved ones gone on before. Death is bringing "rest" to an individual whose life was marked by long, hard, continuous work. And most important of all, death is opening the door to a kingdom of eternal joy, peace, beauty, and union with God.

If these obituaries are to be successful in declaring death a positive good—even if only for those believed to be "redeemed"—they must forge rationales that are equally applicable to the deceased of all ages and all circumstances. These believers must be able to see the same good, for example, in the deaths of a child and of someone who has lived a full life; in the passing of the young, healthy, and productive adult and of a bedridden invalid whose illness severely burdens others.

The death of an infant or child presents a particularly difficult problem. If the deity calls us to death, just as he calls us to redemption, why does he occasionally call so early? In relationship to the scenario of life, sin, redemption, death, and eternity, where does one fit the stillborn infant or the child who dies before reaching the age of accountability? Why would the deity rush to "call home" one who has spent so little time in an earthly existence? The Union Association of Old Regulars is the only association studied that publishes obituaries for infants who were stillborn or who lived only a few days, weeks, or months. A couple of the other associations do publish obituaries for children, but not for infants.

The only rationales put forth fairly consistently in these Union Association statements are (1) that God occasionally sees a baby that is suffering and decides to take that individual directly into heaven, and (2) that sometimes He wants infants and small children as angels to round out or "decorate" his kingdom:

> [Stacey Wayne Deel] was born February 26, 1980, at the Appalachian Regional Hospital at 2:20 A.M. and God called his precious soul to come to be with him at 3:35 A.M. . . . The doctors said he didn't get the right kind of blood circulation to develop right. His lungs weren't developed and he couldn't breathe on his own. They kept him alive as long as they could. But the Lord told him, "Come home and live with me where you'll never have to suffer and can breathe." [42]

> [Misty Dawn Fleming] was born Jan. 7, 1981. Died Jan. 11, 1981. Being four days old, we realize that it is hard for parents to give up their children. It is hard for people to understand why these things happen to them. But God knows all things and does all things well.
>
> Misty is only sleeping now. But some day when God calls her, she could only be another Angel. Because where there is no law there's no transgression. [43]

> One beautiful spring morning as the sun began to rise out of the eastern sky on June 11, 1980, Chad Edward Kiser was born to Freddie and Ramona Kiser. He had to be taken immediately to the U.K. Hospital in Lexington, Kentucky. There they did all they could for him but Jesus knew he had suffered enough in this cruel world and called him home. Home to a place where there's plenty of air for its little lungs. He is dwelling in a mansion that outshines the sun today and basking in God's love. [44]

42. Ibid. (1981), 30.
43. Ibid., 46.
44. Ibid. (1980), 45.

Dead on delivery at the Methodist Hospital, [Jason Edmond Stewart] . . . was the grandson of Mr. and Mrs. Ray Bevins of Elkhorn City, Kentucky and Mr. and Mrs. Autie Stewart of Belcher, Kentucky. We [Leith and Virginia Stewart] waited eleven years for our darling son but the Lord loved him more. He has gone from us to bloom in the Masters Boquet. By the grace of God, we will see little Jason again.[45]

If love could have kept her [Leanne Ramona Dawson], she would not have died. But it seems that she was born to be an Angel for her glow was so bright that surely there is another star in heaven and that light is still shining, only in another place.

She gave us more-love in four short years than some will give in a long lifetime. But sometimes I think that she knew all along that God had special plans for her, for she had a quote that she often said. It made me shutter then and tonight it makes me wonder. For she would often say, "I don't want to grow up. I always want to be little." And tonight, June 28, 1984, somewhere between 9 and 10 o'clock God granted her that wish.[46]

Death is viewed as one of the final steps in a process of selection directed by God. The redeemed pass in body and/or soul directly to heaven. From the perspective of these believers, it becomes a blessing for any who are chosen to pass "over yonder," at whatever time and under whatever circumstances. For the redeemed, death is the beginning of a long-anticipated respite and eternal reward. For the unredeemed, on the other hand, it is the beginning of an eternity far less desirable. "We believe," proclaim the articles of faith of the Mountain District Primitive Baptist Association, "in the resurrection of the dead, both of the just and unjust, and a general judgment and the punishment of the wicked will be everlasting and the joys of the righteous will be eternal."[47] All six Baptist subdenominations believe in these doctrines of eternal punishment and eternal reward. In support of these basic beliefs about a final judgment, these churches point to at least three New Testament scriptures:

When the Son of man shall come in his glory, and all the holy angels with him, then shall he sit upon the throne of his glory:

45. Ibid., 32.
46. Ibid. (1984), 36.
47. Mountain District Primitive Baptist Association, *Minutes* (1976), 21.

And before him shall be gathered all nations: and he shall separate them one from another, as a shepherd divideth his sheep from the goats;

And he shall set the sheep on his right hand, and the goats on the left.

Matt. 25:31–33

Marvel not at this: for the hour is coming, in the which all that are in the graves shall hear his voice.

And shall come forth; they that have done good, unto the resurrection of life; and they that have done evil, unto the resurrection of damnation.

John 5:28–29

And I saw a great white throne, and him that sat on it, from whose face the earth and the heaven fled away; and there was found no place for them.

And I saw the dead, small and great, stand before God; and the books were opened; and another book was opened, which is the book of life; and the dead were judged out of those things which were written in the books, according to their works.

And the sea gave up the dead which were in it; and death and hell delivered up the dead which were in them: and they were judged every man according to their works.

And death and hell were cast into the lake of fire. This is the second death.

And whosoever was not found written in the book of life was cast into the lake of fire.

Rev. 20:11–15

There is some confusion in these obituaries concerning the precise stages through which the redeemed must pass en route to heaven. Some statements clearly depict the deceased, in both soul and body, as already in heaven, this transition having occurred immediately upon death. Others speak of the dead as having gone to a resting place to await the final judgment. And still others suggest that the soul has gone to heaven, while the body is remaining in the grave to await that judgment day. We can see evidence of the confusion in obituaries published in the 1980 minutes of the Union Association of Old Regulars:

If Brother Charles [Ramey] could speak back now he would say—Children it's so beautiful up here, lay everything down and strive for this heavenly land where no sad news ever comes.[48]

Now all we can say is "Sleep on Daddy [Sugar Slone] and take your rest until that great day when God shall awake the dead, then we can all go home with him where trouble will always be a stranger."[49]

She [Virgie Adkins] is in a beautiful land where she will never have anymore sorrows and worries. She left them all behind her and she has joined her Lord where all she will ever know is happiness and peace.[50]

We believe that Mother [Lila Mullins] is resting in Heaven now and if she could speak to us she would tell us not to worry about her, but to worry about ourselves for our day of judgement draws near.[51]

I believe that he [Charley Hopkins Deel] is now resting from all his labors and his soul is taking that sweet rest in the city of God, waiting for the Great Resurrection Morning when that soul and spirit will reunite with that body that is sleeping in the earth. Then the Lord will give him a long white robe and a crown of Glory that will never fade away. He will go to a heavenly home where troubles and sorrow will all be done away with, where all is peace and love forevermore.[52]

This last excerpt apparently best represents the formal beliefs of the Old Regular Baptists relative to death and resurrection. During an interview, Elder Edwin May, moderator of the Sardis Association of Old Regulars, argued that confusion develops in obituaries relative to the issue of resurrection simply because the writers of these documents generally are not the elders of the church but are laymen who get their "beliefs all mixed up." The correct doctrine of Old Regulars, he said, is that at death the soul of a redeemed individual goes directly to heaven, while her or his body remains at rest until final judgment when all of the souls and bodies of the redeemed will be reunited.[53]

48. Union Association of Old Regular Baptists, *Minutes* (1980), 52.
49. Ibid., 63.
50. Ibid., 53.
51. Ibid., 56.
52. Ibid., 59.
53. Interview with Elder Edwin May at his home in Abingdon, Va., 15 Feb. 1985.

On rare occasions an obituary expresses considerable concern about the soul of a departed individual, with the writer being unwilling to affirm an unequivocal conviction that the person in question merited eternal salvation. This occurs only in minutes of those associations that allow obituaries for nonmembers to be published. If an individual has been a church member, the obituary writer automatically assumes the best about the person's fate. But if a writer has very little in the way of assurance that the individual has been redeemed, he or she may hope for the best and pen a statement that withholds judgment either way.

The 1983 minutes of the Union Association of Old Regulars, for example, contain a memorial statement for Thestil Edward Slone, killed in a coal-mine accident at the age of thirty-three. Written by the deceased's uncle, Elder David Slone, the obituary notes that the nephew had been divorced from a first wife and had remarried, producing two children by each union.

Although no details are given for the divorce, this termination of the first marriage may have been the basis for Elder Slone's reservations about the state of his nephew's soul; for Old Regular churches generally exclude from their memberships all divorced individuals "except those who have put away their companion for the cause of fornication."[54] At the point in the obituary when the writer would ordinarily be giving assurance of the deceased's eternal salvation, Elder Slone had the following to say about his nephew:

> Although he did wrong things in life, we all have sin and come short of the Glory of God. He never joined any Church, I have told him you must be Born again. Many times, he would ask me questions concerning the Bible what Jesus said. If he made Peace with Jesus before he died, he is better off, than any of his family and friends left here on earth. . . . To all the family and friends of Thestil Edward be good to one another, and when you can't do any thing good for one, please don't do them any wrong, and make Peace with Jesus while you have life and opportunity.[55]

Evidently Elder Slone hoped that his nephew had done what was necessary to be redeemed but was not at all sure that had happened. Questions were asked about the Bible, the elder said, but substantive action by the nephew may or may not have been taken. Thus Elder

54. Sardis Association of Old Regular Baptists, *Minutes* (1983), 9.
55. Union Association of Old Regular Baptists, *Minutes* (1983), 66.

Slone appears to have done what he felt was the best thing under the circumstances: he wrote an obituary which withheld judgment but left room for hope. That hope may have consoled other loved ones—a father, a mother, the children, and perhaps one or both of the women Thestil Edward Slone married.

Elder Slone, however, did not stop with consolation; he added a measure of exhortation. The remaining family members were urged not to leave their own spiritual conditions in doubt and to "make peace with Jesus" while there was "life and opportunity."

Funerals

> Funeral services were conducted at Crab Creek Primitive Baptist Church by Elders Walter Evans, Dan Smith and Carl Higgins with burial in the church cemetery to await the great getting-up morning when all the saints shall rise to meet Jesus in the sky.
>
> —Obituary for Celia Fields, *Minutes*,
> Little River Regular Baptist Association, 1970

My first experience with a mountain funeral came in the mid-1970s when a close friend and neighbor died. The service was conducted at a small Missionary Baptist church in the western part of Watauga County, North Carolina, and was not, as I learned later, a particularly traditional affair. Nevertheless, two aspects of the ceremony struck me as being somewhat different from funerals I had previously attended.

First, four preachers officiated at this service, and all four spoke at various points in the ceremony. Second, the messages of these preachers were not always strictly eulogistic, but were frequently exhortative. The sermons did not just praise the deceased, comfort the bereaved, and extol the blessings of an afterlife, but instead, at least two of the sermons were heavily evangelistic, calling upon the congregation to take note of the mortality of flesh and to make whatever changes were necessary in their own lives to be ready for death. At the time the rhetoric seemed more fitting for a revival than for a funeral, but later I realized that this preaching approach is very much a part of Appalachian religious tradition.

While the exact customs for funerals vary considerably among the six Baptist subdenominations, and even among the various regions of Appalachia, there are a few common denominators.

First, certain neighborly acts are connected with deaths and funerals in any small community in rural America—food offerings, other deeds of assistance to the family, periods of sitting with the bereaved and the deceased. A death tends to bring out our best—or worst—communal altruism. We are drawn to these intimate, emotional scenes of last farewell out of a fascination with terminated life, perhaps because it is still a great mystery to us how the spark can be there and then suddenly gone, leaving a remnant that looks like the whole but is not. We are also drawn to these events because of our deep empathy for close family and friends, knowing that somewhere down the line a similar set of circumstances awaits us.

So we take our pies, cakes, and casseroles to the home and "sit a spell." We visit the funeral parlor to "pay our respects," admiring the abundance and beauty of the flowers and whispering to others about the peaceful look of the deceased. And we assist the family in whatever way we can, handling some arrangements, baby-sitting, receiving the food offerings, recording names and addresses, officiating at the guest book.

The main way that such customs in mountain communities differ from practices in the typical small town is that in the former, many of the activities, including the display of the body and even part or all of the funeral service, still occur in the home. For example, in many Old Regular church communities the body of the deceased might be displayed exclusively in the family home and in the church, or be first displayed in a funeral parlor and then brought to the home the afternoon before the day of the funeral. This means that people, and particularly close friends and relatives, come directly to the house to visit, to console, and to sit with the deceased, while someone keeps the dead company every hour of the day and night.

All this traffic through the home in turn necessitates a large spread of food and a cadre of helpers to organize, serve, and clean. Visiting children must be kept under control, and members of the immediate family, particularly the surviving spouse, must be watched over and cared for. Women gather on the inside, centering their activities around the kitchen, dining area, and parlor. Men tend to cluster outside, on the porch or in the yard. Occasionally the visiting mourners may engage in hymn-singing and praying, especially when an elder arrives.

The family may also elect to have part of the formal funeral service in the home that evening, with the remainder taking place in the church the next day. This often occurs when it has been determined that a sizeable number of preachers must be included in the ceremonies. Two or three elders, for example, could be selected to preach at the home service and three others to officiate at the larger church service. According to Darvin Marshall this is most often done because the regular church service would otherwise become far too long.

Mountain funerals tend to involve a number of preachers, rather than just one or two. There appear to be at least four reasons for this proliferation. First, many of these churches have not just one preacher, but as many as three, four, five, or even six. Among Old Regulars, Regulars, Union Baptists, and Primitives, an individual church may have several elders, all ordained to preach and all of equal stature within the fellowship. One of these elders, with Old Regulars, may be designated "moderator" of the church, in the sense that he presides over all business meetings of the congregation and handles some other official functions. But, at least with Old Regulars, Regulars, and Union Baptists, there is no other fixed hierarchy among these preachers. Therefore, when someone dies within one of these fellowships, several elders are available to do the necessary preaching.

A second reason for having a number of preachers at a funeral service is to satisfy the varied tastes of the key family members. Usually the deceased will have had a favorite preacher, and that individual undoubtedly will be asked to participate in the service. But the spouse of the deceased may also have a favorite, and so a second preacher will be invited to speak. Other family members may also have their choices, with the result that at least one or two more preachers are asked to participate.

A third reason for the proliferation of preachers may involve political sensitivity: when one particular elder—frequently an aging one—has been close to the family over a period of years, it may be very difficult not to ask him to participate.

Finally, there are situations in which a family feels compelled to have preachers from two or more denominational or subdenomi-

national groups. Over and over again in the Little River Regular
Baptist obituaries, one finds references to funerals presided over
by preachers from a mixture of denominations—Primitive Baptists,
Union Baptists, Regular Baptists, Missionary Baptists, and even in
one case a Methodist.[56] Such occasions do not always go smoothly,
particularly when the Old Regulars are involved. Indeed, Old Regular elders are not supposed to share pulpits with preachers from
other sects or denominations; to do so can result in an elder's exclusion from his church. Darvin Marshall told me of one instance in
which two separate services were fused together: one preacher conducted his service and then left the pulpit, and the second preacher
started all over again—separate singing, separate prayers, and separate preaching.[57]

These subdenominations of Baptists, with the possible exception of the Primitives, have in common a tendency to make funeral sermons at least partially exhortative in nature, "preaching
salvation," even while memorializing the deceased. (The Primitives'
strict Calvinistic stance on election prevents them from ever being
strongly exhortative.)

Missionary and Free Will Baptists are almost always a little more
salvation-oriented in their pulpit rhetoric than are the Regulars,
Old Regulars, and Union Baptists. As we saw in chapter 1, the
latter three groups have preserved some strong remnants of Calvinistic doctrine. But all three do talk about being "born again," and
their preachers frequently remind the unsaved that it is they who
must seek redemption and God, by his "grace," who grants it. The
preaching at many Old Regular funerals differs very little from the
preaching at a regular Sunday service, except that at the funeral the
preacher generally will talk more about the afterlife. The life and
good character of the deceased are covered not in a sermon, but in
an obituary that is read by one of the elders. Written by the family,
this is frequently the same document that will be published in the
association's minutes, or a version of it.

At funerals in Missionary and Freewill churches, and to a large
degree in Regular and Union Baptist churches, when there are two

56. Little River Regular Baptist Association, *Minutes* (1970), 16, 20; (1972), 18,
20; and (1982), 18.

57. Telephone interview with Darvin Marshall, 5 Mar. 1985.

or more preachers, they tend to subdivide duties. One speaker may concentrate on the deceased, while the other or others take a more traditional exhortative role. I do not mean to suggest that altar calls are made and church doors opened at funeral services. I have been told, nevertheless, that these funeral sermons have on occasion resulted in religious conversions.

A Personal Reflection

When I was a child, I had an intense dislike of funerals, primarily because much about them frightened me. When I reached young adulthood this fright turned into revulsion, as I became convinced that people made too much of death and burials, to their obvious financial and psychological detriment.

In recent years I have found these attitudes softening, even changing rather radically. Now I view funerals and all the connected events as very important, even essential and beautiful. I remain concerned about the costs, as some people are driven nearly to destitution to give a loved one the best sendoff possible. But my general impression of what happens at funerals, and particulary at mountain funerals, is now positive.

I like the idea of giving the deceased a dignified but emotional farewell. I also like what is done for the family, what happens in the overall church community, and what I see as a struggle to understand life and death in all their ramifications. I particularly like the unsophisticated obituaries, the individual memorial services, the larger Memorial Days and Decoration Days, and the Old Regular practice of calling out the names of deceased members each year. It must be comforting to know that every year your name will be read, and that there will be those who respond to that reading by saying something good about your life. That is one form of immortality.

CHAPTER 8

Epilogue

It was Sunday, July 21, 1985, when I sat down at my word processor to compose the few pages that would close the initial draft of this work. On my mind that day was the fact that just a week later I would be making my way to Coeburn, Virginia, and from there up a mountain to the Sandy Ridge community to visit the Sandy Ridge Old Regular fellowship's annual communion and footwashing. With this trip I would fulfill a promise I had made the year before when I attended the church's union service. In addition, since the Sandy Ridge fellowship had been more liberal with me than any Old Regular congregations I had encountered at that time, I hoped to get some photographs of the communion and footwashing, and the photographer Joel Poteat was going with me. It turned out, as I have already noted, that there would be an objection to the procedure, and Joel would be able to photograph the preaching service, but not the communion and footwashing.

On that July 21, 1985, I did not know the photographing issue would even arise. But I was still somewhat concerned about the trip because I had been informed that since my 1984 trip to the "Ridge" a slight rift had occurred in this Old Regular congregation, precipitated by some negotiations over a piece of property the church needed for parking. This is the sort of interfellowship dispute that, were it to grow in dimension or intensity, might find its way into the deliberations of an annual association meeting, with the association's moderator appointing a committee to investigate and arbitrate.

Old Regular association moderators have become quite adept at ameliorating local church conflicts. The investigating committee meets with the disputing parties during one of the monthly church business meetings, first obtains from the warring factions a general statement of peace and love, next negotiates a motion to nullify any offending actions that might have been taken as a result of

214

the dispute (the exclusion of a member, for example), and finally arbitrates the issue.

In many ways, these episodes become textbook models of conflict management, beautifully illustrating the effectiveness of third-party arbitration. That is not to say that the method always works, that splits are always avoided, and that peace and love are universally reestablished. But the procedure works often enough to warrant its continued use, and we have seen above one example of a successful conflict resolution, the case of Pilgrim Rest Church.[1]

I refer to the Sandy Ridge situation to emphasize that I am aware that all is not idyllic in these Southern Appalachian Baptist churches. I know that every Southern Appalachian religious setting is not necessarily filled with love, harmony, perfected values, and utopian community. Despite footwashings and flower services, universal human weaknesses—pride, selfishness, the desire for power and influence, the absence of trust—do contaminate these social clusters just as frequently and harmfully as they contaminate others.

Rousseau would have found in these environments much to foster his vision of an uncorrupted nature filled with happy men and women, unfettered by the shallow sophistications of a more "civilized" society. But if he looked closely enough, he would also have found the narrow provincialism and rigid orthodoxy that isolates as it insulates, excludes as it coheres. Individuals, therefore, who have suffered exclusion from one of these fellowships; who, in the course of their work in social service, education, or local government, have encountered the stubborn traditionalism of these people; who have considered the apparent inability of these churches to apply their morality and ethics to a larger social setting where illiteracy, hunger, political injustice, and civil rights abuses flourish; and who have witnessed the fear, distrust, and even hatred that often spring from such severe sectarianism—these individuals might have wondered why I have not advanced an occasional harsh judgment about the beliefs and practices of these six Baptist subdenominations.

I have indeed made those occasional harsh judgments. However, I have worked on the assumption that my readers will have a better understanding of the weaknesses of these traditional religious

---

1. Union Association of Old Regular Baptists, *Minutes* (1983), 8–9.

groups than of the groups' strengths. It has been my inclination, therefore, to depict these groups' practices in a light that is more rosy-hued than not. I confess that bias. Nevertheless, the bias has had a purpose, that of building within my readers a degree of empathy for these folks who have held so tenaciously to the past.

The past is terribly important to these fellowships. Their particular understanding of it has fostered their sense of certainty, of place, of belonging, of heritage, of an ongoing covenant. And the value of this past to them does not diminish with the encroachments of modernity—just the opposite, in fact. "I have lived from ox-carts into the space age," says Roscoe Greene. And when he says it, he quickly adds that for him nothing has substantially changed, that his beliefs are fixed for a lifetime.

I am deeply appreciative that so many of these fellowships have allowed me to intrude on their most intimate spiritual moments, that they have accepted me into their midst not as one of their number but as an empathic visitor. That has often made me feel honored, but it has also communicated to me a sense of trust that I could not violate. The lady at Mount Paran who asked if I intended ever to make fun of her hit a nerve, and that nerve has been tingling just a little for the past twelve years. I hope that she will read this work and be satisfied.

Index

Giving Glory to God in Appalachia was designed by Dariel Mayer, composed by Tseng Information Systems, Inc., printed by Thomson-Shore, Inc., and bound by John H. Dekker & Sons. The book was set in Primer with ITC Novarese Medium Italic display and printed on 60-lb. Glatfelter.